WARS AND SOLDIERS IN THE EARLY REIGN OF LOUIS XIV

Volume 5 – The Portuguese Army 1659–1690

Text and Illustrations by Bruno Mugnai

'This is the Century of the Soldier', Fulvio Testi, Poet, 1641

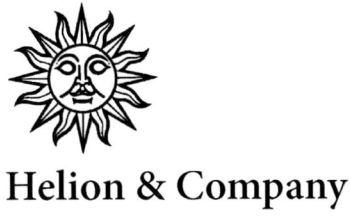

Helion & Company

Helion & Company Limited
Unit 8 Amherst Business Centre
Budbrooke Road
Warwick
CV34 5WE
England
Tel. 01926 499 619
Email: info@helion.co.uk
Website: www.helion.co.uk
Twitter: @helionbooks
Visit our blog http://blog.helion.co.uk/

Published by Helion & Company 2021
Designed and typeset by Serena Jones
Cover designed by Paul Hewitt, Battlefield Design (www.battlefield-design.co.uk)

Text © Bruno Mugnai 2021
Illustrations © as individually credited
Colour artwork by Bruno Mugnai © Helion & Company 2021
Maps drawn by George Anderson © Helion & Company 2021

Every reasonable effort has been made to trace copyright holders and to obtain their permission for the use of copyright material. The author and publisher apologise for any errors or omissions in this work, and would be grateful if notified of any corrections that should be incorporated in future reprints or editions of this book.

ISBN 978-1-914059-28-5

British Library Cataloguing-in-Publication Data.
A catalogue record for this book is available from the British Library.

All rights reserved. No part of this publication may be reproduced, stored in a retrieval system, or transmitted, in any form, or by any means, electronic, mechanical, photocopying, recording or otherwise, without the express written consent of Helion & Company Limited.

For details of other military history titles published by Helion & Company
Limited, contact the above address, or visit our website: http://www.helion.co.uk

We always welcome receiving book proposals from prospective authors.

Contents

Portuguese Chronology 1659–1686   iv
Forword   vii
Acknowledgements   ix
Abbreviations   x
Portuguese Currency   x

1. Portugal Restored   11
2. The Birth of the Modern Portuguese Army   43
3. Portuguese Wars   107
4. Uniforms, Equipment and Ensigns   150

Appendix I: Military Governors, Army Strength, and Orders of Battles   166
Appendix II: Portuguese Infantry *Terços*, 1641–1668   178

Colour Plate Commentaries   188
Bibliography   192

Portuguese Chronology, 1659–1686

1659

14 January	The Portuguese Army of Alentejo defeats the Spaniards in the battle of the Lines of Elvas
30 January	The Spanish army besieges the Portuguese town of Monção; the garrison surrenders on 7 February after a bitter resistance.
17 February	The Spaniards under the Marquis of Viana recapture Salvatierra de Minho
7 November	Peace of the Pyrenees between France and Spain
November	The Spaniards besiege Elvas, but are driven off by António Luís de Meneses

1660

May–June	The Spaniards repulse the attempt by the Portuguese to seize Valença de Alcántara

1661

23 June	Portugal cedes to England the settlements of Bombay in India and Tangier in North Africa as a dowry for Catherine of Bragança, who married King Charles II of England on 24 May 1661
6 August	Treaty of The Hague between Portugal and Dutch Republic, to resolve the colonial struggle in India. Between 1661 and 1663, the Portuguese cede Calcutta, Cranganore, Quillon and Cochim.
11 November	French–German general Friedrich Hermann von Schomberg enters Portuguese service

1662

9 June	The Portuguese garrison of Juromenha surrenders to the Spaniards
September	The Portuguese extend their control on the kingdom of Kongo in West Africa (roughly, modern-day northern Angola with parts of the two Congo republics)

1663

Spring	The Dutch renew the pressure on the Portuguese territories of the Malabar coast, even though this is a violation of the 1661 treaty; a

PORTUGUESE CHRONOLOGY, 1659–1686

	new truce is signed in September.
12 May	The Spaniards under Don Juan of Austria seize Évora
8 June	The Portuguese army under Vilhena and Schomberg score a resounding victory on the Spaniards at Ameixial-Estremoz
24 June	The Portuguese, led by Sancho Manoel de Vilhena and by the Count of Mértola, recapture Évora

1664

7 July	Battle of Castelo Rodrigo, where the Portuguese Army of the Minho under Pedro Jacques de Magalhães defeats the Duke of Osuna
20 June	The Portuguese army seizes Valença de Alcántara after a siege of eight days.

1665

17 June	The Spanish army is defeated by the Portuguese at Montes Claros.
1 October	André Vidal de Negreiros inflicts a devastating defeat on the Congolese at the battle of Mbwila

1666

April–May	Castelo Melhor arranges for Afonso VI to marry Marie Françoise of Nemours
October	The Mughals expel the Portuguese from Chittagong

1667

June–July	Inconclusive Portuguese campaigns in Galicia.
27 November	King Afonso VI, Castelo Melhor, and his Francophile party are overthrown by the King's younger brother Pedro, Duke of Beja, who was to reign as King Pedro II of Portugal. Pedro first installed himself as his brother's regent and then arranged Afonso's exile to the island of Terceira in the Azores.

1668

13 February	Treaty of Lisbon, Spain recognises the independence of Portugal; end of the Restoration War.

1670

April–May	The Portuguese invade the Nsoyo's domains in Congo, but are defeated at the battle of Kitombo

1671

October	An agreement with the Indian ruler of Kanara is signed in Goa; Portugal retains Mangalore.

1672

April–May	The Portuguese from Luanda extend their conquests in the Angolan interior

1674
Pedro II asks for contributions from the Junta dos Três Estados to maintain the border garrisons

1675
April–June   In Brazil, Pedro de Almeida unsuccessfully assaults Palmares, in the interior of Pernambuco

1676
February–May   The Moroccans unsuccessfully besiege Mazagão in North Africa

June–July   Portuguese recruitment and gathering of troops close to the border causes alarm in Madrid

1678
May   Second treaty with the *nayak* of Ikkery for the establishment of the Portuguese enclave in Western India

September   Peace agreement between the Portuguese governor of Pernambuco and the Palmarista chief Ganga Zumba, who is killed by some of his lieutenants who conspired to resume the struggle

1680
Spring   The Portuguese expedition against Palmares fails. Five further unsuccessful expeditions try to seize the Afro-Brazilian stronghold, the last being in 1686.

1681
September   In Angola the governor of Luanda resumes the war against the Mbundu

1683
12 September   Death of Afonso VI

27 December   Death of Queen Maria Francisca of Savoy

Foreword

This book is essential to bring to the public a 28-year conflict between Portugal and Spain, after the latter had annexed and dominated the neighbouring Kingdom between 1580 and 1640. Thorough, with clear and eloquent writing, a respectable number of maps and contemporary pictures, well-endowed with sources and with its high-quality superb illustrations that Bruno has accustomed us to, I was very honoured to have been invited by him to write this foreword. What part of a European History does Bruno Mugnai bring us?

When the Spanish rule ended with the revolt of December 1, 1640, the military potential of the kingdom of Portugal was almost nil, 'resisting only positively', as various sources refer, with the old organisation of the *Ordenanças* which, once re-established and perfected, could constitute an appreciable nucleus of resistance against the long-awaited attempt of the Spanish rulers to reoccupy the throne. This fragility had been aggravated in 1639 by Felipe IV when he ordered the delivery of all the weapons in the possession of the populations in Portugal, but there were other deficiencies: the lack of experience in new tactics, already underway in Europe, allowed by the development of firearms (more muskets than pikes) and there were no experienced chiefs and commanders. Often using his own assets that, it must be said, were large and had been kept by the Spaniards, *Dom* João IV sought, however, to act immediately and, among other measures, re-established the organisation of the *terços* that had been introduced in 1570, appointed a Permanent War Council and a Border Defence Board, created the high positions of Lieutenant General of Artillery, Lieutenant General of Cavalry and Governor of Arms of the provinces, and several captaincies, led by a captain-major and assistants, and finally reorganised the system of *levas*, making military service compulsory for all valid men aged between 16 and 60 years. From these actions arises the first permanent army of Portugal. This reorganisation had, during the period in which they served, two main actors: the Count of Castelo Melhor at government level of the kingdom, from the beginning, and later the Count of Schomberg, a German general come from France.

This War of Restoration was in the shadow of the broader contexts of the Thirty Years' War and had, as we can see in Bruno's book, deep impacts throughout the Portuguese Empire and especially in military issues, turning it into a more global conflict, superiorly dealt with by the author, from the theatres of war to uniforms, armaments, tactics and war strategy, which in the end, allow us to understand how Portugal managed to return to being an independent country. Undoubtedly a book to be read.

Sérgio Veludo Coelho
Ph.D. in History
Military Historian
National Defence Auditor
Portuguese Commission for Military History

Acknowledgements

This book has been slowly growing while I was writing volume 4 of this series, *The Armies of Spain 1659–1688*. Originally, I had the idea of uniting neighbouring Portugal with Spain based on obvious geographic considerations. Although these two states apparently pose symmetry problems in a book divided into two parts, the history of both countries intersects in such a way that it was impossible to deal with one without involving the other. Over time, what should have been only a simple appendix just covering the Restoration War revealed a wealth of ideas and reflections capable of constituting a book in its own right.

Many people have contributed to the growth and conclusion of this book. Therefore, I want to thank those who have been both an inspiration and, like all good friends, a practical help. Firstly, I would thank Nuno Pereira from Lisbon, who has generously supported my project. Equally inestimable is the value of research relating to the Restoration War and the Portuguese army, managed by the talented Portuguese historian and blogger Jorge Penim de Freitas, who periodically made available to fellow enthusiasts the results of his research on the web. His posts left me full of admiration.

Writing this book has created a new passion for Portugal, a country I visited for the first time in 1987, in my youth: a trip that occupies an important place in my life.

BM
Florence, 19 July 2021

Abbreviations

ANTT   Arquivo Nacional da Torre do Tombo (Lisbon)
AIM   Arquivo Histórico Militar (Lisbon)
AHU   Arquivo Histórico Ultramarino (Lisbon)

Portuguese Currency

The *real* (plural *réis*) was the unit of currency from around 1430. The *real branco* (equivalent to 840 *dinheiros*) had become the most common unit of account in Portugal. Meanwhile, the gold *cruzado* had a value of 750 *réis* during the reign of King João IV, then increase to 875 *réis* under King Afonso VI before its demise under Pedro II. Two denominations which did not change their values in this age were the *vintém* of 20 *réis* and the *tostão* of 100 *réis*. The smallest coins were worth 1½ *réis*.

1

Portugal Restored

In the mid seventeenth century, Portugal had a population of about 1,750,000 who occupied a territory of about 90,000 square km, coinciding with the borders of the current state.[1] In general, the demographic situation was more prosperous than in Spain and for this reason some historians have compared Portugal to the United Provinces of the Netherlands, not only in consideration of their extensive colonies, but above all for its commercial fleets that crossed the world's seas.[2] However, due to the Restoration War, there was no demographic increase for many years. The capital, Lisbon, the country's political centre and main commercial hub, had around 165,000 inhabitants, much like Amsterdam. The other major commercial centre of the state, Porto, numbered 20,000 inhabitants and just three other cities had populations of more than 16,000. Most of the population was settled in the central-southern part of the country, in stark contrast to the border regions, which were almost uninhabited due to the war against Spain. The largest frontier city, Évora, was in fact a fortress whose existence was entirely due to its strategic importance. The historic provinces of the kingdom that composed Continental Portugal were Estremadura, Entre-Douro-e-Minho, Trás-os-Montes, Riba-Côa, Beira and Algarve. In the Atlantic Ocean, the Portuguese retained Madeira, Cape Verde and the Azores Islands, which were useful stopping off points for America and Africa, even though the inhabitants depended strongly on Lisbon for subsistence.[3]

Portugal's social classes were distributed in the traditional seventeenth-century hierarchy, with nobles and clergy who retained privileges and local power over the bourgeoisie and the lower class 'third state', or *povo* (commoners). The nobles, who took an active part in the events of December 1640 and the establishment of the new Bragança dynasty, included few

---

1 Colin McEvody and Richard Jones, *Atlas of World Population History* (New York: Facts on File, 1979), p.102. In 1700, the population had grown to two million.
2 *The New Cambridge Modern History*, Vol. V – *The Ascendancy of France, 1648–1688* (Cambridge: Cambridge University Press, 1964–68), p.384.
3 Grain shortages sparked popular disturbances in Ponta Delgada in 1643 and 1695. There were also repeated supply crisis in subsequent years. See Anthony R. Disney, *A History of Portugal and the Portuguese Empire* (Cambridge: Cambridge University Press, 2009), vol. II, p.97.

WARS AND SOLDIERS IN THE EARLY REIGN OF LOUIS XIV - VOLUME 5

Above: Portugal. Facing page: Brazil in 1644.

PORTUGAL RESTORED

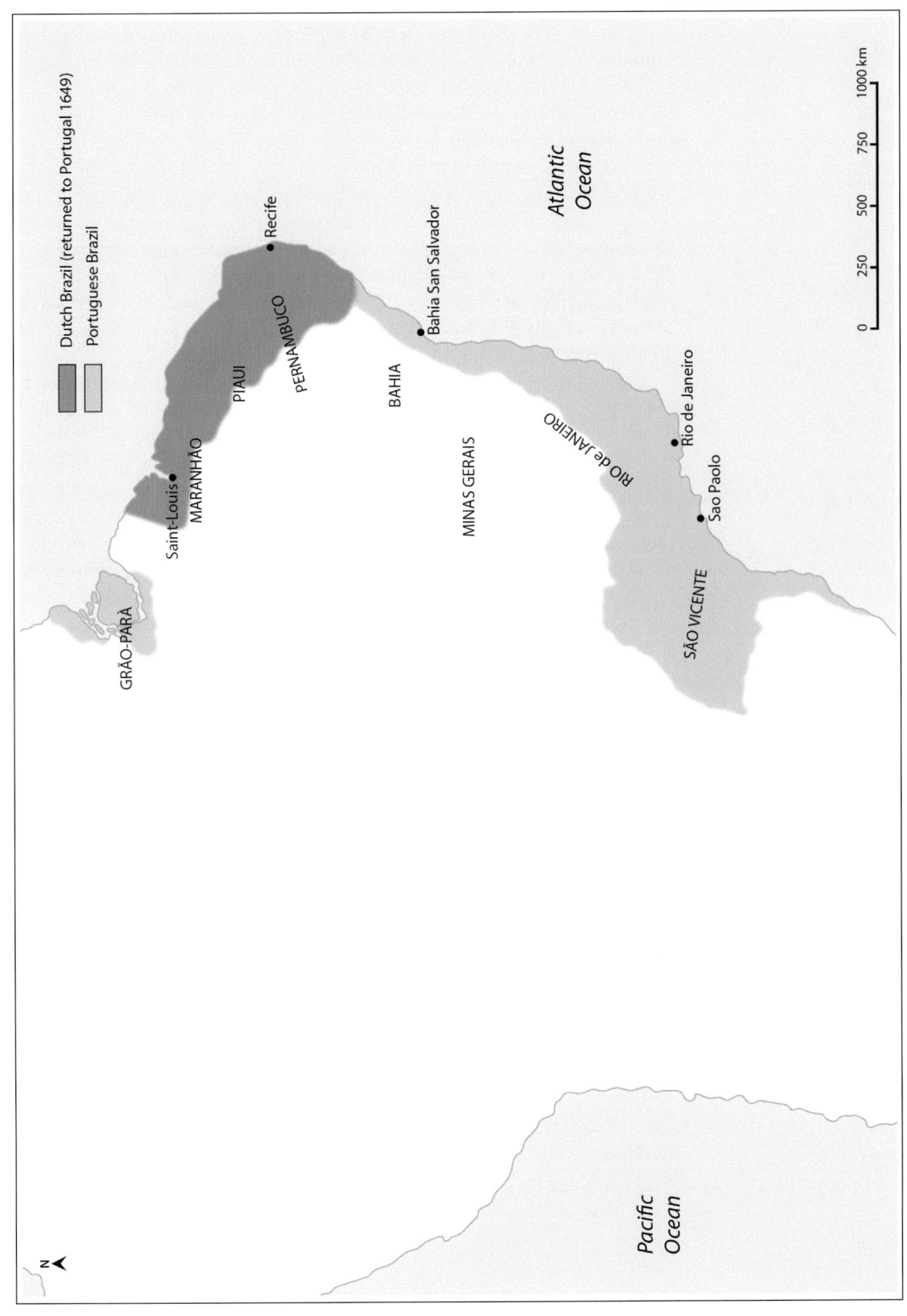

grandees. Most of them were relatively youthful *fidalgos*, many being second sons. There were also Portuguese businesspersons of substance, mostly New Christians (primarily Sephardic Jews who had converted to Christianity), who managed important interests in Spain, extending in some instances to the Habsburg court.

The Bragança government was wary of these New Christians and moved against those whom it deemed too close to the enemy. The King confiscated their property in Portugal and in the colonies where he could, but there is no evidence of any organised, broadly-based capitalist support for a return to Habsburg rule. While apparently no commoners played an active part in planning the Restoration of December 1640, several trusted leaders in Lisbon were given advance notice of what was afoot and responded with their unreserved backing.

Throughout the long years of struggle that followed, popular support for the Braganças in both towns and countryside never seriously wavered. This was of fundamental importance, since it was the third estate that provided the military recruits and the tax revenue that made the national war effort even possible. However, support to the new dynasty and political goals differed strongly between town civilians and countryside villagers. This was a direct consequence of the state's economy. Overall, three quarters of Portuguese territory was uncultivated and depended heavily on trade with foreign countries and colonies for agricultural supplies. The centre of the Portuguese economy was its sea routes. After the establishment of the overseas empire, Portugal adapted its economic structures to the new situation. Like the Dutch, the Portuguese had also created a private commercial company that held a monopoly on the export of various goods, with two naval squadrons of 18 warships which took the name of *Companhia do Brasil* and *Companhia das Índias Orientais*.

Portugal's vast colonial empire stretched from South America to China. Brazil was the largest Portuguese overseas territory, with a population that had grown rapidly in the seventeenth century, although it was concentrated mainly on the coast. The interior was still almost unexplored, and a theatre of war for the actions of the *bandeiras* who faced native resistance to colonial rule. In the 1640s, a dispute with the Dutch had slowed down Brazil's growth, but at the end of the century, the population increase returned to pre-war levels. Around 1650, about 750,000 inhabitants lived in Portuguese Brazil,[4] mostly Africans with their European masters, equal to about a fifth of the population,[5] which included 100,000–150,000 baptised mulattos and indigenous natives registered as Portuguese subjects.[6] Colonial Brazil was divided in a variable number of *capitanías*, which comprised territories with

---

4   McEvody-Jones, *Atlas of World Population History*, p.306.
5   In the mid seventeenth century, Brazil was probably home to between two and three million of natives. Evidence for such estimates is fragmentary but fair estimates, particularly considering the Brazil's size. Assuming a demographic collapse of up to 50 percent during the first hundred years after contact, that does little to change the picture. Further reading: Langfur, Hal, 'Recovering Brazil's Indigenous Pasts' in *Native Brazil. Beyond the Convert and the Cannibal, 1500–1900* (Albuquerque: University of New Mexico Press, 2014), p.9.
6   *The New Cambridge Modern History*, Vol. V – *The Ascendancy of France, 1648–1688*, p.388.

different administration and status. In the 1660s, there were 19 *capitanías*, reduced to seven in 1709.[7] The colonial capital and largest 'Portuguese city' after Lisbon, São Salvador da Bahia de Todosos Santos, was home to 8,000 Europeans for a total population of about 40,000. Further towns, like Rio de Janeiro, São Paulo and Recife, were increasing in population and size as a result of the development of the Brazilian economy, which largely depended on African slaves.

The Portuguese Empire in Africa had expanded from the enclaves of the *Costa dos Escravos* (Slaves' Coast) made up of harbours along the ocean routes, which included the settlements of Cabo Verde, Guinea, Benin and São Tomé, with a total of 25–30,000 free inhabitants. To these territories were added extensive Continental possessions located within the current African states of Mozambique and Angola, with the latter representing the largest reservoir of servile labour for the sugar cane and tobacco plantations in Brazil. In these colonies, the free population, European or otherwise, probably amounted to less than 80,000 inhabitants. The western Portuguese possessions in Africa formed a viceroyalty managed by a governor based at Luanda. The African possessions also included the fortified harbours of Tangier and Mazagão (today El Jadida), in Morocco, the only Portuguese outposts in this area after the loss of Ceuta, which was retained by Spain after 1641. The *capitão general* (captain general) resided in Tangier and at about this time it was a city of probably some 10,000 to 12,000 inhabitants, roughly the same size as a large provincial centre in Portugal, while Mazagão was home to half of this number.[8] In 1641, Lisbon also held some possessions in the Arabian Sea. Muscat, in eastern Arabia, was the main harbour for securing the trade in the area along with Matrah, while Mombasa and Malindi in east Africa supplied further safe harbours to the Portuguese merchants on the seas to the north-east of Africa.

---

7   The history of the Brazilian *capitanias* is marked by constant subordination, annexation and division. New donor captaincies were carved out of territories which were too vast and difficult to administer directly and small captaincies, nominally in private hands, but often abandoned by their holders, were annexed by larger or more successful Crown captaincies. Some complications resulted from captaincies being merged and recreated with the same name but representing altered regions. In the 1660, at least a few of the later captaincies were islands or capes of negligible size. In some cases, new captaincies were created as administrative divisions or sub-captaincies of existing ones before becoming autonomous territories. Disney, *A History of Portugal*, vol. II, p.233.
8   Disney, *A History of Portugal*, vol. II, p.233.

WARS AND SOLDIERS IN THE EARLY REIGN OF LOUIS XIV - VOLUME 5

Above: Mozambique. Facing page: Central Atlantic Africa

PORTUGAL RESTORED

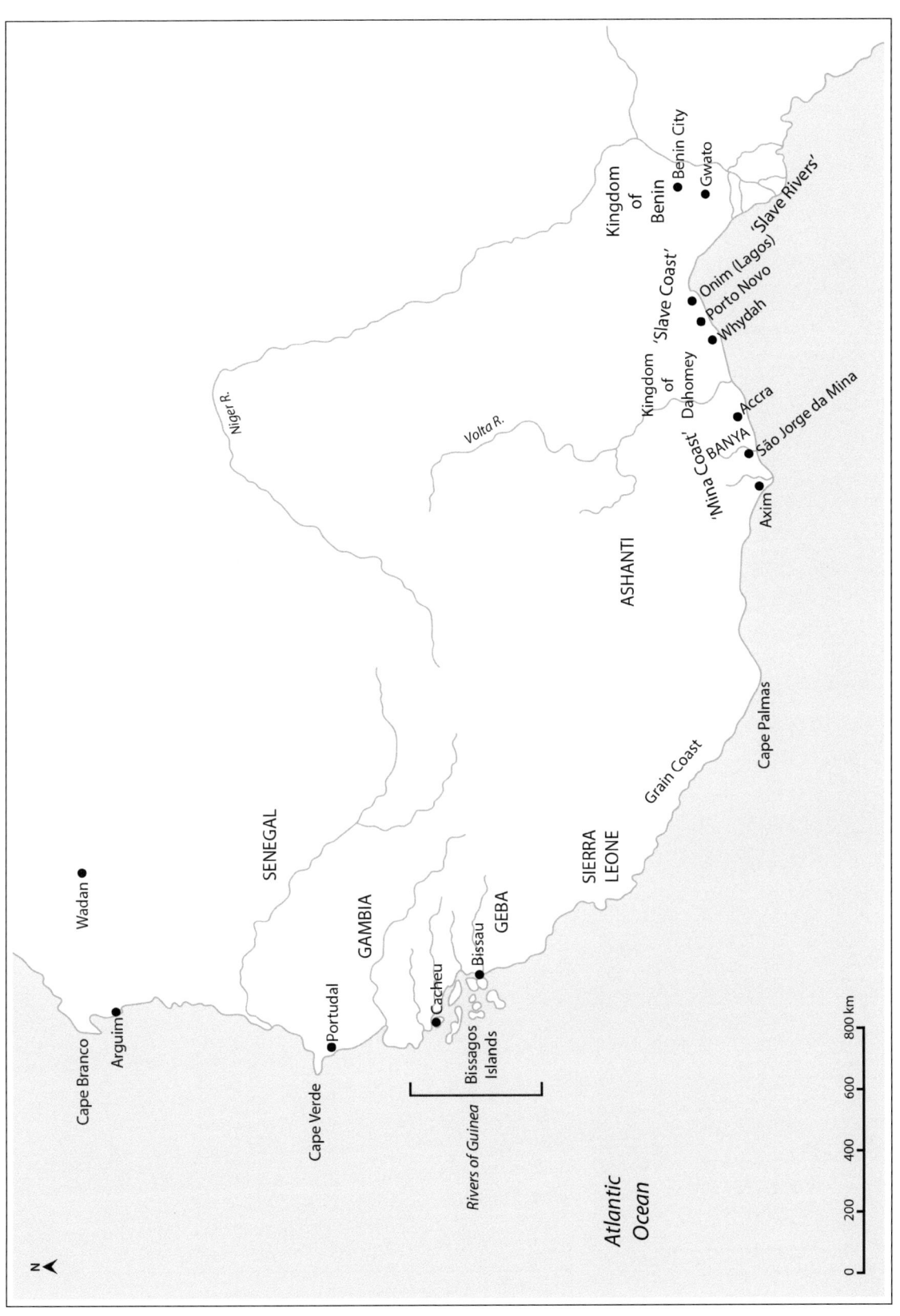

WARS AND SOLDIERS IN THE EARLY REIGN OF LOUIS XIV - VOLUME 5

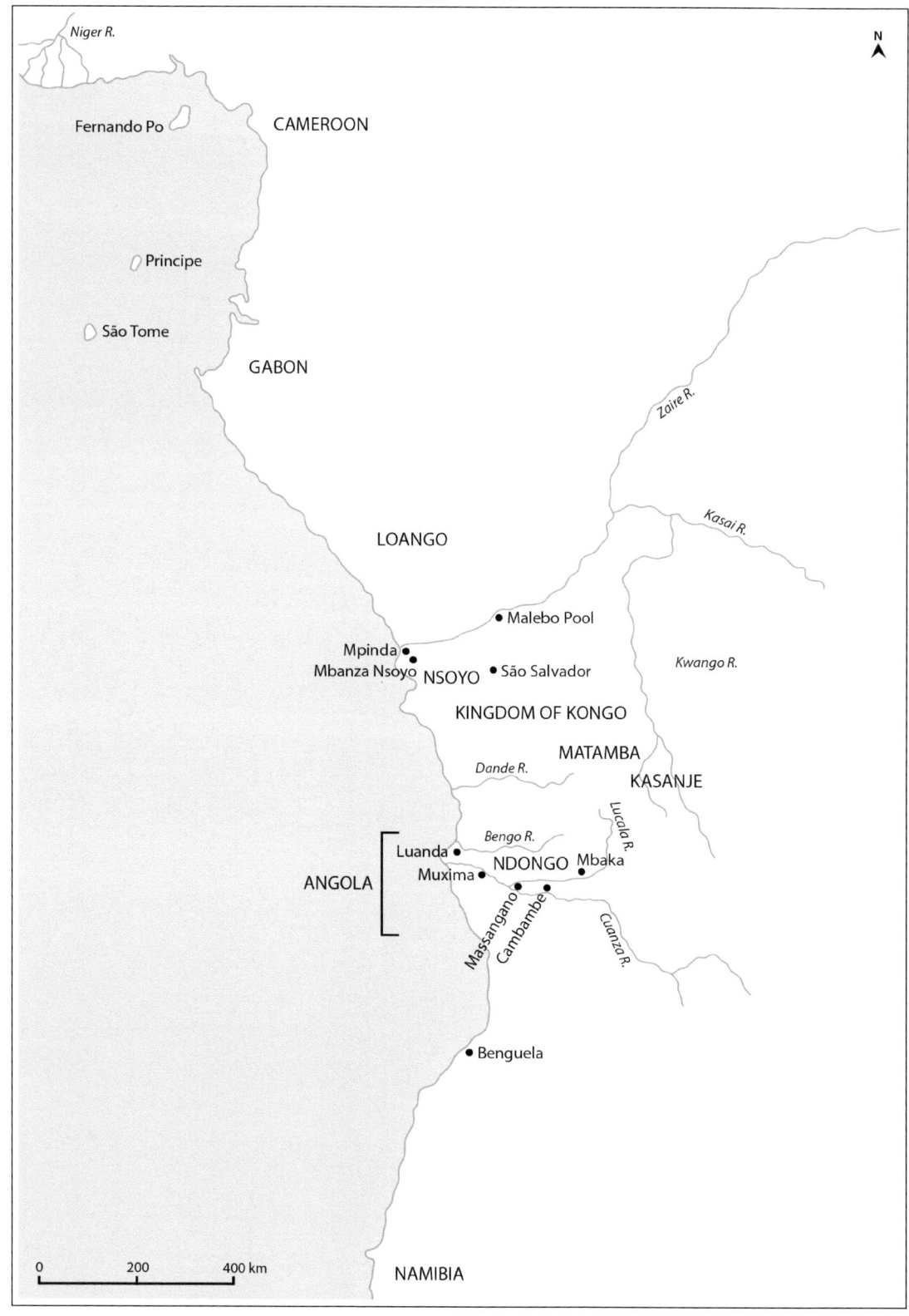

South Atlantic Africa

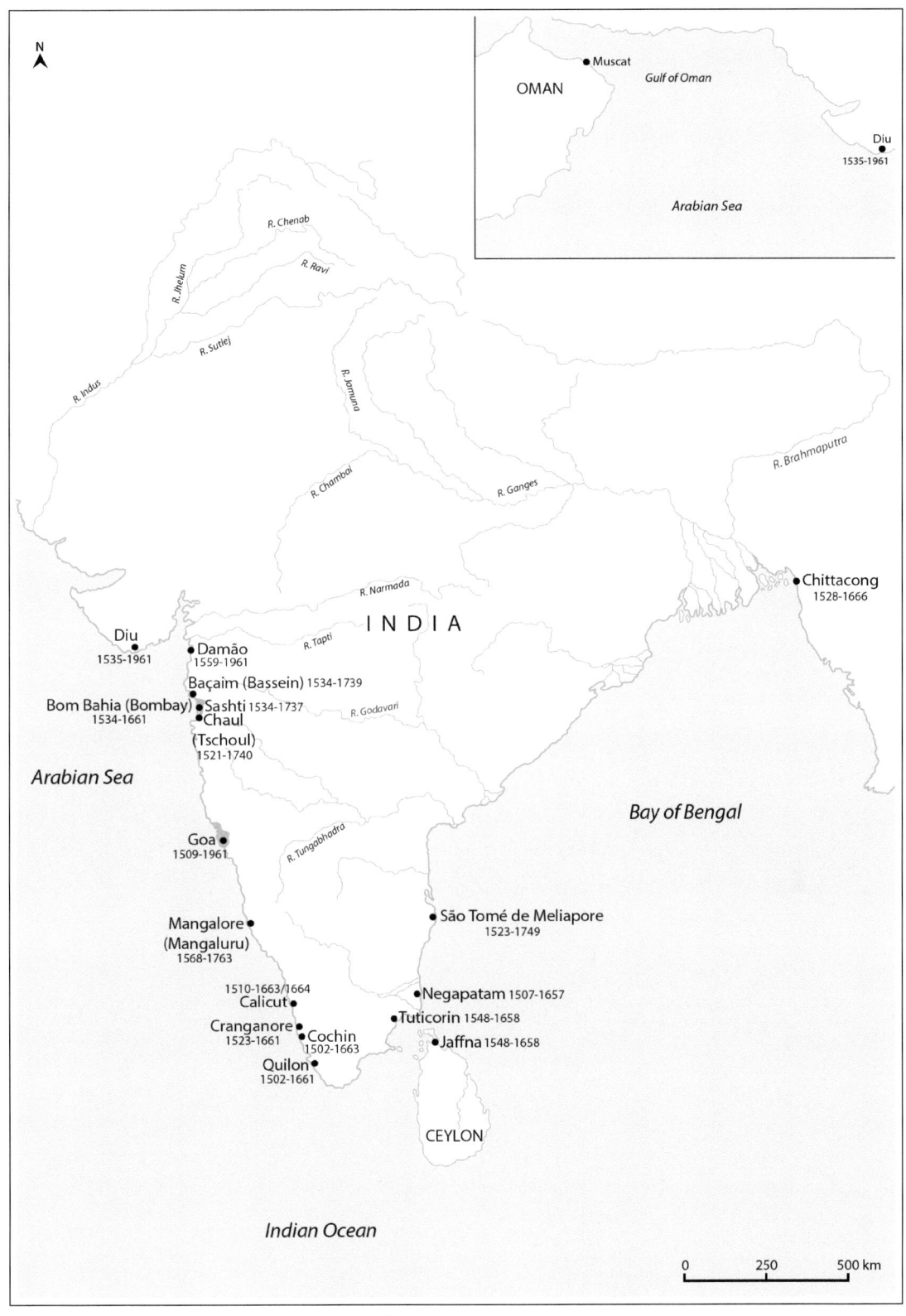

The *carreira da Índia*: Portuguese India and Muscat

WARS AND SOLDIERS IN THE EARLY REIGN OF LOUIS XIV - VOLUME 5

Portuguese Possessions in Eastern Asia

Bird's eye view of Goa, capital of Portuguese India, in a seventeenth-century print (author's archive). In the 1660s the Portuguese *Estado da Índia* formed a vice royalty with Goa as capital, from which were ruled all the territories from Diu to Chittagong. The other captaincies in Asia were East Timor with Lifau, Isla da Flores in the Sonda Sea, and Macao in China. (Cidade do Santo Nome de Deus de Macao)

The last main Portuguese colonial domain extended along the *carreira da Índia* through the Cape route and had less than three million inhabitants.[9] The axis of this empire had its centre in the sophisticated Indian city of Goa, proudly celebrated as 'the Rome of Asia', and where the governor and viceroy of the *Estado da Índia* had his residence. Across this region, Portugal also held a series of fortified harbours and enclaves stretching from Diu Island in western India to East Timor, including the *capitanías* of Daman, Bassein, Scarfty, Bombay, Chaul, Basrur, Honnavar, Mangalore, Calcutta, Cranganore, Cochin, Quillon, Tuticorin, Negapatam, Mylapore, Chittagong, Ceylon, Flores Island, Macau, Malacca and Lesser Sundra islands.

---

9   In the sixteenth century, the Portuguese seized the Sultanate of Gujarat, with Daman (1531, formally annexed in 1539), Salcete, Bombay (today Mumbai), Vasai (occupied in 1534) and Diu (acquired in 1535). These territories became the *Província do Norte de l'Estado da Índia*, with an extension of 100 km on the coast from Daman to Chaul. The province was governed by the Portuguese Viceroy residing in the fortress of Chaul. These domains formed the first colonial settlements, known as *Velhas Conquistas*. Mumbai was ceded to England in 1661 as a wedding present from the *infanta* Catarina of Bragança, Princess of Beira.

Each possession was governed by the respective captain general appointed from Lisbon. Until the eighteenth century, the Portuguese governor of Goa had authority over all Portuguese possessions in the Indian Ocean, from East Africa to Southeast Asia.[10] Therefore, the governor of Goa also dealt with the *Capitanìa General do Moçambique* which included Quelimane, Tete, Quiloa, Nova Sofala, Sena, Querimbe with the Islands of Cabo Delgado, Forte Jesus of Mombasa, and Mascate. By the mid seventeenth century, Goa and the other Portuguese possessions in India were in decline and had perhaps 50,000 inhabitants in all, of which 10,000 Europeans.[11]

In 1641, the loss of Malacca reduced the Portuguese influence in Asia, but this decline was offset by a burgeoning Macau, where a few hundred Chinese converts to Catholicism and another 6,000 non-convert Chinese lived together with 1,000 Portuguese families concentrated at *Cidade do Santo Nome de Deus de Macao*. This *capitania* had an overall population of perhaps 50,000 inhabitants including the native subjects.[12] The most remote Portuguese *capitanía*, East Timor, had just a fortified harbour manned by a Portuguese garrison, which constantly faced the Dutch presence in the other side of the Island.

The Portuguese Government

In December 1640 the only legitimate Portuguese dynasty was restored to the throne of Lisbon. This event represented the return to a state and government system that interrupted the Spanish domination that began in 1580.[13] The 60 years of inclusion of the Portuguese kingdom in the Spanish monarchy had produced substantial changes from a social, economic and political point of view. Now, the political separation from the Habsburg monarchy meant that Portugal lost its formal status as part of the Spanish economic bloc but regained its capacity to develop an independent trade policy. Moreover, the Restoration had important repercussions on relations between the Portuguese aristocracy and the two crowns. The proclamation of the new Portuguese king was in reality a coup organised and staged by a group of nobles, determined to restore what they considered to be Portugal's traditional order.[14]

---

10 This 'Imperial asset' in India and Africa lasted until 1752, when a new governorship was established for Mozambique and the eastern African domains. In the late 1600s, Portuguese South-East Africa possessed just five centres of significance: Ciudad do Mozambique, Quelimane, Sofala, Sena and Tete, all located in the central region.

11 Jonathon Riley, *The Last Ironsides. The Portuguese Expedition to Portugal, 1662–1668* (Solihull: Helion & Company, 2014), p.33: 'The low point of Portugal's fortune in the East came between 1625 and 1640, when in only one of those years were more than three ships sent to India.'

12 Disney, *A History of Portugal*, vol. II, p.392.

13 *The New Cambridge Modern History*, Vol. V – *The Ascendancy of France, 1648–1688*, p.389: 'An abundant politico-legal literature sprang up to prove the legitimacy of the Restoration, to secure recognition from foreign powers, and to establish the authority of the new regime at home.'

14 Anthony R. Disney, *A History of Portugal and the Portuguese Empire* (Cambridge, Cambridge University Press, 2009), vol. I, p.222: 'They (the Portuguese pro-Bragança nobles) had no intention of altering the constitution, still less of disturbing long established social relationships

PORTUGAL RESTORED

The Acclamation of King João IV, by Veloso Salgado (Military Museum, Lisbon). João Duke of Bragança arrived in Lisbon from Vilaviçosa on 6 December 1640. Nine days later he was formally proclaimed King of Portugal before a large gathering of nobles and dignitaries. On 28 January 1641 the Portuguese *cortes* held its opening session at which João was duly sworn in as king. This act in itself was highly significant for it involved exercising a power strictly exclusive to ruling monarchs. The successful installation of the Bragança regime emphatically did not represent a revolution but was rather the triumphant culmination of a coup d'état.

The events took many of the leading lights of the Portuguese clergy and aristocracy by surprise. On one hand, the fact that Felipe IV of Spain (and III of Portugal) had given gifts and benefits to the Portuguese nobility to gain their support to the Spanish government, meant that when news reached Madrid that don João, Duke of Bragança, had been proclaimed king of Portugal, the numerous Portuguese *fidalgos* who were at the Madrid court declared themselves willing to offer their services to the Spanish king for the reconquest of Portugal. On the other hand, the Portuguese aristocracy who instead sided in favour of the Bragança obtained a series of privileges aimed

---

based on privilege. Their principal aims were to sever the union, put a stop to Olivares' alleged innovations and restore 'customary' government under a resident Portuguese king.'

João IV, King of Portugal (1604–1656) Don João was a rather reluctant central figure in all the unfolding drama of the Portuguese Restoration. When he became king in 1640 at the age of 36, he was precipitated into an unfamiliar and dangerous world. His background was that of a country gentleman who before his elevation to the throne had never left Portugal. Indeed, he had seldom ventured from the ducal seat at Vilaviçosa. A decent and pious man, he had a fondness for music, was always cautious in his movements and remained firmly traditional in his values. (Unknown artist, Museum of Évora, Portugal)

at consolidating their support for the reborn kingdom, redefining the distribution of power. This led in due course to a redistribution of Portuguese titles and the rise to prominence of several new families. Some titles disappeared altogether or became 'Castilianised' and hence removed permanently from their former Portuguese context. One way or another, all noble opposition to the Bragança monarchy was either crushed or excised.

In January 1641, the *Cortes* met to legitimise the new king and reintroduced the ancient instruments of government that had existed before 1580. As occurred in several *Ancien Régime* monarchies, the Portuguese kings had to negotiate with this assembly. Tension between traditional devolved rule and royal centralism had been endemic in medieval Portugal giving rise to serious internal conflict. Though less violently confrontational than in the past, this dichotomy was still a basic reality of Portuguese life, where the *Cortes* opposed the King's centralist views until the next century.[15]

The Portuguese *Cortes* consisted of representatives of the three Estates who met separately: the great lords and landed nobility; the archbishops, bishops and prelates; and two deputies each from 92 large and small towns. The latter formed the *Estado dos Povos*, which had an important role in the opposition to the King's absolute rule. In turn, each province of Portugal had its own *camara*, which managed the local administration. All the deputies in the *Cortes* were elected by a meeting of the municipalities consisting of *fidalgos* (noblemen), magistrates, citizens, representatives of the guilds and the municipal judges, the latter elected by property owners.

Nobles and ecclesiastical dignitaries were often chosen as urban deputies.[16] The *Cortes* would be called if the King wanted to introduce new

---

15 Disney, *A History of Portugal*, vol. I, p.235.
16 *The New Cambridge Modern History*, Vol. V – *The Ascendancy of France, 1648-1688*, p.392: 'The machinery of State was firmly in the hands of the great nobility, the high clergy and the judges. Between the monarch and the people stood a bureaucracy well organised in the essential branches of war, justice and finance. But this structure embraced the remnants of feudalism and local rights: on the one hand, Commanders of Military Orders and those who had in their gift lands, revenues and appointments; on the other, the *camaras* (municipalities) with their judges, and elective village judges. It was, however, the landed proprietors and merchants with a certain income who made up the *camaras*, and in the large towns these were presided over by a nobleman. Elections were triennial. In the chief towns the representation of guilds was organised

taxes, change some fundamental laws, announce significant shifts in foreign policy, like the ratify of treaties with foreign states, or settle matters of royal succession, issues where the cooperation and assent of the towns was thought necessary. Changing taxation, especially requesting war subsidies, was the most frequent reason for convening the assembly. As the nobles and clergy were largely tax-exempt, setting taxation involved intensive negotiations between the royal council and the delegates at the *Cortes*. New laws could not be introduced without the approval of the *Cortes*, specially convened at Lisbon, and even the heir to the throne had to take the oath during a session of the *Cortes*. They had to decide doubtful cases of succession, and the king had to consult them in grave matters of state, vital to the national interest.

The Spanish kings reduced the importance of the *Cortes*, and during the entire period of Habsburg rule the *Cortes* had met only four times. Between 1641 and 1688, however, they met eight times, always in Lisbon, playing an important part in the reorganisation which followed the Restoration. After 1641 the political role of the *Cortes* had become far less important. As a result, Portugal prefigured an already absolute state, with a hereditary monarchy and a bureaucratic machinery, which was restored in 1640, though better organised thanks to the administrative improvements under Spanish rule. Though the role of the *Cortes* became irregular, its influence did not completely disappear, and the Estates maintained their control in several matters, the army included. Therefore, after 1641, Portugal oscillated between two forms of government: the one by the Councils and High Courts, with the King restricted to appointing their members and to a very general guidance and supervision, and the government by the King and his secretaries, with the Councils and High Courts as principal instruments in the administrative machine. After the Restoration, there was no actual ministerial government, the functions of ministers being discharged by secretaries of state, *Vedores da Fazenda* (Superintendents of Finance), and presidents of Councils and High Courts. During periods of personal rule by the monarch these functions were discharged by some favourite secretaries and councillors, and in either case an important part was played by the royal *Despacho*, those who took documents to the king for signature.

The Secretariat of State, a position dating from the sixteenth century, controlled the broad lines of domestic, colonial and foreign policy, as well as the army and navy. At the end of 1643 the King separated it from the Secretariat of *merces e expediente*, which dealt with the appointment of officials, officers and magistrates up to a certain rank, and from the *Secretariat da assinatura*, dealing with the signature of documents coming from the Councils. The Secretary of State ensured continuity in government: Pedro Vieira da Silva, for instance, held the post from 1642 to 1662. However, the head of the government was either a minister favoured by the king, or, from 1662 to 1667, the *escrivão da puridade* (confidential secretary), a post

---

in the *Casa dos Vinte e Quatro* which, subordinated to the Senate of the *camara*, was responsible for the economic administration and for the upkeep and policing of public places.'

Dom Luís de Vasconcelos e Sousa, 3rd Count of Castelo Melhor (1636–1720). Appointed as the King's secret notary in 1662, Castelo Melhor overcame the difficulties which had hitherto beset Portugal in the war against Spain, reorganising the troops and entrusting their command to competent generals. Consequently, the Portuguese Restoration War entered a victorious phase for Portugal (1663–65) and Spain began peace negotiations. Agreement proved difficult to attain and meanwhile the internal political situation in Portugal deteriorated, Castelo Melhor and his Francophile party losing ground to the Anglophile party. The King was obliged to dismiss him on 9 September 1667, in a palace coup organised by the King's wife Maria Francisca of Nemours and brother Pedro. Shortly afterwards, the King himself was also deprived of power. Castelo Melhor went into exile in Paris and then London, but in 1685 he was permitted to return to Portugal and two years later, to court. On the accession of João V in 1706 he was appointed as a councillor of state, and he continued to occupy a prominent position until his death. (Author's archive)

revived by the Count of Castelo Melhor but abolished on his banishment.[17] The Council of State, established in 1569 and continuing the old King's Council, was the supreme political organ, deciding the issues of war and peace, and making the highest civil, military and even ecclesiastical appointments. The great lords had the title of councillor even when they did not perform the duties. Among the members there were dukes, marquises, counts, archbishops and bishops, but hardly ever magistrates or other commoners.

The *Conselho da Fazenda* (Council of Finance) directed the financial, economic and mercantile administration. It was headed by the three *vedores* (Superintendents), all noblemen, representing specific interests. It consisted of three to five legally trained councillors, a Procurator Fiscal, and four secretaries. Subordinate to this council were the Court of Accounts, the *Casa da India*, the mint, civil shipyards and depots, consulates, the customs and other branches of the revenue, and finally the Brazilian Trading Company with its successor, the *Junta do Comercio do Brasil*. In 1643, the Colonial Council replaced the ancient Council of India. Under a president selected among the high nobility, which comprised six councillors (two noblemen and four lawyers), a secretary and two clerks. It was concerned with the government of all overseas possessions, excepting the administration of justice, the organisation of the merchant fleet, and colonial mercantile policy, except where Brazil was concerned. One of the most urgent tasks that awaited João IV after the 1640 coup was to contact the Portuguese overseas settlements and secure their adherence. Special couriers were therefore hurriedly dispatched to all corners of the empire, the sensational news reaching Bahia in February 1641, Goa

---

17 Luís de Vasconcelos e Sousa, 3rd Count of Castelo Melhor (1636–1720) was a Portuguese royal favourite who, as effective Governor of Portugal from 1662–1667 during the reign of Afonso VI, was responsible for the successful prosecution of the war against Spain, and the Spanish recognition of Portugal's new ruling dynasty in 1668. The King appointed Castelo Melhor his *escrivão da puridade*, a position in which the favourite was able to exercise the functions of first minister.

in September and distant Macau in May 1642. In 1643, having won the loyalty of Portugal's overseas possessions, João IV went on to create a new *Conselho Ultramarino* (overseas council) to take responsibility for administering them.

Since the war against Spain required new financial efforts, and since the *Cortes* of 1641 and 1642 maintained the control of finances, the *Junta dos Três Estados* was also established in January 1643, as a permanent organ representing nobility, clergy and towns. The *Junta* replaced the existing economic commission established in 1641 and had its residence in the Royal Palace in Lisbon. Initially the *Junta* managed the taxes accepted by the *Cortes* of the previous year, but soon, all military spending was controlled by the *Junta*, and therefore took care of every economic aspect concerning the army, and not just the collection and distribution of taxes, and therefore extended its action to all the military expenditure.

The *Junta* had the task of fixing and apportioning war taxation and of supervising the financial administration of the state. Its scope gradually broadened, taking in some sectors of commerce; but its original functions in civil matters were slowly reduced to control of the less important taxes. After 1643, senior commanders, officers, engineers and fortifications, hospitals, ammunition and supplies, commissars, supply of horses for the army and artillery and further issues passed under the direct control of this council, causing the *Junta* to quickly become an actual royal court responsible for the administration of the army, namely the main organ of consultation and administration of the monarchy in matters of war. Its creation was the result of a commitment by the Crown to the *Cortes*, equivalent to those the King had taken in connection with the recruitment of troops for the army. As a result, the increase in taxes needed to cover war expenses allowed the *Cortes* to take direct control of the army and military spending. The *Junta dos Três Estados* alongside the aforementioned Council of Treasury also supervised the activity of the *vedor general do exército*, the official in charge to control the expenditure at all the levels of the Portuguese military.

Finally, the *Conselho da Guerra* (Council of War) was soon established on 11 December 1640 and received its statute three years later. The council dealt with military affairs concerning the organisation of army and navy and

Luís de Meneses, 1st Marquis of Marialva and 3rd Count of Cantanhede (1596–1675), portrayed by Feliciano de Almeida (Collection of the Uffizi Museum, Florence). In 1667, a group of prominent nobles opposed to Castelo Melhor, including as leaders the Marquis of Marialva and the Duke of Cadaval, began to prepare for a palace coup. Probably from the start these nobles sought out and secured the support of Afonso's younger brother, Prince Pedro. They could certainly also rely on the backing of Queen Marie-Françoise and her circle, for she despised her unfortunate husband and may have already begun a relationship with Pedro. In November 1667 this increasingly confident opposition prised the hapless Afonso from Castelo Melhor's influence and procured the minister's dismissal. Cadaval and his collaborators then intensified pressure for a more comprehensive solution to Portugal's constitutional and dynastic crisis, seeking the replacement of the inadequate Afonso VI by Prince Pedro.

submitted the issues to the King for his consent. The council comprised an unspecified number of councillors, with one adviser, one *promotor de justiça* (prosecutor of justice) and one secretary. All the councillors of state had the right to attend, but the regular members were the military governors of the provinces, senior commanders, generals of artillery, the captains of the fleet, the viceroy of Brazil (when present), and two judges of the Supreme Court. It also functioned as a high court of military justice of first instance for the regular troops and an appeal court for the auxiliary troops.

This council proposed the officers appointed to the army and navy, and their confirmation, supervised fortifications, naval armaments, ammunition depots, discipline, foundries and hospitals, and was responsible for the conduct of war in strategic matters. The Portuguese territory was divided into governorships, which performed the main function of military headquarters. From north to south they were Entre-Douro-e-Minho, Trás-os-Montes, Beira, Riba-Cáo, Alentejo, Estremadura, and Algarve. Alongside the war council, further military matters were managed by the *Mesa da Consciencia e Ordens¸* in charge of the administration of the Military Orders and consulted by the King on matters of religion and conscience, including the confiscation of the property of people condemned by the Inquisition.

The other state matter, that of justice, was the responsibility of the aristocracy, which managed the *Desembargo do Pago* (the Supreme Court), sited in Lisbon and composed of one president with six *desambargadores* (judges) selected from the *fidalgos* and the clergy. Below the *Desembargo*, the Lisbon *Casa de Suplicagao e Relagão* (the Court of Appeal) dealt with all civil and criminal cases in southern and central Portugal; the cases in the north of =dom came to the *Casa do Civel e Relacão* of Porto/ There was also a military tribunal in charge of offences which were not punished by disciplinary means, but the supreme court extended its authority over the army, judging officers and soldiers for offences occurred outside their active service.[18]

Portuguese War Fronts

The Restoration of 1641 caused considerable repercussions at the international level, since the events of Portugal intersected with an extensive network of European relationships, including the trade with the colonies and foreign markets. Though after the uprising Portugal returned to being an independent state, the political and diplomatic implications connected with the new situation necessarily had to be redefined. The new monarchy had to pursue its goals moving on very dangerous ground. On the diplomatic front, Portugal's main effort was the recognition of its own political and dynastic

---

18 Fernando Dores Costa, 'Governadores das armas, mestres de campo e capitães-mores no Alentejo durante a Guerra da Restauração: inovações na administração e centrosperiféricos de poder', in *Centros Periféricos de Poderna Europa do Sul (Sécs. XII–XVIII)* (Lisbon: Publicações do Cidehus, Edições Colibri, 2013), p.209. In 1648, despite the protests, the War Council and João IV did not recognise the officers the privilege of not being tried by the Supreme Court because of their authority 'which could cause negative effects and public backbiting'.

independence, and the preservation of its overseas domains. In fact, the ability to defend the state militarily also depended on the good performance of overseas trade, which was dangerously undermined. Portugal's strategic location, and a steady demand especially in northern Europe for some of its products, help to find a solution.

Portugal possessed a long coastline along the main Atlantic shipping route from the North Sea to the Mediterranean and was therefore conveniently accessible to the seafaring nations of western Europe. Its agricultural products and salt could be readily exchanged for the woollens and other manufactured items of more industrialised countries. Portugal could also supply its trading partners with rare and exotic products from its overseas empire, while that empire itself was beginning to be recognised as a worthwhile market for European exports. However, after the Restoration the government inevitably looked to expand commercial relations with European countries outside the Iberian Peninsula along the Atlantic Ocean.[19] Portugal's Atlantic choice brought immediate benefits and marked a decisive turning point in its colonial history.

Portugal's struggle to regain its position in the community of nations was inevitably long and tortuous. Despite the widespread popularity of the new regime its situation in the early months after the coup was highly precarious. In August 1641 a noble conspiracy to assassinate João IV and return the Habsburgs to power was uncovered in Lisbon. Its instigators were probably in contact with other Portuguese nobles in Spain, although the extent of Madrid's direct involvement is uncertain.[20] The 1641 conspiracy shows clearly that the elite, particularly the greater nobility and higher clergy, remained for some time quite divided over the Restoration. The Bragança king was acclaimed with enthusiasm in the overseas domains, and the smooth transition of loyalties was much facilitated by strong support from the Jesuits and the absence of Spanish troops. Only in Tangier, Mazagão and Ceuta, possessions geographically close to Spain, and heavily dependent on Spanish supplies, was the issue seriously in doubt. But in the end Ceuta alone stayed with Felipe IV.

The successful outcome of the Restoration, and its widespread acceptance throughout the Portuguese empire, did not alter the fact that the country was woefully ill-equipped in 1641 to conduct the war of independence that was now inevitable. In the years between 1640 and 1668, the Portuguese monarchy had to face problems on whose solution the economic stability of the country depended. Portugal was, in fact, engaged on several fronts with more than one enemy. The strategic scenario certainly could appear paradoxical to contemporary readers, and probably seemed no less puzzling in the 1640s as well. Before beginning its war with Spain, Portugal was

---

19 The strategic scenario of Europe modified the pattern of Portugal's trade with its own empire, as the focus shifted more and more from maritime Asia to Brazil and Atlantic Africa. See Disney, *A History of Portugal*, vol. I, p.243.
20 The prime mover appears to have been the archbishop of Braga. However, some of the greatest nobles in Portugal were also involved, including the Marquis of Vila Real and his son the Duke of Caminha. Both these grandees were arrested, condemned and then publicly beheaded. Another personage implicated was the New Christian merchant Pedro de Baeça, who had lent heavily to the Habsburgs. He too was arrested, tried and hanged.

Francisco de Moura y Melo y Cortereal, 3rd Marquis of Castel Rodrigo (1610–1675) Viceroy of Sardinia and Catalonia until 1663, and Governor of the Spanish Low Countries in 1664–68. He was another of the Portuguese noble families happily inserted into Spain before the restoration of the Braganças, and together with many other aristocrats he was exiled from Portugal. Among the Portuguese who served in the army of the Monarchy with the rank of general after 1641 there were also Don Francisco de Melo, Gregorio de Brito, Simon Mascarenhas, Felipe da Silva, Pablo de Parada and Luís da Silva de Vago. (Author's archive)

engaged in the overseas domains against the Dutch Republic, which in turn was the arch-enemy of *Los Austrias*.

This strange triple war continued until 1648, when finally, Spain recognised the independence of the United Provinces. There was thus a mutually profitable truce in Europe, but this did not apply overseas. Moreover, the Peace of Westphalia left Portugal isolated and engaged by sea against the Dutch assaults in Brazil and Africa, and on land against the attempts of reconquest by the Spaniards. In the East, despite the accord of 1635 between the English East India Company and Portugal, the Dutch gained the advantage; the Cape route ceased to be the axis of the Portuguese trade.[21] In the Atlantic, however, the Portuguese won the upper hand. Despite the loss of São Jorge da Mina in Benin, Angola and São Tomé, taken by the Dutch in 1641, they were regained in 1648 with a successful Portuguese-Brazilian expedition. This event decided the fate of Brazil since the slave trade returned into Portuguese hands.[22]

In South America, the Dutch had to evacuate the Maranhão province in 1644, after a revolt by Portuguese and natives which lasted 18 months, and they never managed to control Bahia. In fact, their domination of the north-east, conquered in 1630–1635, lasted for only 10 years. Pernambuco rebelled in 1645, and the Dutch were defeated at Tabocas by João Fernandes Vieira. Guerrilla warfare began and some help came from Portugal. In March 1648, the Portuguese under Vieira and André Vidal de Negreiros won the first Battle of Guararapes, and the reinforcements brought by Francisco Barreto secured a second victory in February 1649. Since the

---

21 Although Portuguese trade in Asia was severely threatened by the more competitive Dutch East India Company, the large Portuguese families kept their business with the colonies going while still making large profits. Among these, the Viceroy of the Portuguese Indies, Luís de Mendonça Furtado and Albuquerque, amassed a fortune in eight years thanks to the commercial revenues from China and Mozambique. See *The New Cambridge Modern History*, Vol. V – T*he Ascendancy of France, 1648–1688*, pp.389–390.

22 The Restoration War, even though relations between Spanish America and Brazil and the rest of the Portuguese overseas dominions were not completely interrupted, seriously damaged trade. Trade relations remained alive between Brazil and the Spanish viceroyalty of Peru even after 1641, especially with regard to the import of African slaves, managed by the Portuguese *asientistas*, but after the loss of São Tomé and other territories in Africa conquered by the Dutch, this traffic was considerably reduced and only slowly resumed after 1668 and peace with the Spanish Habsburgs. In particular, Portugal continued, though with more difficulty than before, to enjoy reasonable access to Spanish American silver. See in Disney, *A History of Portugal*, vol. I, p.243.

Painting by an unknown artist illustrating the Second Battle of Guararapes (National Historical Museum, Rio de Janeiro). The two battles of Guararapes were fought between the Dutch and the Portuguese in the province of Pernambuco. The first confrontation occurred on 18 and 19 April 1648, end the second and decisive followed on 18 February 1649. The Portuguese deployed a small army with few regular soldiers, the main force being formed by local militia. Though the Dutch West India Company fielded a larger, better-equipped force, they suffered shortage of supplies and poor discipline, as most of their army was made up of mercenaries from Europe. The Dutch commanders were also unused to fighting the elusive Portuguese, who took advantage of their knowledge of the terrain. The Portuguese victory marked the end of the Dutch presence in Brazil. The victorious commander, Francisco Barreto de Meneses, earned the epithet of *Restaurador de Pernambuco*. Note in the painting the Portuguese troops organised in ethnic corps including native soldiers and Africans with firearms, swords and bucklers.

creation of the Brazilian Trading Company, merchant ships enjoyed safe passage between Portugal and Brazil. In January 1654 the Dutch forces in Brazil capitulated.[23]

Guinea and Angola had formed the main trade link between Europe and South America, bringing Portugal considerable gains, but although Lisbon still controlled those possessions, after 1641 the Dutch pressure was eroding Portuguese rule in Benin and Cabo Verde. In the same year, the Dutch launched new offensives in the Atlantic and the Indian Ocean, which concluded with the occupation of Luanda in Angola, which was the key Portuguese base for the slave trade, and therefore for the survival of Brazilian plantations. Portugal also lost several ports and possessions in Asia. In 1641, the Portuguese forces in Malacca were finally defeated by the Dutch. This domain had constituted the centre of the Portuguese trade with China.

---

23 The Dutch defeat in Brazil has been investigated by scholars from over the world. The Anglo-Dutch War of 1652–1654 certainly hampered the Dutch in South America. Furthermore, the Dutch had a high proportion of northern European mercenaries, who suffered greatly from the Brazilian climate. Finally, the Portuguese took advantage of the spontaneous and fierce resistance of settlers and natives to the Dutch domination.

All these losses inflicted a severe blow to the Portuguese economy, but despite the involvement in the war against Spain, Angola was reacquired in 1648. The decisive, and epic assault seizing the colony came from Brazil thanks to the Captain of Rio de Janeiro, Salvador Correia de Sá, who reached Luanda with Portuguese and native troops, besieged the town and regained it for Portugal exactly seven years after its loss.[24] However, the colonial war against the United Provinces did not finish, forcing Portugal to divert more resources for defending its overseas empire. In 1641, a ten-year truce had been signed and came into force in Europe immediately, but this was not proclaimed in Brazil until mid 1642, and in Asia the truce took effect only in 1644. However, though peace with the Portuguese suited the Dutch Republic well enough in Europe, the Dutch East and West India Companies both preferred to prolong hostilities in order to maximise their gains. As a result, the truce was often broken. The Portuguese-Dutch hostilities were still continuing as a consequence of both India companies' expansionism, but the war had begun as a consequence of the United Provinces' struggle to break away from Spain, and a now independent Portugal had little reason to continue it. In 1652–1654 the ill-defended Portuguese fortresses at Basrur, Mangalore and Honnavar on the Kanara coast were all seized by the *nayaks* of Ikkeri, with Dutch backing. Meanwhile, the sultan of Bijapur briefly invaded the Goa territories and held the capital of Portuguese India under threat until 1655.[25]

Under these circumstances, and given the struggle against Spain in Europe, it is hardly surprising that the Portuguese court, including the King himself, believed Portugal had little hope of forcing the Dutch out of Brazil, and still less of expelling them from the possessions in Africa and Asia. In 1652, war had broken out between the United Provinces and England, forcing the Dutch to concentrate their fleet in the North Atlantic. Nonetheless, in order to maintain peace with the Dutch, João IV had been prepared if necessary to give up Pernambuco and even contemplated abandoning Brazil altogether. Instead, the Dutch garrison in Recife surrendered on 26 January 1654, and the Dutch West India Company were expelled from Brazil by the end of the year.

These victories greatly exceeded all expectations, but the almost unexpected success did not put an end to the colonial emergency. The

---

24 Luanda was defended by 1,200 Dutch troops. When a Dutch force of 300 soldiers returned from the interior to help their garrison of Luanda, they also surrendered to the Brazilian-Portuguese, but their allied warriors of Queen Ndjinga engaged the expeditionary force of Salvador de Sá. After a series of skirmishes, the Africans were defeated as well. Then the captain sent a force to Benguela where the Dutch garrison surrendered. Salvador Correia de Sá also sent a fleet that recaptured the archipelago of São Tomé e Príncipe from the Dutch. See also in Lourenço, Paula, *Battles of Portuguese History – Defence of the Overseas* – Volume X (2006).

25 In this period, the Portuguese domains in India were left adrift, and without firm leadership or effective input from the homeland and were given over to the hands of men unwilling to make the sacrifices necessary to uphold the empire. Crown control was only restored to Goa in late 1655, when the Viceroy Count of Sarzedas arrived from Lisbon. Sarzedas, who at one point wrote in his diary that every single fortress in his viceroyalty urgently needed help, faced an all but impossible task. Further reading: de A.T. Matos and L.F.R. Thomaz (eds) 'A carreira da Índia e as rotas dos estreitos', in *Actas do VIII seminário internacional de história indo-portuguesa. Angra do Heroísmo* (1998), p.27.

The complex curtain walls that protected Muscat on both its seaward and landward sides, in the painting of António Bocarro. These impressive fortifications demonstrate the great lengths to which Portugal went to defend its presence east of the Cape of Good Hope. In this area the Portuguese also held further minor forts at Matara and Curiate. Through the loss of Muscat in 1650, the Portuguese were deprived of their major stronghold in the Persian Gulf region. (Author's archive)

struggle continued in Asia, where between 1656 and 1658 the Dutch in turn seized Negapatam and Tuticorin in India and completed the conquest of Ceylon seizing the fortress of Jaffna, the last Portuguese possession on the island and another important axis for trade with eastern Asia. This was the last major campaign of the Portuguese-Dutch colonial war since a new truce was signed in 1658. But it was not until 1661 that the Dutch agreed to give up all their Brazilian claims, in return for a massive Portuguese indemnity of four million *cruzados*, a request to which Portugal agreed signing the Treaty of the Hague on 6 August 1661.[26] There followed much difficult haggling before a peace applying to all war theatres was signed in 1663. Even then, disagreements over implementation dragged on for several years, and the Dutch insisted on retaining the Portuguese possessions in Kerala and Kanara, which they had seized after a further agreement had been signed in 1663.[27] In 1665, the latent state of war with the United Provinces of the Netherlands forced the Brazilian governor to intervene again in Angola, in order to secure the domain from the Dutch. Moreover, additional threats also came from the Indian sultanates, which conquered the Portuguese harbours of Calcutta in 1664, and Chittagong in 1666.

A further source of danger came from the emerging Arab Omani naval power in the Persian Gulf. In 1648, the Omanis sailed to seize Mombasa, Portugal's main possession on the Swahili coast, and two years later assaulted Muscat, the principal Portuguese base in the South Arabia region. Neither

---

26 Disney, *A History of Portugal*, vol. II, p.230.
27 These possessions included the harbours of Cochin, Quillon and Cranganore.

place was given up lightly. Muscat was captured by the Omanis only on the fourth attempt, having previously been invested in 1640, 1643 and 1648. Mombasa survived a further siege in 1661 but remained constantly under threat from Oman.[28]

The loss of key places in Africa and Asia forced the new ruling house to define a survival strategy. Furthermore, Portugal was confronted not only with a daunting military challenge, but with formidable diplomatic obstacles. Spain vigorously opposed recognition of the Braganças in every European court. Portugal, which had not possessed any independent foreign policy for over half a century, began the war against Spain with few experienced diplomats. The envoys were required urgently not only to seek recognition, but also to secure desperately needed foreign assistance. After 1641, in every diplomatic negotiation, a strategy oriented to achieve foreign support in the national interest was carried out. João was particularly hopeful of succour from France.

In the years immediately preceding the coup, French agents had visited Portugal, encouraged revolt and promised backing. France's subsequent recognition of the Bragança rule, and its support for the Catalan rebels, which helped tie down Castilian forces away from Portugal's border, were of great assistance. In 1648, the Peace of Westphalia redesigned the international political scenario, leaving Portugal needing to seek allies against Spain both to be able to safeguard its independence and to avoid being isolated in the power games of the European states. It was therefore essential for the Portuguese to maintain market profitability at a high level in an attempt to attract new alliances with commercial guarantees and privileges. João IV tried to strengthen the alliance with France from which he obtained military support, but when he proposed a formal Franco-Portuguese alliance, the French, unwilling to be too committed against Spain, fudged the issue, and a somewhat ambiguous relationship between the two kingdoms persisted for years. The second natural ally of Portugal was England. London soon recognised the new Portuguese government in 1641 and offered naval aid to drive the Dutch out of Portuguese domains in exchange for trade privileges guaranteeing free trade in Portuguese ports and possessions. On the other hand, relations with Rome and the United Provinces of the Netherlands were more difficult, despite the truce signed with these latter on 12 June 1641, which had given new impetus to Atlantic trade.

In 1656, shortly before his death on 5 November, João made a desperate bid to secure a French alliance. He offered the hand of his daughter Catarina, along with a dowry of one million *cruzados* plus either Tangier or Mazagão in Africa, to the young Louis XIV. But the offer was not accepted. After the death of João IV, the regency passed to his wife, Queen Luísa de Gusmão, who continued her husband's important diplomatic campaign to strengthen the alliances, especially with the Louis XIV, always under Cardinal Mazarin's guiding hand. The skilled Portuguese diplomat, João da Costa, Count de

---

28 In 1696, after a prolonged and desperate resistance, Mombasa surrendered. This loss ended any pretence of Portuguese hegemony along the northern East African coast.

Soure, was sent to Paris to begin negotiations with a free trade offer with the colonies and money to fuel his action. The proposal, however, was rejected again by Mazarin.

Three years later, the Peace of the Pyrenees sanctioned the end of hostilities between Spain and France. The treaty caused strong indignation in Portugal and was considered like a betrayal of the pro-French policy warmly supported by the Queen. One consequence of the treaty of the Pyrenees was to force the Portuguese regency to rely more on its other ally, England. The failure to include Portugal in the 1659 treaty greatly worried a faction of the *fidalgos* closest to the court who feared of being isolated from Europe. In 1660, Portuguese agents gained authorisation from the Cromwellian Protectorate to buy arms and horses and recruit up to 12,000 men in England.[29] Shortly afterwards Charles II was restored, England was again a monarchy and its relations with Portugal grew warmer.

Just a few weeks before her exile the Queen Regent proposed the marriage of her daughter Catarina with Charles II. Shortly after Afonso VI's coming of age, Luís de Vasconcelos e Sousa, 3rd Count of Castelo Melhor, saw an opportunity to gain power at court by befriending the mentally deficient king. He managed to convince Afonso that his mother was plotting to steal his throne and exile him from Portugal. As a result, the King asserted his right to rule and dispatched his mother to a convent. Then Afonso appointed Castelo Melhor, his *escrivão da puridade*, a position in which Vasconcelos was able to exercise the functions of first minister, and because of the weakness of the King, he became the virtual dictator of Portugal. The negotiations with London were carried out by Francisco de Melo and Torres, 1st Count de Ponte and Marquis of Sande, considered one of the most brilliant diplomats of Portugal. It was precisely through the treaties with England of 1654 and 1661, and with the royal marriage between Catarina and Charles, celebrated on 31 May 1662, that Portugal broke its isolation. This wedding brought to England the possession of Bombay in India and also the poisoned chalice that was Tangier in North Africa. Moreover, the marriage to a Protestant

Charles II Stuart and Catherine (Catarina) of Bragança in a print celebrating the Royal Wedding in 1662. Portugal's bridal diplomacy favoured the international recognition of the Bragança as legitimate kings. Shortly after the wedding of Charles II and Catherine, Portuguese diplomacy secured the alliance with France with the union of Afonso VI and Marie-Françoise de Savoye-Nemours in 1666. When the coup deposed Afonso VI in 1668, Marie-Françoise could not have been left in limbo, while sending her back to France would have strained relations with Portugal's major ally and would require the refunding of her dowry. The council of state and the *cortes* were acutely aware of the urgent need for an heir, and the solution arrived from the Queen and Afonso's brother, Pedro, when in 1668 Marie-Françoise gave birth to a daughter, Isabel Luísa Josefa. This young princess was sworn in as heir presumptive in 1674, but only after a conspiracy to kill Pedro and Marie-Françoise and restore Afonso VI had been crushed the previous year. After this incident, Afonso was brought back from exile in the Azores and confined in the palace at Sintra until his death. (Author's archive)

---

29 John Lynch, *Spain under the Habsburgs*, vol. II (Oxford: Blackwell, 1969), p.156.

Afonso VI (1643–1683) in a portrait dated to early 1660. When João IV died in 1656, the future of the House of Bragança was still far from assured. João's promising eldest son, Dom Teodosio, had died three years before, so the late king was succeeded by his far less suitable second son, Afonso VI. The Prince was both physically and mentally handicapped, probably as a consequence of meningitis contracted in infancy, which seems to have left him a hemiplegic. At the time of his accession he was only 13 years old – and in accordance with his father's wishes Luísa de Guzmán, the Queen Mother, was made regent. She maintained the key functions and policies of the previous administration and held firm to the ongoing struggle for Portuguese independence, notwithstanding her own Spanish origins. (Author's archive)

monarch was deeply unpopular among the Portuguese aristocrats who favoured an alliance with France. From this period, an Anglophile party and a Francophile party developed at the Portuguese court.

However, the alliance with France was not over. Substantial military aid continued to be delivered to Portugal from France to face the Spanish offensives after 1659. The link between Lisbon and Paris was strengthened in November 1665, when Louis XIV proposed the marriage of Prince Dom Afonso with the princess Maria Francesca of Savoy, Duchess of Nemours and Aumale. The future queen arrived in Lisbon on 2 August 1666 followed by further French military aid. Habsburg hopes of regaining Portugal rapidly faded at Montes Claros and the death of Felipe IV not long afterwards removed a major obstacle to reconciliation. With England mediating and France now agreeing that the time to end hostilities had arrived, the details of a comprehensive treaty were at last thrashed out. This was signed at Lisbon on 13 February 1668, Spain recognising Portugal's independence and the two old antagonists affirming mutual respect and friendship.

The turbulent years that followed did not break the link between Paris and Lisbon. After Afonso VI was deposed and his marriage to the French princess annulled, a regency assumed the government in the name of Afonso's younger brother, the infant Dom Pedro, who became king in 1683. Despite her desire to return to her homeland, Maria Francesca agreed to marry Dom Pedro on 2 April 1668, when the peace treaty with Spain had already been signed. After the secret French-Portuguese treaty of 1667, the alliance with France was strengthened in the 1670s, always with an anti-Spanish perspective.

From this moment on, Portugal had to deal with an economy that was going through structural difficulties due to the international situation linked to trade with the colonies. However, from the 1670s, Portuguese status among the European states, and with it the future of the Bragança dynasty, became steadily more secure. This happy turn of events placed the continuity of the monarchy beyond reasonable doubt and was in stark contrast to the bleak situation in neighbouring Castile, where the once mighty Habsburgs were now represented by only the childless and feeble Carlos II.

The last two decades of Pedro's reign were untroubled by any major political crises. In its external relations, Portugal continued to maintain a policy of studied neutrality, carefully avoiding involvement in international disputes, but the signing of the secret treaty of 1667 with France marked Portuguese policy in the last decades of the seventeenth century. The bilateral relations with Spain were constantly characterised by mutual suspicion. Despite the idea of involving Portugal in an 'Iberian League' sketched out with little conviction by Madrid in the aftermath of the Lisbon peace, the reports from the ambassadors, their letters and the issues discussed in Madrid and Lisbon give a good example of the mutual distrust.[30]

During this period, both governments faced internal tensions that did not facilitate political detente. The strategic situation and the possible alliance between Lisbon, London and Paris benefited French interests, since any idea of attack or instability on the border between the two peninsular states would have diverted military resources from an increasingly weakened Spain, and therefore increasing the prospects of a French victory in Flanders, Italy or Catalonia. In turn, England would benefit from it, turning to the offensive against the Spanish and Dutch colonies in America and Africa. Madrid's concerns were understandable, especially after the spring of 1672, when the Spanish ambassador in Lisbon had uncovered the 34 points of the secret treaty signed in 1667. Louis XIV promised Portugal full assistance in case of a new war against the Spaniards and was trying to draw Lisbon into a grand anti-Dutch and Spanish alliance, offering as inducement the enticing possibility of recovering some of the *Estado da Índia*'s many losses.

In this regard, the Louis XIV offered a squadron of six men-of-war to support the Portuguese attempts to recover the colonial possessions seized by the Dutch.[31] In early 1673, the Portuguese court discussed with little interest strategies and geopolitical options proposed by Louis' diplomatic efforts. The negotiations to involve Portugal in a new war against Spain and the Dutch Republic continued even after the start of hostilities, with France and England allied against the United Provinces. However, the unwillingness of Prince Dom Pedro to compromise the peace signed in 1668 made Louis XIV's plans for Portugal a non-starter. New tensions emerged when the deposed Afonso IV sought support for his cause in Spain.[32] At the

---

30 Rodríguez Hernández, Antonio José, 'Miedos de Guerra y Ecos de Frontera: la posición de España ante una alianza franco-lusa durante la Guerra de Holanda (1672–1679)', in *Historia Moderna*, Serie IV, vol. 25 (2012), p.118.

31 *Ibid.*, p.119: 'The incoming struggle was the one against the Dutch Republic, and therefore France wanted the unconditional support of Portugal, and this would have helped to cause a rift between the two states, as the United Provinces and Spain were two 'inseparable' allies, as it was written in the ninth point of the 1667 secret treaty.'

32 In Lisbon, the internal turmoil amplified by the controversial and general forgiveness of the converts led to the birth of an opposition movement in favour of the ousted Afonso IV. In September 1673, the conspiracy that attempted to assassinate Prince Pedro was discovered, and some of the people involved confessed that the Spanish ambassador in Lisbon could also be involved. But despite the existence of some relationship between the diplomat and the conspirators, it does not seem that he was really involved and with this event and Spanish involvement turned out to be non-existent. See in Disney, *A History of Portugal*, vol. I, pp.232–233.

court in Madrid the idea that France continued to interfere with Portuguese politics was still being discussed. At the beginning of October 1673, many thought that France would benefit the most from the conspiracy, giving the Portuguese a good excuse for a new conflict.[33] Indeed, documents captured by Spanish spies and informants reported that Portuguese representatives in Paris ignored the French suggestions. Meanwhile, French agents spread the news that the 'Castilians had violated the peace with the perfidy of the conspiracy orchestrated in Lisbon against Prince Dom Pedro'.

However, in 1674, signs of the poor progress of the Franco-Portuguese alliance were also known in Madrid, and the onset of a crisis in relations between Paris and London made the formation of the triple anti-Spanish league less and less difficult. Nonetheless, tensions and suspicion between Portugal and Spain did not finish and involved the diplomats of both in a game of intelligence gathering to get to understand the development of events and highlight the slightest signs of a resumption of hostilities.[34] A further threat occurred in 1675, but before the end of the year, the relative tranquillity came to an end. Fears of a resurgence of conspiracy ideas against Pedro II, in which Spain might be involved, combined with news concerning the strengthening of the Portuguese army and the increase of the navy. This last fact had not gone unnoticed by the Dutch, who tried to persuade Prince Pedro to explain the reason for such unusual preparations for war. The Portuguese replied that the only reason was to preside over the border fortresses so that they could maintain their strength, while the Portuguese navy prepared to fight against the Muslims in the Arabian Sea.

Effectively, the colonial naval situation worried Lisbon, especially in the Indies, and showed a huge distrust towards the Dutch and their designs in Asia. These uncertainties continued for a few more weeks. The sight of a Portuguese squadron sailing through the Straits of Gibraltar caused panic among the local Spanish authorities, fearing that they might even be on the way to besiege Ceuta, or that its destination was to join the French in the Mediterranean.[35] However, the Portuguese fleet headed towards the Muslim bases in North Africa and even for the time being the peace was not broken. The state of alarm did not end in the following months, as the restoration works in some Portuguese border fortresses were interpreted by Madrid as a sign of the impending war. In the following months, every act carried out across the border continued to be carefully examined. Therefore, the new recruitment drives in Extremadura

---

33 Rodríguez Hernández, *Miedos de Guerra y Ecos de Frontera*, p.125: 'The Duke of Albuquerque feared the rupture between the two countries, which would no doubt be supported and paid for by France. There were also alarming rumours that in just eight days the French Navy could land a detachment of 5,000 or 6,000 soldiers in Lisbon to attack Spain along with the Portuguese.'

34 In the context of the fight between spies, the Spaniards made use of the information collected in Lisbon by the Italian abbot Giovanni Domenico di Masserati, sent as a representative of the King of Spain in Portugal, who collected a large amount of very detailed information about the Portuguese policy worthy of a secret agent of great talent.

35 Rodríguez Hernández, *Miedos de Guerra y Ecos de Frontera*, p.126: 'The fleet's destination did not become known until it arrived off Alicante, because the Portuguese commanders had received the order to read the plans at that time. Furthermore, to confuse the Moroccans, Prince Pedro ordered those ships to use the French flag when crossing the Strait of Gibraltar.'

and Galicia for the Spanish army were seen as a threat in Lisbon until the final destination was revealed. However, nothing happened and although in May 1677, rumours about an imminent war against Spain were circulating in Lisbon, the shaky peace was not interrupted.[36]

This left the door open to Spanish acceptance of a Portuguese mediation for a truce with France, but the military mobilisation ordered by Lisbon raised numerous doubts and old fears, such as the possibility that new Portuguese claims would be introduced based on some points of the 1668 Peace Treaty, such as the restitution of Ceuta in North Africa, a fortress that had already sparked bilateral tensions during the years of peace.[37] In fact, the Portuguese gave an ultimatum, stating that if by 15 June they did not obtain a positive response regarding the peace mediation process, they would considered this answer enough, leaving open the option for beginning action against Spain. It does not appear that this was a mere diplomatic boldness, as it had its echoes on the border.

In June, very disturbing news reached Madrid from Galicia, indicating that in Villanova de Cerveira there were the Portuguese infantry officers who publicly said that if Lisbon's request was not granted, they would cross the Spanish border. Faced with this Portuguese threat, Spanish acceptance of the mediation was not long in coming, even if the Portuguese justification for the ultimatum did not seem too harsh. Effectively, Madrid could object that Portugal had not communicated its mediation plan to the allies. In fact, and belatedly, the mediation was communicated to the Austrian emperor indirectly, since Portuguese diplomats had acted in an uncoordinated manner and above all, there were none of Lisbon's diplomats in the courts of Central Europe, as was also the case with most of the states allied with Spain such as Denmark and German states. Imperial acceptance was achieved through Papal mediation, while the belated approval of some German princes was formulated through the governor of the Spanish Low Countries.

France tried new means to induce Portugal to go to war against Spain, but by the spring of 1678, peace negotiations were continuing, restricting French diplomatic action in Lisbon. The new situation and the newfound calm allowed for Spanish-Portuguese military collaboration for first time in the face of a common enemy, the Muslims of North Africa. Already, at the end of June 1677, and after the conclusive acceptance of the Portuguese mediation, there was a formal request from Spain for a collaboration to help the city of Oran, which had been under siege by the Muslims since 1676. The city was in dire need of grain, supplies and soldiers. The emergency was so serious that collaboration was also requested from Genoa and the United

---

36 *Ibid.*, p.139.
37 *Ibid.*, p.140: 'In mid–1677, the secret treaty established between Portugal and France ten years earlier would have expired, and even if never fulfilled it was still valid. It is possible that the Portuguese government, aware of this, used the mediation project to prevent the renewal of the agreement, thus freeing itself from French pressure, a stratagem that it was able to exploit very well, The Portuguese were also aware of the delicate situation in which it found itself Spain with its financial and military problems.'

Provinces. The relief of Oran was successfully concluded, and the Portuguese participation resulted in a naval squadron and infantry landing in force.

In the 1670s, Portugal exploited its position to gain its own international diplomatic autonomy and free itself from French protection, and notwithstanding the failure of the Portuguese peace mediation in 1678, the diplomatic role of Lisbon began to be considered in Europe. However, some tension with Spain returned during the short Luxembourg War in 1683–1684 and until the end of the century both states continued to closely observation the other's military policies and activities.

Further Portuguese involvement occurred in the colonies, especially as a consequence of the slave trade.[38] Initially, Portuguese-procured slaves destined for Spanish America came chiefly from Upper Guinea; then they came from the Slave Coast, via São Tomé. Meanwhile, Portugal's plantation colonies in Brazil had from the 1650s also imported African slaves through new *asientos*. The slave trade had become set on a new, irreversible course of growth. But, by the time it had gathered momentum, Upper Guinea and the Slave Coast was no longer the principal suppliers, leaving this bitter primacy to Angola. This region became the theatre of slave trade on a very large scale, which involved the Portuguese garrisons of the coast's settlements in sporadic encounters and skirmishes, and even actual pitched battles in 1665 and 1670.

Although the Portuguese steadily lost ground in Upper Guinea, aggressive rivalry between the European powers made all of them keen to possess fortresses in the region. But fortresses, along with the monopolies they were intended to impose, were disliked by African rulers. However, despite the decline of the settlements at Cacheu and Bissau, Portugal struggled to maintain its share of the slave trade in Upper Guinea, where foreign competition was particularly intense. Eventually, in the late seventeenth century, in an effort to improve its competitive position, the Portuguese tried to re-take the initiative. They abandoned the traditional approach of selling fixed-term monopolies to contractors and began instead to experiment with chartered companies. A company for the Portuguese West African trade was duly instituted in 1664; but it quickly failed. Subsequent companies were launched in 1676, 1682, 1690 and 1699; but all were under-capitalised and proved short lived. In the same years, Portugal tried to strengthen its position in Benin with an agreement with the Kingdom of Dahomey for the supply of African slaves from the region and especially from Congo.

From the 1670s, Portuguese colonial interests were concentrating on Brazil and West Africa, while other possessions appeared more like 'pearls on the crown' than useful domains. At this regard, there were many of the King's councillors in Lisbon who considered the North African outpost of

---

38 In order to obtain more gains from the slave trade, in 1641 King João IV distributed *asientos*, or monopoly contracts, for the America slave trade. The first *asiento* allowed for the importation of 4,250 slaves per year, but this figure was too far from the much higher actual need for slave labour. Again, the King issued new *asientos* to allow the gathering of more African slaves. See also Malyn Newitt, *The Portuguese in West Africa, 1415–1670* (Cambridge: Cambridge University Press, 2010), p.22.

Mazagão as unnecessary for the state. After the ceding of Tangier to England, this isolated fortress in Morocco was the only Portuguese port in the region. The town had spent the years following the Portuguese Restoration in relative tranquillity until the 1670s. In 1675, the Moroccan throne had passed to the new Alaudite dynasty, which with Sultan Mulei Ismail had inaugurated a policy of reunification of the country and the consequent expulsion of foreigners from their outposts in Africa. After the departure of the English from Tangier in 1684, the sultan was not slow to threaten Mazagão too, who suffered episodic Moroccan assaults from as early as 1676 and remained under threat until 1770.

The shift of Portuguese colonial interests towards the Atlantic Ocean consequently also influenced their bases in the Arabian and Indian oceans. In this area, the constant threat was in the shape of the Dutch. Portuguese-Dutch relations east of the Cape continued to be tense for some time, with controversy persisting over whether or not the Dutch East India Company was obliged to hand back Cochin and Cannanore, both having been taken after the 1663 treaty with the United Provinces had been negotiated in Europe.

Eventually a revised Portuguese-Dutch agreement was struck in 1669 by which Portugal accepted that these two places would continue under Dutch East India Company control, at least for the time being. In return, the Dutch reconfirmed the peace. However, when peace with the Dutch in the eastern seas finally arrived, Portuguese trade and traffic between India and Europe had been drastically reduced. For over two decades an average of less than one ship a year had been arriving in Goa from Lisbon, and even fewer had made the return voyage. Then, throughout the last third of the seventeenth century, a modest revival began. Sailings via the *carreira da Índia* became more numerous, more regular and, with the return of peace, more reliable. The Portuguese viceroys took steps to resume the trade, though the results achieved were hardly spectacular.[39] Meanwhile, the trade with Indian ports south of Goa had been quickly re-established. A series of agreements was signed in 1671, 1678 and 1701 with the *nayak* of Ikkeri, still the principal ruler of coastal Kanara. The Indian prince restored their *feitoria* at Mangalore to the Portuguese, which was important especially for Goa's external rice supply.

The insecurity of Portuguese possessions in Asia had also increased with the arrival of a new competitor in the region. In 1664–65 France signalled its intention to become a significant participant in Asian maritime trade by forming, under the inspiration of Jean Baptiste Colbert, Louis XIV's minister of finance, the *Compagnie Royale des Indes Orientales*. The arrival in India of the French presented the Portuguese with yet another option, similar to the one in Europe against Spain, because here their common interests could be

---

39 Disney, A History of Portugal, vol. II, p.305: 'During 1668–1680 crown pepper exports to Lisbon averaged some 350 quintals annually, less than 5 percent of what they had been in the first half of the century, Clearly, if the India-Portugal trade in the late seventeenth century had depended on the pepper monopoly alone, it could not have survived. Portuguese trade with India slowly recovered during this period, and it did so less by resuming the patterns of the past than by changing in response to new circumstances. One of these was that in Goa, as well as in Macau and many parts of Asia beyond, there was now a rapidly growing demand for Brazilian tobacco.'

Pedro II (1648–1706) ruled Portugal first in Afonso's name from 1667 to 1683, then as king in his own right from 1683 to 1706; a total of 39 years, longer than any other Portuguese monarch since the fifteenth century. On coming to power his political priorities were to consolidate his regime and secure the succession. The *cortes* met in January 1668 and quickly confirmed the legitimacy of his takeover. (Author's archive)

combined against the Dutch. In return of French support to recover control of the outposts seized by the Dutch, Paris asked Portugal to cede to France at least one of its Asian maritime bases. As happened in Europe, the regent Prince *Dom Pedro* wisely rejected these overtures. As Pedro II recognised, the French proposal came far too late, and its supposed benefits were too risky and uncertain.

Having just ended the long war with Spain in Europe and secured a firm peace with the Dutch east of the Cape in 1669, Lisbon saw no tangible advantage in entering into new hostilities, especially as the junior partner of an untried ally. Portuguese caution soon proved justified, for the French in India failed to establish a base and Colbert's company achieved no lasting success. Pedro's refusal to join Colbert's anti-Dutch coalition ended any lingering hopes among realistic Portuguese that the *Estado da Índia*'s losses of the past half-century might still be regained by force. More importantly, it also marked the beginning of a long-standing Portuguese tradition of maintaining de facto neutrality with all other European powers in maritime Asia, without, of course, prejudice to the underlying Anglo-Portuguese alliance. This tradition served the Portuguese domains in Asia well. While Portuguese relations with other Europeans in Asia would thenceforth often involve considerable intrigue and mutual suspicion – and even occasional hostile confrontations and 'incidents', for the next century actual war was always carefully avoided. Significantly, there were also no further losses of Portuguese possessions in Asia to European rivals.

2

The Birth of the Modern Portuguese Army

In 1641 an ill-prepared Portuguese David was going to face a tormented but not exhausted Spanish Goliath. In the aftermath of the uprising that had brought the Bragança dynasty to the throne, Portugal did not have a stable army. Although the Portuguese struggle to regain a secure position in the community of nations was inevitably dangerous and tortuous, the raising of a national army in such a short time is almost unique in European military history. Continental and regional powers had begun the transformation of their military units into permanent bodies, while Portugal built its own army from nothing. In this respect, the Portuguese army is a very interesting subject of investigation, becoming as it did an advanced military organisation that would remain almost unchanged until the next century. At first, military organisation was rudimentary, and there were desperate shortages of equipment and horses. Border fortresses had long been neglected, and many of the kingdom's most experienced soldiers served the Habsburgs in Catalonia or Low Countries. The only professional unit formed by Portuguese subjects was the *terço da Armada Real*, raised to provide the marine troops for the fleet.[1] Further local troops were gathered in the militia, which often served under Spanish officers. In the 1640s, Spaniards, Flemish Walloons, Italians and Germans composed the majority of regular forces in Portugal, while native Portuguese represented just 2.9 percent.[2] In the overseas domains, there were weak Portuguese garrisons formed by regular soldiers, supported by a militia-type organisation similar to the one that existed in Portugal, but only in Brazil there were trained units of significant size.[3]

---

1   In 1641 there was also a Spanish infantry *tercio* named *Portugal*, but the composition was mixed Spanish Portuguese.
2   Gabriel Espírito Santo, *Montes Claros, 1665: a Vitória decisiva* (Lisbon: Tribuna de História, 2003), p.27.
3   Frederic Mauro, *Le Portugal, le Brésil et l'Atlantique au XVII siècle – 1570–1670* (Paris: Fondation Calouste Gulbenkian – Centre Cultural Portugues, 1983), p.126.

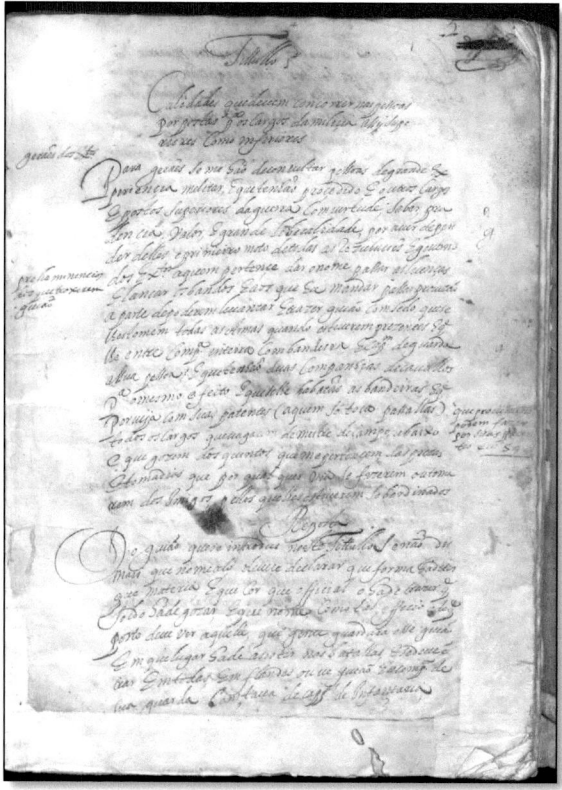

Part 5 of the *Ordenanças Militares*, dealing with the qualities of the soldiers, with the annotation made by Joane Mendes de Vasconcelos. He was a prominent general and a member of the War Council in the opening phases of the Restoration War. He belonged to a family of captains and military writers, and was regarded as an officer with extensive military experience acquired on European battlefields in the service of the dual monarchy and in Brazil. Joane Mendes was commissioned by João IV to leave his observations and comments on the *Ordenanças Militares* of 1643. Although the observations were never published, the practices followed, and much of the later printed regulations, demonstrate his influence or in certain cases the continuation of the reforms that he sought to introduce in the Portuguese army. (*Ordenanças militares discutidas entre ossres. Joanne Mendes de Vasconcellos*, Library of the Portuguese Army, Lisbon)

After the proclamation of the new dynasty, the ancient *Ordenanças* were revived to assemble the army.[4] This institution originated in medieval Portugal, but in the 1640s it had to be revised to adapt in the new situation. Originally, all the male subjects aged 16 to 60 available for the service in the army and fleet were registered in the *Ordenanças*. João IV aimed to gather these troops and appoint officers from the aristocracy, which was in turn registered in another ordinance, to command them. Without other means of raising an army, the general levy of the *Ordenanças* represented the only useful source of men for a restored Portugal. From this pool of recruits, regular soldiers could be also raised in order to form permanent *terços pagos* (professional infantry units) and cavalrymen. Further infantry corps composed by auxiliary troops called *milícias* or *auxiliares* could also be created. At the King's wish, the army was to number 20,000 foot and 4,000 horse, a strength considered in line with the armies of the major Western European powers. These forces became the first and second line of the Portuguese army, and the *Ordenanças* were eventually employed as a home guard. Joining the regular and auxiliary force, the Council of War was able to gather more than 30,000 foot and 7,800 horse assigned to the field army as well as in the frontier garrisons.[5] In order to manage this force, the War Council prepared a regulation, which was submitted to the King on 15 August 1643, known as the *Ordenanças Militares*. This regulation, although never published, constituted the basis of the Portuguese military until the beginning of the next century.

However, in 1641 the power of the King was not the same as that exercised by the Portuguese monarchs before 1580, and the optimistic expectations were soon disappointed by the actual economics of running the state.[6] To mark

---

4　The first *Ordenanças* were established in 1570 under the reign of Sebastião I, after several attempts to create a system of military organisation controlled by the King, carried out during the reigns of Manuel I and João III, which would replace the municipal militia.

5　Claudio de Chalby (ed.), *Synopse dos Decretos remettido sao extinto Conselho de Guerra* (Lisbon, 1869), vol. I, p.8; decree of 12 May 1641.

6　King João IV was considered a rebel by Felipe IV of Castile, with all the consequences that this status gave him abroad as well as in Portugal. In the first days of his reign, the new King had to rely on

the beginning of a new rule, King João IV had abolished 'the illegal and unjust taxes' introduced during the Habsburg rule.[7] However, having removed a major sources of revenue at the time when war against Spain became imminent, new fiscal measures were needed. The *Cortes* approved the imposition of a new tax, the *décima*, which had to be paid for three years, or however long the war lasted.[8] After 18 months, the annual subsidy proved to be inadequate, forcing the King to reconvene the *Cortes* to ask for an additional increase in taxation. The opposition of the *Cortes* posed new obstacles since they deemed it impossible to find enough resources to maintain an army of such size. The *Cortes* of 1642 reduced the regular strength and established further limitations to recruitment.[9] As a result, the first line regular infantry formed five, later 10, 'regular' *terços* (regiments) organised the same as the Spanish *tercios viejos*. The cavalry had to deploy 40 independent companies, regarded as elite units. Finally, 300 professional artillerymen under a command staff quartered in Lisbon completed the field army.[10] However, the mustering of troops proceeded slowly, due to the inevitable organisational obstacles dictated by the emergency. At the end of the summer of 1641, only 3,000 foot and 400 horse were ready to march on campaign.[11] One year later, the army assembled in Alentejo numbered 9,392 men with a significant force of cavalry equal to 21 percent of the army, but still far from the expected 12,000 foot and 1,500 horse authorised in 1642.[12] Conditioned by economic expediencies, before 1657 the standing army never deployed more than 10,000 men. Despite the efforts made by the Braganças, and the skills of the Portuguese commanders, the situation

---

    a strong internal aristocratic and ecclesiastical opposition. In the early days of the Restoration, he did not know if it was larger throughout the whole Portuguese population. To impose its legitimacy, it had to compromise with the aristocracy and the bourgeoisie on matters of military recruitment, especially with the latter, represented by the *Estado dos povos* to which the King had to grant many privileges such as the exemption from any form of compulsory military service. See also Nuno Lemos Pires, 'Guerra global portuguesa: a restauração', in *Revista de História das Ideias*, Vol. 30 (2009), pp.337–353.

7 Lorraine White, 'War and State Development in 17th Century Portugal', in Enrique Hernán Garcia and Davide Maffi (eds), 'Guerra y Sociedad en la Monarquia Hispanica. Politica, estrategia y cultura en la Europa moderna, 1500–1700' (Madrid: Labirinto Ediciones, 2006), vol. I, p.292.

8 In theory this was an annual imposition of 10 percent on income which was supposed to be paid by all the three estates, including the nobility and clergy, who were traditionally exempt from taxation.

9 '*Auto* of the *Cortes* celebrated in this city of Lisbon, 19 September 1642', by the *Estado do Povos*. The text of the resolution is very clear: 'Since the Kingdom has allegedly contributed with the money for twenty thousand foot soldiers and two thousand eight hundred horses, nor the peoples, nor will the peasants be obliged to serve in arms on the borders, except on specific occasions which are declared in the regulation of services for the same Kingdom, and removed the auxiliaries, and other persons from every company (of ordinances) in all counties and reformed and armed in such a way that without oppression of the peoples they will help on occasions and in places where it is needed.'

10 AHM, *Alvará dos privilégios que Sua Majesta defoi servido conceder aos soldados auxiliares, capitães e outras pessoas da mesma milícia*, dated 24 November 1645.

11 ANTT, *Conselho de Guerra, Consultas*, M. 2, letter dated 12 July 1641.

12 White, Lorraine, *Guerra y revolución militar en la Iberia del siglo XVII*, in 'Manuscrits' 21 (2003), p.82.

of the army was for a long time a painful one, and the Spanish strategic decision to consider Portugal a secondary front clearly saved Portugal from a potentially ruinous invasion. The shortfall in revenue from the *décima* was becoming unsustainable. Of the 1.7 million *cruzados* approved by the *Cortes* in 1645, only one million was collected in 1646, while between 1647 and 1651 there was an annual deficit of half million *cruzados*.[13] The *Cortes*, and more precisely the representatives of the popular class, continued to exert a strong opposition to the increase in expenditure for the army, and therefore conditioned its size. Despite these limitations, the King had succeeded in getting an increase in the regular force. After 1642, the number of the regular infantry and cavalry had progressively increased, devising every time new financial expedients and additional taxes, but in 1646, the *Cortes* established a limit to the war contributions. These resources could sustain a much smaller force than expected. Furthermore, the revenue for the army had to be distributed according to the season, since the *Cortes* gave permission to maintain a force of different sizes depending on the time of year. In the five months between June and October, coinciding with the period of large-scale military campaigns, three-fifths of the money was sent to the army, and the remainder was paid over the next seven months. Since there were invariably costs to be deducted from these sums each month, and other extraordinary expenses, the funding for the army remained conditioned by constant uncertainty. In this scenario, the treatment of soldiers' pay was controlled by the seasons, since they received their wages for seven or eight months, and only bread in the remaining period. The military economic plan voted by the *Cortes* established that in summer – actually five months – the army would have deployed its full strength, and in the winter a little more than one third of the total would be under arms. Excess soldiers could be discharged and then re-enlisted depending on the likelihood of war. The field army could gather 10,650 infantry and 2,495 cavalry in summer, while 6,250 and 1,448 respectively remained in service in the seven months from November to May. However, all these figures were on paper only, since as usually occurred the actual effective forces remained far less for most of the time. In July 1646, in Alentejo, the area strategically most exposed to an invasion, there were 7,606 infantry and 1,531 cavalry, excluding officers. On 8 October 1646, the Count of Alegrete referred to the presence in Alentejo of 5,980 soldiers and 609 officers. A further 2,000 men were garrisoned in Olivença, Juromenha, Campo Maior and Ouguela, and finally 800 sick soldiers were in Elvas.[14] On 14 January 1648, the senior member of the War Council Joane Mendes de Vasconcelos, pointed out that the last muster registered just 4,661 professional soldiers. A couple of months later the number had dropped to

---

13 Fernando Dores Costa, *A guerra da Restauração 1641–1668* (Lisboa: Horizonte, 2004), p.245 and 250. The differences were due to the refusal of the clergy to contribute, and the nobility's avoidance of financial obligations.
14 *Cartas dos Governadores da Província do Alentejo a El-Rei D.João IV e a El-Rei D. Afonso VI*, vol. II (Lisbon, 1940), pp.126–127.

THE BIRTH OF THE MODERN PORTUGUESE ARMY

Infantry fighting at the Battle of Ameixial, 8 June 1663. Oil painting on lead. (Collection of the Visconde de Fonte Arcada, National Library of Lisbon)

3,800 infantry in nine *terços*.[15] The councillor also noted that subsistence was more difficult in Alentejo, where prices were higher, and all the officers serving in this province insisted on receiving full pay for the whole year, because otherwise 'none of them would be able to escape the famine and this would have undermined the service to the monarchy.'[16]

Every sign of a possible accommodation between France and Spain reflected the rapid growth of troops enlisted to face the expected Spanish offensive. In the muster of 12 October 1657, the field army numbered 12,326 men, and increased to 17,195 a year later. In the following years, the regular force never decreased below 10,000 men, except in 1659, when just 9,500 'regulars' were gathered on the border of Extremadura.[17] In 1661, the Army of Alentejo deployed 10,000 foot and 3,500 horse as a response to the increasing Spanish threat.[18]

According to the contemporary authors, in 1663, the overall strength of Portuguese army numbered 30,000–32,000 infantry of the first and second line, divided into 28 regular *terços*, 35 auxiliary *terços*, and 7,000 regular horsemen, supported by 'a magnificent train of artillery' and finally further 1,500 auxiliary horsemen.[19] The tones of exaltation at these numbers hid the truth, since in reality the Portuguese army continued to suffer from the shortage of troops. This problem, and the pressing requests for more troops, were submitted to the monarch at the beginning of every campaign. In May

---

15 Fernando Dores Costa, 'Governadores das armas, mestres de campo e capitães-mores no Alentejo durante a Guerra da Restauração: inovações na administração e centro speriféricos de poder', in *Centros Periféricos de Poderna Europa do Sul (Sécs. XII–XVIII)* (Lisbon: Publicações do Cidehus, Edições Colibri, 2013), pp.202.
16 *Ibid.*, p.203.
17 Lorraine White, *Guerra y revolución militaren la Iberia del siglo XVII*, p.82.
18 *Ibid.*
19 Geronimo de Santa Cruz, *Declaracion que por el Reyno de Portugal ofreceel doctor G. De Santa Cruz a todos los Reynos, y Provincias de Europa* (Lisbon, 1663), p.48. The author did not mention the militiamen, who were 'difficult to number, because countless'.

1663, on the eve of the victory at the battle of Ameixial-Estremoz, the anxious military governor of Alentejo, Sancho Manuel de Vilhena, wrote: 'How different is the number of people with find from the one we imagined, a lack that Your Majesty should remedy calling for troops from other provinces, as I informed Your Majesty through repeated letters, since without people it is impossible to make war'.[20] The emergency triggered a decisive war effort. In 1664, the Army of Alentejo deployed the unprecedented figure of 24,000 first-line soldiers, including French and English troops.

Though these figures represented a very significant result for a country that had raised a regular army in a very short time, Portugal was always forced to resort to various expedients in order to continue the struggle. Fortunately for Lisbon, the limited availability of troops on the Spanish side also made the emergency less pressing, at least until 1659. The first phase of the war was marked by intense activity, gathering information to determine the strength of the enemy. This intelligence gathering also took place on the Spanish side, and each time the news concerning the arrival of more enemy troops reached the headquarters, the mobilisation of further troops began to face the possible threat. For this task, the Portuguese commanders resorted to the second-line troops, the aforementioned *auxiliares* recruited on a territorial basis. The formation of this category lasted several years and very closely resembled compulsory military service. The *auxiliares* included all the young married and unmarried subjects between 18 to 40 able to bear arms. They received payment corresponding to the military service supplied; exemptions were rare and depended on the need for men. Each sector of the border fielded its auxiliary infantry financed by the respective province. The training and maintenance of these contingents to a state of acceptable efficiency was undoubtedly a success for Portugal during the Restoration War. Although this infantry closely resembled the Spanish provincial *tercios*, the Portuguese model was more successful, both from a military and economic point of view. The most exposed province of Alentejo deployed the largest contingent, but the other provinces also contributed with their forces. In 1659, pressed by the expected Spanish offensive, the Council of War submitted a proposal to reform the army to the King, in order to increase the number of the first-line troops, and to establish a better organisation of the auxiliary infantry, forming permanent units, like the regular *terços*. The reform project had been prepared by General of Artillery Pedro Jacques de Magalhães, who personally set out the plan. This was a major military reform introduced in the army during the War of Restoration. The presence of the auxiliary troops became more and more needed, and in the next decade the Crown increasingly resorted to using these troops. In 1660, among the forces gathered in Alentejo, numbering 14,700 foot and 1,290 horse, half of them were *auxiliares*, and also in the following major engagements they represented a significant percentage of the field army. For the campaign of 1663, culminating in the victory of Ameixial-Estremoz, the field army mustered in May deployed 12,582 foot, of which 6,105 were *terços*

---

20   ANTT, *Conselho de Guerra, Consultas*, 1663, M. 2, letter dated 9 May 1663.

pagos from Alentejo, 1,799 from other provinces, 1,381 foreign mercenaries, and the remaining 3,297 were *auxiliares*.[21] Although these troops were not immediately available, since they were officially reservists, in the crucial years between 1662 and 1665, the Portuguese commanders claimed to be able to mobilise a significant number of the auxiliaries in barely two weeks.[22] The double structure of the Portuguese army remained a constant throughout the war, and ultimately, it was one of the most successful contributions towards winning the final victory.

The peace of 1668 provided the opportunity for a radical reform of the army. Portugal maintained a small standing army and continued its selective draft system. Only a few professional infantry *terços* remained in service at full strength, like *Armada*, *Lisboa*, *Principe* and others among the oldest of the army. The overall strength of the regular force was reduced to 8,000 men, but the international situation did not permit too much in the way of demilitarisation. In the 1670s, a prudent King Pedro II submitted the plan to the *Cortes* to increase the regular force for deployment in the colonies and in North Africa, as well as to deploy a field army enough strong to secure the border with Spain. In 1676, four new infantry *terços* were raised, equal to 6,000 men, while a further 300 horsemen joined the cavalry quartered in Lisbon. Despite the considerable economic burden required by the permanent troops, and the policy of neutrality maintained by Pedro II in the following years, the Portuguese regular army gradually increased its strength, and in 1696 deployed 20 regular infantry *terços*. The cavalry remained organised in single companies until 1705, while the artillery formed a regiment, which later assumed the title of *Terço da Corte*. These latter formed the garrison of Lisbon and performed the honour-guard service alongside the marine infantrymen of the *terço da Armada*. It should be noted that Portugal, unlike nearly every other kingdom, did not have household troops or Royal Guards. The only unit comparable to a Life Guard was the small company of *Arqueiros* who formed the palace guard and escorted the King during state ceremonies.

Commands

The king formally held the supreme command of the army: the War Council submitted for his approval all the appointments to the higher command, and the subordinate ranks also received the king's endorsement. The king also had authority over the army in the overseas domains. Here, each *capitania* housed a *capitão-general* appointed by Lisbon, who was usually also the viceroy or governor. However, at the operational level, the *governadores de armas* managed

---

21 ANTT, *Conselho de Guerra, Consultas*, M. 23, C. 85 (9 May 1663). The auxiliaries came from Santarém, Vilaviçosa, Avis, Portalegre, Évora, Campo de Ourique, Beja and the Priorato de Crato; the regulars, belonging to other provinces were 310 from Trás-os-Montes, 457 from Algarve, 532 from Estremadura and 500 from Beira. The foreigners were 237 Italians and 1,144 English mercenaries.
22 Fernando Dores Costa, 'Formação da força militar durante a guerra da restauração', in *Penélope: revista de história e ciências sociais*, XXIV (2001), p.90.

the command of forces in the field in each respective province in Portugal. As commander-in-chief, each *governador* had the direct access to the king or the War Council for submitting and discussing military matters of his province and the strategic situation in wartime. The military governor benefited from a large degree autonomy and managed the military affairs like a contemporary field marshal. He also extended his authority over recruitment. The command of a governor could be extensive, depending upon the number of subordinate outposts and commanders attached to him. He controlled the updating of the *Ordenanças* from which the army drew the soldiers. Among his specific duties, the governor controlled the service of the *capitanias* of his province and submitted their appointment to the War Council, as well as the officers of the field arm being put forward to the appointment of a command or promotion.[23] According to the Ordinances of 1643, the qualities required to a governor were 'affability, magnanimity, and disinterest in personal gain.'[24] Military knowledge was also required, but he must also have been a skilled politician. Although the length of a term of office was not established, rarely did a governor remain in his post for more than three or four years, but he could reassume the office another time, alternating the rank with another duty. Between 1647 and 1658, André de Albuquerque Ribafria held the post of *governador de armas* in the province of Alentejo three times, as did the influential Count of Vila Flor, Sancho Manuel de Vilhena, in Beira between 1647 and 1663. Several *governadores de armas* continued their career in the colonies as viceroys, like João de Vasconcellos e Sousa, Count of Castelo Melhor, who governed Brazil between 1650 and 1654. The governor had his residence in the main fortress of the province and at the same time he was the commander of the local garrison. He also held the command of all the garrisons quartered in the province, which usually were commanded by the respective *mestre de campo*. In the early years of the conflict against Spain, the involvement of the garrisons was quite sporadic, but years after, when the war entered its decisive phase, the border fortresses where commanders participated in the war operations elsewhere found themselves without a military leader. Thus, in April 1661, the War Council, through the Count of Atouguia, warned the King of the need to appoint a vice-governor in the most exposed border fortresses, so that they would be in place when the governors and other commanders joined the army on campaign. Six fortresses were identified: Castelo de Vide, Campo Maior, Juromenha, Mourão, Moura and Serpa. However, four months later, despite the positive reaction to the premiss, no deputy commanders had been appointed for these posts.[25] Since the beginning of the war against Spain the primary strategy was based on the defence of the borders, and the concept of joining the direction of all military affairs under a single commander-in-chief was never considered.

---

23 Fernando Dores Costa, 'Governadores das armas, mestres de campo e capitães-mores no Alentejo durante a Guerra da Restauração: inovações na administração e centrosperiféricos de poder', in *Centros Periféricos de Poderna Europa do Sul (Sécs. XII–XVIII)* (Lisbon: Publicações do Cidehus, Edições Colibri, 2013), p 202.

24 Aires, Cristóvão, *Historia Organica e Politica do Exercito Português* (Lisbon, 18i908), vol. IV, pp.59–60.

25 Dores Costa, *Governadores das armas*, p.204. In Elvas, when the Comte de Atouguia went on campaign, he autonomously appointed the *mestre de campo* Luís de Menezes as vice-governor.

Furthermore, it was politically difficult for the Crown to entrust such a delicate task to a single commander in a such highly influential position in Portugal after 1640, in order to avoid dissent from the other governors in command. But despite this, the military governor of the Alentejo was, more than others, held the greatest honour and burden commanding this key sector throughout the war. Even when in 1643 King João IV took the command of the field army, the governor of Alentejo directed the operations as commander of the Army of Alentejo. The same applied to the authoritative Friedrich Hermann von Schomberg, the only foreigner to hold the position of military governor, who commanded in Alentejo from 1662.[26] The military governors retained many of the perks reserved for the Spanish viceroys, and they were escorted on active service by a mounted lifeguard company under a lieutenant with 30–40 men.

Each governor had a senior field officer under his command with the rank of *mestre de campo general*. Officially, he was the senior commander of the infantry in the province's army. Like the governor, this officer had to be considered for his virtues, but also for his military knowledge. Before gaining the rank of *mestre de campo general*, it was necessary that he had held other command posts, after having served 'with valour and sagacity, and reputed to be able to master theoretical and practical matters, because only the officers with these requirements are preferred for this rank.'[27] The *mestre* was in charge both in garrison and in the field, and replaced the military governor of the province when the latter was absent or assigned to another task, or where the position of governor was vacant. Usually, the *mestre de campo general* put forward candidates for the ranks of *ajudantes de tenente de mestre de campo general* (lieutenant adjutant), *preboste general*

Friedrich Hermann von Schomberg (1615–1690), portrayed in 1678 (Bibliothèque Nationale de France, Paris). Notwithstanding the prickly relationships with some of the Portuguese military leaders, and the tight constraints imposed on him by limited manpower and material resources, Schomberg was able to achieve significant improvements in military organisation, training and tactics in the Portuguese army. After serving for 35 years in the French army, in 1685 he resigned the service as *Marechál*, and joined the service of Brandenburg. In 1688 the Elector lent him and a mercenary corps to William III for the campaign in Ireland against James II. In April 1689 Schomberg was naturalised as English, but three months later he was killed at the Battle of the Boyne.

---

26 To avoid rank disputes with the Portuguese officers, King Afonso VI gave Schomberg the title of Count of Mertola and grandee of Portugal.

27 *Ibid*. In his comments on the military ordinance of 1643, Joane Mendes de Vasconcelos clarified all the more important requisites for the rank of *mestre de campo general*: 'It is necessary to entrust this rank to the most experienced commanders, and among them, to the candidates with the longest experience in the infantry.'

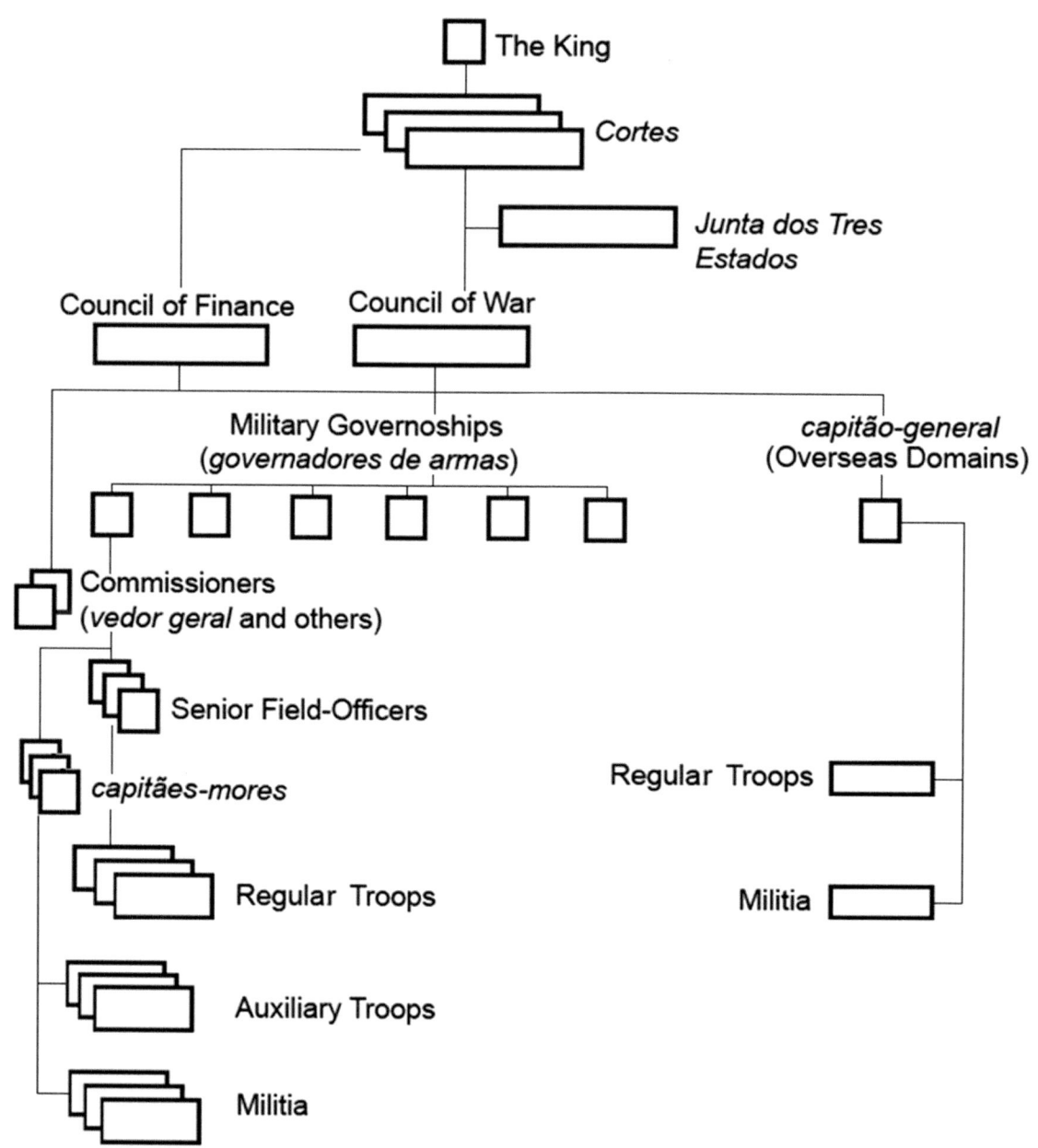

The chain of command in the Portuguese army. (Author's graphic)

(general prevost), *tambor geral* (drum major), *capitão de guias* (captain of the guides), and *furriel da corte* (quartermaster major), who made up the military headquarters of each province. Furthermore, he approved the official appointed by the General Auditor. Like his Spanish counterpart, the *Mestre de Campo General* had a small company of 'mounted arquebusiers' to protect his person.

The other main senior ranks of the Portuguese army were the *capitão-general da cavalaria* (captain general of cavalry), later *general da cavalaria*, and the *tenente de mestre de campo general* (general lieutenant of infantry). Since in the 1640s the cavalry deployed fewer numbers than the infantry, the cavalry general was subordinate to the *mestre de campo general*. Furthermore, the commander of the cavalry in a province was not always an actual general. When manpower was low, as was the case in the early years of the war, especially in the northern provinces of Portugal, the command of the cavalry was usually held by a lieutenant general, a commissioner general or even a captain. There were occasions when this specific command position, held with a rank less than general, was designated as senior commander of the cavalry. Being a post of such importance, the senior member of the War Council, Joane Mendes de Vasconcelos, was surprised that the chapter concerning the general of the cavalry in the Military Ordinances of 1643 did not allow for lieutenant generals to ascend to the higher rank 'immediately and preferably.'[28] Later, when the war evolved into raids and ambushes usually performed by the cavalry, the rank of *general da cavalaria* assumed its proper seniority, becoming the third in command of the Portuguese command staff.

In fourth position of the Portuguese army's hierarchy was the *tenente de mestre de campo general*. As the title implies, he was the assistant to the senior commander of infantry in a province, and in turn had one or more adjutants. His duties were to exercise and distribute all the orders received from the *mestre de campo general* and to manage in the field the communications between senior officers. In his comments on the Ordinances of 1643, the always keen observer Joane Mendes de Vasconcelos refers to this post in the following terms: 'Lieutenants of the *mestres de campo* should always consult with the senior officers, but never with captains of infantry, for not being equal with these latter, since the captains ascend to this rank.'[29]

Directly under the cavalry commander, there was the *tenente general da cavalaria* (general lieutenant of cavalry), who served similarly to the

---

28 A contradiction to which the experienced councillor made prompt reference and correction in his comment: 'There is no record in this title (chapter of the ordinances) of people who serves as cavalry lieutenant general being consulted as cavalry commanders. Any commander should be sure that the advice of these officers has to be considered in the war councils, because they are to be preferred to all others and to have the precedence over other positions. The ordinance gives cavalry captains and mestre de campo the possibility of becoming generals, and also omitting the position of general commissioner. All this despite the knowledge that the lieutenants possessed the qualities best suited to serve as generals.' See Jorge Penim de Freitas, *A cavalaria na Guerra da Restauração: reconstrução e evolução de uma força militar, 1641–1668* (Lisbon: Prefácio, 2005), pp.74–75.
29 Rede de Bibliotecas de Defesa Nacional, *Ordenanças militares discutidas entre ossres. Joanne Mendes de Vasconcellos* (1643).

correspondent rank of *tenente de mestre de campo general*. However, the division between infantry and cavalry commanders was more apparent than real. Although the cavalry commanders most often came from mounted units, access to the senior ranks was open to all army's officers. In Chapter 15 of the Military Ordinances of 1643, Joane Mendes de Vasconcelos outlined that the *tenente general da cavalaria* (lieutenant general of cavalry) also could come from the infantry, promoting the most valiant *mestre de campo*. It would have been convenient, he added, because the lieutenant generals often went into operations with mixed forces of cavalry and infantry, and therefore it was necessary for them to know the best way to employ both arms. This rank had the particularity that it could also held by company officers. Furthermore, the rank could be held by an officer with another rank, such as foreign colonels. However, these cases were not very frequent. After 1643, in every province there was a cavalry captain appointed as lieutenant general, but not in Alentejo, because this province quartered the largest army, and consequently more cavalry which required a senior commander. As the conflict progressed, the increase in cavalry strength caused a consequent increase in the number of experienced officers with this rank. Ideally, the first level in the structure of the cavalry should include one general, two lieutenant generals and four general commissioners; although in some cases, one lieutenant general may have been sufficient to ensure command of a few cavalry in the smaller provincial armies. In the early years of the Restoration War, some foreign officers were appointed to the rank of lieutenant general. In Beira, the French Jacques Talonneau de La Popelinière died in combat in March 1644, holding that rank since he had arrived in Portugal two and a half years earlier with the rank of captain of horse. Dutch cavalry officer Jan Willem van Til served as lieutenant general in Alentejo in 1645. Among the French officers, Achim Avaux de Tamericurt became of the best in this rank. He served in Alentejo and Beira from 1662 to 1668. With him, Jacques Talonneau de la Popelinière became *tenente general* in the province of Trás-os-Montes, after climbed through the ranks from private soldier, after serving in Portugal from 1646 to 1658.[30] Among the Portuguese, some skilled cavalry commanders such as João de Mascarenhas Count of Sabugal, Dinis de Melo de Castro and João da Silva, held the rank of *tenente general da cavalharia* in the decisive campaigns which occurred after 1659.

Although the military ordinances of 1643 sought to give the Portuguese army a distinct character, the Spanish influence persisted in the terminology of ranks. The most obvious case was the one represented by the *comisáriogeral*. As for the cavalry captains, the commissioners could be appointed to the rank of *tenente general da cavalaria*.

Since there were no cavalry regiments in the Portuguese army, except among the foreign forces, the general commissioners were especially designated to command the foreign cavalry corps. This placed them almost at the level of the colonels, but these latter were generally the owners of their

---

30 Freitas, 'Guerra da Restauração', *O outro Jacques Talonneau de la Popelinière, official francês de cavalaria ao serviço de Portugal (1646-1658)* (11 November 2009).

THE BIRTH OF THE MODERN PORTUGUESE ARMY

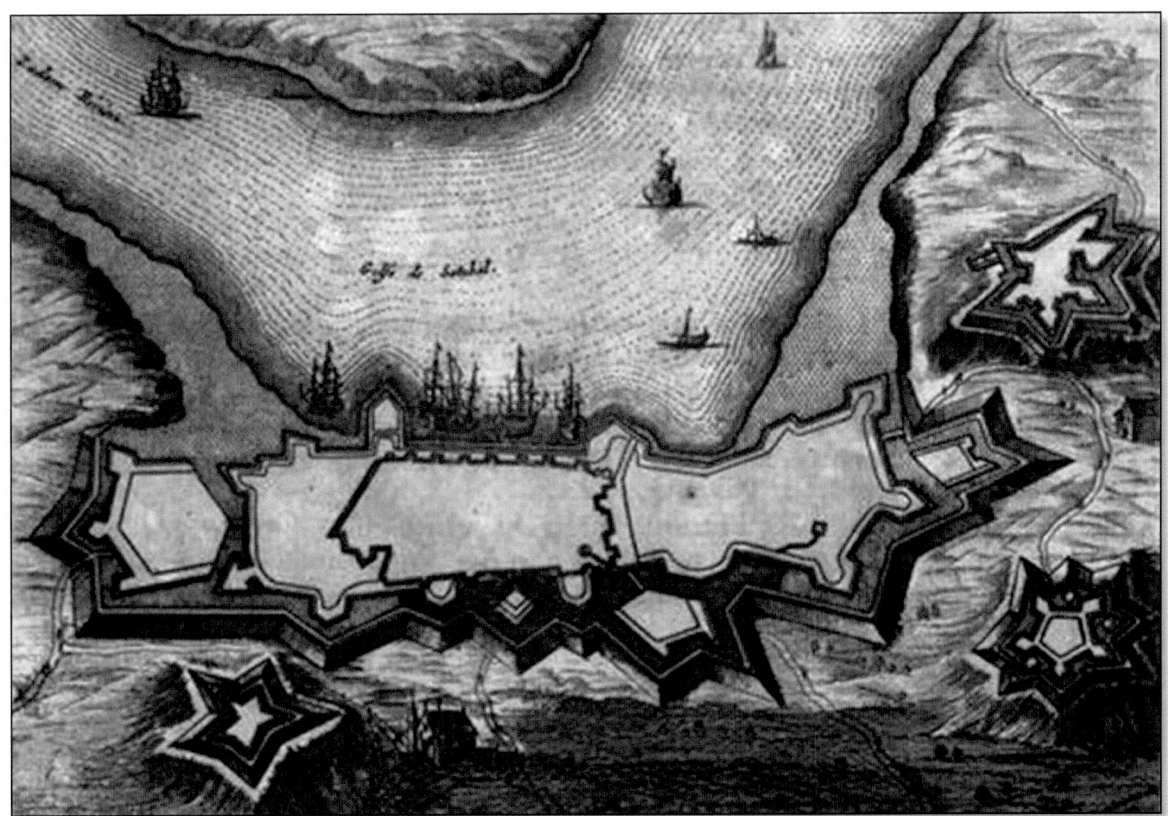

The fort of São Filipe de Setúbal, also known as Castelo de São Filipe, was one of the strongholds defending Lisbon and its harbour. Between 1649 and 1655 the fort received improvements allowing the artillery to effectively guard the port of Setúbal. (Author's archive)

regiments, and therefore they considered themselves superior to the general commissioner when both officers served together on campaign. In Portugal in 1643, there was a need to assign the extraordinary rank of colonel to a general commissioner, who existed only in the Army of Alentejo, and then he was authorised to impose his authority over foreign colonels, who could otherwise choose to refuse to obey him. However, the rank of *comisáriogeralda cavalaria* remained subordinate to that of lieutenant general.

In the following years, further ranks were introduced. In the 1650s, the rank of *general de artilharia* was created for the major garrisons, but not only as commander of artillery, because to this rank were appointed commanders of the *terços* as a special recognition, as occurred in the Spanish army. Theoretically, the rank identified an officer with knowledge in siege warfare, therefore, in the general staff were often more than one general of artillery present. In the same period, the rank of *tenente general de artilharia* was also introduced, for the officers who actually dealt with the direction of the artillery, especially in the costal fortresses or large border garrisons.

At the beginning of 1663, the *sargento-mor de batalha* (sergeant major of battle) was also created in the Portuguese army after the insistence of Sancho Manuel de Vilhena, Count of Vila Flor. The rank was immediately introduced in the Army of Alentejo, and the first officers appointed were Diogo Gomes de Figueiredo e Bobadilha and João da Silva de Sousa. The Count argued with the War Council in favour of the creation of the new rank, referring to the existence of the *General Wachtmeister* in the armies of the Emperor, an imitation of which was also created in the Spanish army,[31] because it was considered 'of great convenience for the good service on campaign.'[32] However, the actual reasons for introducing this rank were different. While the Spanish rank tried to solve the problem of hierarchy among the various senior officers involved in the field, in the Portuguese case the issue was more complex. In this specific case, the *sargento-mor de batalha* was a rank introduced specifically to reduce the authority of Schomberg. In fact, the susceptible Vila Flor, who had become *governador de armas* of Alentejo sometime earlier, feared that Schomberg would be appointed as *mestre de campo general*, as he effectively did on 15 March 1663. Vila Flor did not wish to have Schomberg as his subordinate on campaign, and with a stroke of the pen, he tried to overthrow his *mestre de campo general* by giving him the new rank in order to reduce his influence.[33] However, the result was in practice irrelevant and brought with it even more complexity within the chain of command. Not only did the rank of *mestre de campo general* continue to exist, but the *sargento-mor de batalha* performed similar functions to the *tenente de mestre de campo general*. In theory, a *sargento-mor de batalha* would be directly subordinate to a captain general or lieutenant general of the army, or more often to the *governador de armas*, namely to the senior commander of an army. In practice, this rank also became a subordinate to the *mestre de campo general*.[34]

The Portuguese general staff at the Battle of Montes Claros contained all the senior ranks. The commander-in-chief position was held by the *governador de armas*, Luís de Meneses Marquise of Marialva, with Friedrich von Schomberg as *mestre de campo general*. The Count of São João served as *general da cavalaria*, Pedro Jacques de Magalhães as *tenente de mestre de campo general*, and Luís de Meneses was the *general da artilheria*. Miguel Carlos de Távora, Diego Gomes de Figueiredo, and João Silva de Sousa were the *sargentos-mores de batalha*, in charge of the command of the first and second line of infantry, in addition to the infantry reserve. Further senior officers held the command of different corps of the field army. Both wings of cavalry of the first line were under the respective *general da cavalaria*: Dinis de Melo e Costa on the right, and Pedro Cesar de Meneses on the left. The second lines of cavalry were under the *tenente general* Luís da Costa on the right and António de Maldonado on the left. The *comisáriogeral* António de Sequeira Pestana held the command of the cavalry reserve.

Other posts introduced over the years, or at least conclusively regulated, were the officials in charge of the administration, which formed the *vedoria general das tropas* (general survey of troops), established in August 1645, in order to coordinate the activity of financial control for the army. This office

---

31 In this regard, even before 1653 the Marquis de Aytona had proposed the introduction of the post of *sargento mayor de batalla* in the Spanish army, with authority over all the *maestres de campo*, following a precedent introduced in Flanders. Molinet, Diego Gómez, *El Ejército de la Monarquía Hispánica a través de la Tratadística Militar, 1648–1700* (Madrid: Ministerio de Defensa, 2007), p.80.
32 ANTT, *Conselho de Guerra, Consultas*, 1663,M. 23, letter attached to the *consultas* of 20 February.
33 Freitas, *O Combatente durante a Guerra da Restauração*, p.65.
34 Aires, *Historia Organica e Politica do Exercito Português*, vol. IV, p.49.

operated closely with the royal treasury and the *Junta dos Três Estados*, which had regulated the activity with a specific law, known as the *Lei das Fronteiras* (Laws of Borders). This law constituted the basis for the *Regimento do vedor geral*, issued a few weeks after its establishment. The *vedoria* dealt with every financial operation concerning the army and appointed the officials to control the regulations in matters of expenditure, such as the payment of wages, the purchase and distribution of supplies, and the registration of officers and soldiers mustered, as well as the cost of military transport. The *vedoria generaldas tropas* remained in charge of the administration of the Portuguese army until 1763. There was a *vedor general* in each province; the first one was appointed in Alentejo and began work in February 1642. In the following November, he undertook the first accurate muster of the troops, in order to prevent the chaos that reigned in the matter of military spending, mainly with regard to the payment of the soldiers, and to improve the machinery of army finances. The *vedorgoral*'s regulation consisted of 84 chapters, dealing with the control of the *listas* (troops), *livros* (register), musters, cavalry and *fazenda* (finance), but only for infantry and cavalry, because the artillery had its own *vedor*, who was usually appointed in the larger garrisons. As was frequent in this period, each chapter extended to other matter, and in many cases, there was no rigorous organisation.[35] Among these, the *vedor geral* had to inspect the stores of foodstuffs, to ensure they were safe, and the goods could be preserved without corruption. The regulation continued in the same verbose tone:

> He [the *vedor general*] will also inspect the artillery and ammunition, if there is no vedor of the artillery, ordering that the gunpowder be protected from humidity, and that the weapons be clean and well preserved. He will make sure that the pikes are placed correctly, and that the pole are greased with linseed oil or aloe water, so that the woodworms do not corrode them, and that the guns are distributed by the cavalry so that they do not give the same soldier two guns. of different calibre, cause of grave when he is in engaged combat.[36]

Other duties concerned logistics, promotions, hospitals, desertions and discipline, which must have forced the *vedores* into industrious activity. The *vedoria geral* interacted with the *ministros de soldo and fazenda*, the officials responsible for the use of funds allocated to the army in each province, which belonged to the personnel of the Royal Treasury. The *vedor geral* was a non-military position and it was held by civilians, like other officials of the administrative apparatus, such as the general accountant, the *pagador general* (general payer), the legal officers, and the *comisários de mostras* (muster commissioners). The *vedor geral* oversaw the work of four *comisários de mostras* (muster commissioners), in charge of certifying every month the strength of garrisons and field units and transmitting the data to Lisbon. Here, four *amanuenses* (administrative officials), managed the keeping of these

---

35 Freitas, Jorge Penim de, *O vedor general do exército*, in 'Guerra da Restauração, Blog de História Militar dedicado à Guerra da Restauração ou da Aclamação, 1641–1668' (12 September 2008).
36 Ibid., *Regimento do Vedor geral*, 29 August 1645 (26 September 2010).

records. The commissioners were therefore constantly on the move to carry out musters of all the garrisons. The regulation pointed out that in the absence of the commissioner's certification, no payment was made.[37] The *vedor geral* received the money for the military expenditure of his province, which were paid irregularly and rarely in sufficient quantity. As a result, many soldiers received nothing for months, sometimes more than two years, as happened in the last phase of the war against Spain. This inconvenience was known as *privilégio da primeira plana*, a custom that was widely criticised by the military throughout the war, from senior commander to private soldier, but which even royal intervention in 1653 failed to address this disgraceful situation.

The *junta das fronteiras* was another military office under the joint control of the *conselho de fazenda* and the War Council, in charge of the restoration and construction of fortresses. This office dealt with the extensive network of fortifications that included not only the border ones, but also the 18 major fortresses protecting the coast, especially Lisbon. The harbour of the capital and its access were defended by six forts, including, among the main ones, São Felipe de Setubal, Cascáis, Peniche, São Sebastião da Caparica, and the monumental Torre de Belem, each manned by a permanent infantry and artillery garrison. The threat of Spanish naval action against the Portuguese coast, as well as the risk of an invasion from the sea, was not underestimated. The recurrent naval battles fought in the Atlantic contributed to the continued high the level of attention paid to coastal defence.[38] Moreover, the harbour at Lisbon was subject to a blockade in 1650, then in 1657, 1658 and again finally in 1666, and the capital even faced an attempted Spanish landing. After the restoration of 1640, the *junta* prepared a detailed description of all the fortresses with their armament and the contents of their arsenals, which in some cases dated back many decades. The successful modernisation and enlargement of the fortifications was another decisive Portuguese success in the war against Spain. The border was protected by modern defences, which guaranteed the strategic security of the most exposed areas. In the *junta das fronteiras* there was a *tenencia*, a post usually was held by a general of artillery, who managed the work of coordinating the administration alongside the *vedoria geral*.

All the affairs relating to military justice within the army answered to the *prebostegeral*, who dealt with these matters like the holder of the corresponding Spanish rank. This officer was promoted from the rank of captain of infantry, according to the Military Ordinances project of 1643, although Joane Mendes de Vasconcelos, in his writings, warned that considering the temperament of the Portuguese, it seems that it is enough to be elected as adjutant. The Portuguese general also mentioned that the *prebostegeral* had an escort formed by a company of mounted *archbuzeiros*, with two lieutenants and a

---

37 *Ibid.*
38 Naval battles occurred in the Atlantic Ocean between the Spanish and Portuguese fleets starting from 1641, when the first significant encounters occurred off the Algarve coast. Further naval engagements involved the two fleets in 1644 against off the Algarve, the Azores and Vigo in 1650, Cabo de Roca in 1652, Madeira in 1654, Mazagão, in the Mediterranean, in 1656, Nazaré in 1660, Vigo and Douro in 1664, and Lisbon in 1665.

chaplain, who accompanied him with the executioner, 'because everything is necessary for the brief execution of a death sentence.'[39] After the reform of the Portuguese cavalry of 1664, the company of the *prebostegeral* continued to serve on a permanent basis and comprised a minimum of 40 horsemen. Chapter 36 of the Military Ordinances stated that the exercise of the office included the verification of execution of orders and bans, patrolling of roads and pathways, and assigning places in the encampment for the suppliers. Some of these functions are not much different to the ones performed by military police in modern times.

The Portuguese chain of command included another important rank, who managed personally the provincial military resources: the *capitão-mor* (captain major). He was responsible for recruiting, training and equipping the troops from the *Ordenanças* (militiamen) in his province's cities, towns or villages.[40] This office had been instituted in 1570, when the king appointed a land officer in each province of Portugal, with the rank of captain. According to the sixteenth-century regulation, each *capitão-mor* was responsible for his own company of *Ordenanças*. In each province there was also a *sargento-mor*, who assisted in commanding the companies from the same province, organised in the *terço da ordenança*. In the next century, with the rise of the regular army, the *capitão-mor* moved from a military position to an office that could be performed by an officer with any rank, whether he was in the regular army or militia. Nevertheless, the office maintained the prestige of earlier times, because in addition to the aforementioned tasks of recruiting, training and commanding the *Ordenanças*, the *capitão-mor* also held the military governorship of the district, if there was no officer specifically appointed to this task. Furthermore, when between 1645 and 1646, the militia and the auxiliaries became two separate organisation of the original *Ordenanças*, the *capitães-mores* acquired a key position in each district. They were also involved in the capture and return of deserters, and many times their actions were evaluated precisely for the results obtained in this task. Since military personnel of various provenance could hold the title of *capitão-mor*, *mestre de campo* or cavalry captains could be also occasionally appointed to this office. In 1663, in the province of Beira, there were officers of very mixed provenance. In Castelo Rodrigo resided the *tenente de mestre de campo general* António Ferreira Ferrão; Castelo Bom housed the infantry captain António de Figueiredo, a veteran from the army of Flanders; finally, Segura had Diogo Freire, already *capitão-mor* of Idanha, transferred because he performed very badly with the population of that village. As the captains had control of enlistment and in practice decided the assignment of recruits to the auxiliary corps, they exercised considerable power over communities. There were several disputes caused by the action of the *capitães-mores*, the echo of which forced the War Council to intervene. The problems emerged

---

39 Freitas, *Regimento do Vedor Geral*, 29 August 1645.
40 There is some confusion regarding the *capitão-mor*, and it is not uncommon to find in essays, or even valuable academic works, a reference to the designation of *capitão-mor* as a military rank during the War of Restoration. It would have been, but before 1640. See Dores Costa, *Governadores das armas*, pp.205–206.

not only about the abuse of power of these men, but primarily due to the strong competition of the emerging popular classes against the aristocracy, from which mostly the captains came. The emergency caused by the war facilitated these officers in the construction of a net of relationship between the government and the common people, placing themselves above any other authority.[41] The power that the *capitães-mores* had locally was in fact considerable. They chose the officers of the *Ordenanças* and for this reason, they had a great influence in the communities and were often envied. Being the provincial authority directly responsible for the administration of the recruitment lists, the captains decided who was exempt from military service and who was not, who belonged to the *milicias* and who to the *auxiliares*, holding almost a power of life or death. The internal balance of the Portuguese society could be subverted by the importance acquired by a *capitão-mor*, and by his power to give orders to all, nobles as well as their subjects, forcing both to obey the contingencies of the war. The councillor and former military governor of the province of Beira, Álvaro de Abranches, summarised the topic by writing:

> These men (the capitães-mores) were used to being petty kings in their provinces and the military mobilisation of Your Majesty's subjects gives them the power to dispose unlimitedly of people.[42]

In 1641, with the granting of patents to appoint the *mestres de campo* in charge of recruiting the soldiers, the core of the officer class of the modern Portuguese army was formed. However, in Portugal, as in practically any contemporary army, the career advancement of officers depended entirely on the internal organisation of infantry *terços* and cavalry companies. All officers were designated according to their position in the unit, and therefore there was a *primera plana* (major staff), which included the commanders of an infantry *terço*, which was separated from the officers assigned to the companies. The aristocrats usually had access to the rank of officer by virtue of their birth. Once they entered the army, often as simple cadets, they climbed the ranks according to the vacancies available and of course, whether their service had been positive. Vacancies depended on the careers of the senior officers; therefore, if there was not much progress in the higher positions up to general,

---

41 *Ibid.*, p.206. One of the most serious controversies involved the Torres Novas' *capitão mor*, Manuel de Vasconcellos. The captain was accused of having prosecuted some residents and having assigned them to the *auxiliaries'* infantry to take revenge for some of their excesses against his authority. Vasconcellos defended himself from the calumny of those who accused him, claiming to have intervened in full compliance with the royal laws. His action was also condemned by the village representatives, who insinuated that the captain had been induced to intervene by Jacinto de Vasconcellos and his brother-in-law Alvaro Lopez Correa. They were the same ones who had prevented another candidate from taking the post of captain. In his letter, the Manuel de Vasconcellos identified the causes of the hatred towards him 'as an effect of the zeal and readiness with which I carried out royal orders and fulfilled my obligation as a true and faithful Portuguese vassal, as I always had done.' The dispute became so strong that the War Council even suggested to the King that he move to Torres Novas and settle the quarrel.

42 ANTT, *Conselho de Guerra, Consultas*, Consulta M. 105 *sobre o capitão mor de Viseu João Paes do Amaral* (26 April 1646).

then the career advancement lower down the hierarchy was necessarily delayed, especially since the commanders almost always held the command of a *terço*. In Portugal the rank of *mestre de campo* followed the same pattern established in France and Spain, and it held great prestige. However, since the King was the actual master of the army, the terço as well as the company did not belong to the *mestre de campo*, who therefore was rather a commander-administrator. This resulted in less income, but the *mestre de campo* could turn to other forms of filling their own purses. The most common among these not always legal practices was to advance money to soldiers, who often waited for months their wages, but at a reduced rate, and then to collect the full amount when the government finally paid the arrears.[43]

The rank of *mestre de campo* existed only in the infantry and corresponded to the rank of colonel. Though the rank of colonel was formally held by the commanders of Lisbon militia, which were usually registered as *regimentos*, the terms *mestre de campo* continued to identify all the officers holding the senior rank of a regular infantry *terço* as well as the ones of auxiliaries and militia. According to the Military Ordinances of 1643, to ascend to the rank of *mestre de campo* it was necessary to have served for 12 years in the army, of which four had to be in the rank of captain.[44] However, nobility and other 'people of quality' were exempt from this apprenticeship, which in practice meant that the *terços* could be commanded by members of the nobility without the necessary, or any, military experience. In this case, the *sargento-mor* (Major), who was second in command, held greater responsibilities on campaign. As commander of his *terço*, the *mestre de campo* moved on horseback, although there were officers who preferred to fight dismounted in the heat of the battle.

The vast majority of the *mestre de campo* were of Portuguese nationality, however there were some foreign officers. Along with the Sicilian-born Pietro Pissingo (or Opecinga), another Italian reached the rank of commander of an infantry *terço*. This was the Roman Giovanni *João* Tranquillo Vannicelli, a person halfway between adventurer, professional soldier and trader. He passed with ease from commander of an Italian *tercio* in the Spanish army of Milan between 1648 and 1649, to colonel of a regiment raised in Hamburg for Portugal in 1650.[45] Five years later, Vannicelli was promoted to the rank of *tenente general da cavalaria* in the Army of Alentejo and in 1662, he was among the officers who asked the King to be allowed to retire from active service, 'because he does not think to be able to serve Your Majesty any more'.[46] Vannicelli remained in Portugal together with other members of his family as associates in the Brazilian sugar business.

---

43 This abuse was attributed, along with other crimes, also to the Scottish *mestre de campo* David Caley referred to below.
44 Rede de Bibliotecas de Defesa Nacional, *Ordenanças militares discutidas entre ossres. Joanne Mendes de Vasconcellos* (1643).
45 ANTT, *Registo Geral Merces*, Livro 19 (December 1650).
46 ANTT, *Conselho de Guerra, Consultas*, M. 22 (6 March 1662). Vannicelli is here described as a 'Venetian'.

Much less successful was the career of the Scot David Caley. In 1641 he arrived in Portugal accompanied by another officer, the Englishman Christopher Potley. Both had long military careers, having served for 30 years in the armies of Sweden and Denmark. Potley had achieved the rank of colonel, while Caley, who had followed the same route, had become lieutenant colonel. They proposed to King João IV that they form two infantry regiments, receiving in exchange the rank of colonel and the pay of foreign commander, which was double that paid to the Portuguese *mestre de campo*. The King was willing to pay an even higher salary if they were able to get him two regiments formed by British mercenaries, but it was not possible to achieve the project as the officers had intended, who nevertheless both entered the Portuguese army. In August 1641 Caley and Potley accompanied the *governador das armas* Martim Afonso de Melo on his journey to Elvas, when the future Count of São Lourenço took the command of the Army of Alentejo for the first time. They served as volunteers, waiting for a command to become vacant in one of the *terços* of the provincial army. On 28 October 1641 Caley was slightly injured during the assault on Valverde, or perhaps in the subsequent looting, being the first offensive operation performed by the Portuguese army into Spanish Extremadura. Meanwhile, the coveted employment as a commander did not arrive, and in June 1643, exasperated by the tardiness of the payment of wages, Potley returned to England, leaving Caley in Lisbon with the other foreigners looking for a suitable position in the Portuguese army. The perseverance of the Scot was rewarded a few months later, when in September he received the patent of *mestre de campo* of one of the auxiliary *terços* recruited in Estremadura. Caley marched to Alentejo to return to Valverde. The town fell again into Portuguese hands, as well as Villanueva del Fresno, renamed Vila Nova de Portugal. It was here that Caley's *terço* remained in garrison. At the end of the campaign the unit was disbanded, and the Scottish *mestre de campo* spent the following months in the castle of São Jorge in Lisbon. In 1644, he held the command of another auxiliary *terço* and served in Alentejo until March 1645. After spending some months in Beira, two disciplinary proceedings were undertaken against him. Then in 1646 he was finally appointed to the command of one regular *terço* and assigned to the garrison of Olivença, where he was put under investigation because of his alleged poor behaviour during the Spanish assault on the town. Possibly Caley was the victim of previous intrigues or disagreements with other Portuguese officers. The soldiers refused to testify against Caley and the King himself did not authorise his removal from command of the *terço* until the investigation was concluded, despite the insistence of the *governador das armas* of Alentejo, Martim Afonso de Melo Condé de São Lourenço, who argued that the Scot could desert to the Spanish. In October 1648, with the investigation ongoing, Caley and his wife left Olivença and went to Lisbon. Precisely a year later, a royal decree dismissed him from the army and he was free to return to Scotland. However, in March 1650 he was still in Lisbon, miserable and sick, as he says in a petition sent to the War

Council.[47] There is no more information about him, therefore it is very likely that he finally left Portugal in April or May 1650.

Infantry Organisation

The *terços pagos* of the Portuguese infantry were permanent units formed by professional soldiers, who were enlisted for a determined period, which before 1668 usually coincided with the duration of the war. Between 1641 and 1642, there were 10 regular infantry *terços* deployed from north to south: one in Entre-Douro-e-Minho, two each in Beira and Estremadura, and five in Alentejo.[48] In its continuing policy of increasing the army, the Portuguese monarchy managed to increase the number of infantry despite opposition from the *Cortes*. Between 1643 and 1646, five new *terços* were raised, in Alentejo, Minho and Algarve, followed by further 13 before 1659. Every expedient was considered to circumvent the limitations imposed on recruitment by the *Junta*, including the initiative of private individuals, who agreed to recruit companies. Other initiatives involved the guilds of bankers and traders, like the *Terço da Armada da Bolsa*, raised in Lisbon in 1658, or the *Terço novo da Câmara do Porto* in 1659. In the early 1660s, the number of infantry corps increased significantly, with *terços* appearing under the designation of *terços novos*, due to the split of some of the old *terços*. Although some of these units had a short life, being assembled for a limited period, the overall strength of the infantry continued to increase until 1665, when the province of Riba-Côa recruited a *terço* of infantry to serve in Alentejo for a single campaign.[49]

The *terços* became the largest administration unit of the infantry and presented the same features of the Spanish *tercio*, from which the Portuguese *terço* was clearly derived. The establishment of 1643 replaced the original plan to field 2,000 men. After this date, each *terço* numbered 1,596 men not including the *primera plana*. This comprised the aforementioned *mestro de campo* and *sargento-mor*, with two *ajudantes* (warrant officers), and one *tambor mor* (drum major). Under the major staff there were 12 companies of 133 rank and file. Each company fielded a major staff composed of:

---

47 Freitas, 'War abroad: English, Scots and Irish officers in the Portuguese Army, 1641 to 1657', in *Arquebusier*, vol. XXIX/III, 2005, pp.2–11. 'Caley claimed he had not received money after his dismissal, because he had been unjustly accused of not having distributed the equipment to his men in the 1643 campaign. The War Council was sympathetic to the foreign officer: 'because as he is a foreigner and at the same time, he did not know the language or the styles of this Kingdom.'
48 Condé de Ericeyra Luís de Meneses, *Historia de Portugal Restaurado* (Lisbon, 1679), vol. I, p.85.
49 Although not impossible, it is a difficult task to trace the history of the first Portuguese *terços*, because the dispersed and incomplete nature of primary sources, like the *Livros de Registo do Conselho de Guerra*, or the *consultas* and decrees of the same council, as well as the inaccuracy of references to certain units in the narratives of the war campaign, as happened even in Meneses's famous *Historia do Portugal Restaurado*. Also, several works printed in the following century are not always reliable. Gastão de Melo de Matos, in the 1940s, drew an outline of the organic history of the regular and auxiliary *terços* recruited in Entre–Douro-e-Minho, which however did not have continuity for the other provinces.

1 *capitão* (captain) with a page-boy
1 *alferes* (ensign)
1 *abandeirado* (colour Bearer)
1 *capelão* (chaplain)
2 *sargentos* (sergeants)
2 *tambores* and 1 *pífaro* (drummers and fife)
1 *Armeiro* (gunsmith)
1 *Serralheiros* (blacksmith)

The combat force of each company comprised 40 *piqueiros*, 60 *mosqueteiros* and 25 *arcabuzeiros* divided in five tactical squadrons, each commanded by a *cabo de esquadra* (corporal). The *mestre de campo* was also the captain of the first company, which therefore did not have a captain, and the command on the field was always delegated to the *alferes*. In total, a *terço* numbered 480 pikemen, 720 musketeers and 300 arquebusiers. This was the establishment recommended by the regulations, but between what the expected paper strength and the number of soldiers actually available, there were always differences. One of the most common differences was in the number of companies. The original fixed number of 10 companies, proposed before 1643, posed some difficulties, because for organisational necessity it was considered better to form *terços* aggregating more companies, since the number established would have left out many *companhias soltas* (free companies). However, the decrees of the War Council were imperative in imposing a maximum of 10 companies. A compromise succeeded, and in the first years of war, the *terços* fielded between 10 and 12 companies, depending on the total availability of companies in the provinces.

A new organisation was introduced between 1645 and 1646. Now the *terço* comprised a regular *primera plana* with eight ranks:

1 *mestre de campo* with one or more page-boys and adjutants
1 *sargento-mor*
2 *ajudantes*
1 *ajudante supranumerário*
1 *tambor mor*
1 *cirurgião* (surgeon)
1 *capelão* (chaplain)

The last two ranks, however, were not always present, given the lack of people who had the required skills or knowledge. The first company always belonged to the *mestre de campo*, and now deployed one ensign, one sergeant, one *abanderado,* and two musicians, The remaining nine companies each had the same ranks as above, plus the captain commander of the unit with one *pagem de gineta*. This latter was a young cadet who carried the *gineta* (spontoon), namely the distinctive weapon of the captain, when the officer was in charge of leading the company. The *pagem de gineta* received the same pay as a private soldier, while in contrast the *abanderado*, who usually was another boy, received less pay. The *terço* still deployed 10 companies divided in four platoons with four *cabo de esquadra* and 96 private soldiers, comprising

THE BIRTH OF THE MODERN PORTUGUESE ARMY

30 pikemen, 48 musketeers and 18 arquebusiers. The *terço* numbered now 76 officers and NCOs belonging to the *primera plana* and company staff, and 40 *cabos de esquadra* with 960 soldiers, for an overall strength decreased to 1,076 men.[50] Obviously, these were the theoretical strength and organisation. In fact, there were strong differences among the *terços* even in the ones from the same province, especially in the number of personnel belonging to the major staff, which numbered cadets and other officers appointed by the *mestre de campo*.[51] The established organisation was intended for the calculation of expenses and for paying the troops, since the military administration only referred to the full strength. In Portugal, as well as in Spain, the *terço* had become the larger administrative unit of the infantry, but here the organisational pattern maintained the original tactical role, and this ambiguity led to some contradictions. No seventeenth-century commander was willing to trust the theoretical figures of the forces in the field, since the actual number of soldiers almost always differed from the total declared on the paper. In this regard, Portuguese sources are very explicit. Some muster lists, sent to the War Council after the reviews, show the tremendous variations existing between the professional *terços*. The musters executed between September 1660 and September 1661 in the army of the province of Alentejo depict the situation of the units on the field, and in the latter period the 10 *terços* comprised 855 officers and NCOs, including the supernumeraries, and 4,789 soldiers, for 5,644 men at all. Luís de Meneses' *terço* was closest to the establishment strength with 1,017 men, but of the remaining, only three fielded more than 700 men, while the other *terços* were below the strength deemed acceptable. On the last page of the list, the *vedor geral* laconically noticed that several soldiers were absent from the companies without permission to return to their homes.[52]

According to some contemporary scholars, during the campaign of 1662, the regular Portuguese *terços* deployed on average a full-strength force of

Infantry *capitão* with buckler and sword, 1665. Reconstruction after the figures depicted in the *azulejo* representing the Battle of Montes Claros, preserved in the palace of the Marqueses de Fronteira in Lisbon. (Author's reconstruction)

---

50 Gastão de Melo de Matos, 'Notícias do têrço da Armada Real (1618–1707)', in *Anais do Club Militar Naval* (Lisbon, 1932), pp.27–28.
51 Aires, *Historia Organica e Politica do Exercito Português*, vol. IV, p.69.
52 ANTT, *Conselho de Guerra, Consultas*, 1661, M. 21: *Relação dos Officiais e Soldados de Infanteria e Cavalaria que se acharãoneste Exercito – ultima mostra* (22–23 September 1661).

600–700 rank and file.[53] In the last phase of the war, the strength of the *terços* considerably varied again. In 1663, the infantry engaged at Ameixial-Estremoz, deployed the *terço* of Trás-os-Montes with 310 men, the one of Algarve with 432, Cascáis with 532, and Beira with 500.[54] Months later, the Spanish spies reported in detail that the seven unidentified Portuguese *terçoa* camped in the environs of Évora fielded from 251 to 724 men.[55]

Coeval sources, although partially, allow to establish the percentage of soldiers actually armed with firearms and the ones equipped with pikes, showing a variable percentage depending by the province of provenance, but with little differences. The inventories of weapons registered in the arsenals between 1647 and 1654,[56] show that in the *terço* there were at least two third of soldiers with firearms, with a proportion of muskets oscillating between 33 and 49.5 percent, and the harquebus between 20.2 and 32.5 percent, leaving to the pikemen a percentage between 30.3 and 34.5 percent.[57] Some sources supplies more than one information regarding the presence of musketeers, arquebusiers and pikemen in a wide range of percentages until the early 1660s. According to the detailed Spanish report of the Portuguese infantry at Évora in 1663, each *terços* fielded a very different number of musketeers, arquebusiers and pikemen, and in some case, there are no arquebusiers or just a couple of pikemen.[58]

In the next decade, the infantry organisation turn to the French model, and progressively the soldiers with firearms were unified in a single musketeer specialty.[59] However, the differences of strength among the *terços* continued until the end of the war. In the 1670s, the regular infantry did not modify the basic organisation, but some change occurred in the units embarked on the fleet, which were equipped only with firearms. In 1676, four new *terços* were recruited in Lisbon, Setúbal and Cascáis, each with a field strength between 1,400 and 1,500 men.[60] In the same years, the auxiliary *terços* were also called to arms, as a response to the reciprocal diffidence between Madrid and Lisbon. However, the presence of the regular infantry on the border remained low key, limited to guarding the strategic outposts

---

53 Jonathan Riley, *The Last Ironsides. The English Expedition to Portugal, 1662–1668* (Solihull: Helion & Company, 2014), p.53.
54 Dores Costa, *Formação da força militar durante a guerra da restauração*, p.91.
55 BNE, *Sucesos 1663*, pp.122–123. Thanks to Francesco Pellegrini for this notice.
56 Today preserved in the Portuguese Military Historical Archive of Lisbon.
57 Freitas, 'Infantaria: o equipamento das companhias', in *Guerra da Restauração* (30 March 2008).
58 BNE, *Sucesos 1663*, pp.122–123; see also in the Appendix.
59 Until the end of the century, the Portuguese army retained just two type of infantrymen, musketeers and pikeman, and did not raise grenadiers until 1701. In this year, the King of Portugal asked Louis XIV to send him a company of grenadiers to serve as a model for his army. On 14 August 1701, the French King consented the formation of a company of 50 men, which took the name of *Compagnie de grenadiers du Portugal*. See also in Victor Louis Jean François Belmont, *Histoire de l'infanterieen France par le lieutenant-colonel Belhomme* (Paris. 1893–1902), vol. II, p.352.
60 Antonio José Rodríguez Hernández, 'Miedos de Guerra y Ecos de Frontera: la posición de España ante una alianza franco-lusa durante la Guerra de Holanda (1672–1679)', in *História Moderna*, Serie IV, vol. 25 (2012), p.139.

with the minimum necessary number of soldiers. In 1677–1678, for instance, the border fortress of Villanova de Cerveira garrisoned 600 foot in total.[61]

As was the case in the Spanish army, the largest tactical formation of the infantry was the *esquadrão*, which usually combined companies to form corps of 300–500 men. The Portuguese infantry fought in a similar way to their Spanish enemies and like the latter based its strength on good cohesion and the depth of the ranks. The presence and experience of infantry of other nationalities brought some improvements in tactics and firing system. The relatively small numbers of the Portuguese army made it possible to standardise regulations and tactical discipline, and this made things easier for the commander in the field. The *Ordenanças Militares* of 1643 remained in place, and much of the infantry regulations printed later demonstrate its influence, or in certain cases, the continuation of the advances that preceded the original project in which it sought to standardise tactical discipline.

The history of the Portuguese army has been investigated quite thoroughly thanks to the increasing access to the archives, but many gaps remain regarding the pedigree of the first units. It is possible to follow the evolution of a *terço* if the research is based on the name of the field commander, since the units were usually designated by the name of the *mestre de campo*. However, even the issuing of a commission does not guarantee that an officer held command of the *terço* to which he was appointed. Especially in the first years of the war it is possible to find the registration of several commissions for the rank of *mestre de campo* without any direct link with a unit. The second part of the *Livros de Registo do Conselho de Guerra* is dedicated exclusively to this type of document, where the holders never got to exercise the designated command. Another difficulty is the occasional exchange of units between officers by mutual agreement, after they had already been in charge of a *terço* for a period of time, often quite short. Not a very common practice, however it happened, as reported at least on one occasion. In the *consulta* of the War Council which met on 22 April 1664, a request from the *mestre de campo* Manuel Lobato Pinto was discussed, in order to exchange the command of a *terço*. Pinto had been appointed to the *terço* previously commanded by Pietro Pissingo, but he had not served in that unit before moving to Monforte to attend to the restoration of the fortress. From there he went to Vilaviçosa, to assist in the restoration of that town's fortifications. While there, he learned of his appointment to the rank of *mestre de campo* of the *terço* held by Pietro Pissingo. The *terço* of Diogo de Faro was quartered in Vilaviçosa, now under the command of Francisco Henriques. After an agreement with Henriques, Lobato Pinto proposed to make the exchange. The War Council were favourable to the request, as both the *mestres de campo* agreed on it and because it did not jeopardise the service of the royal troops. The King himself gave his consent on 30 April 1664. In this way, the *terço* belonging to Pietro Pissingo went to Francisco Henriques, while the one in Vilaviçosa passed to

---

61   *Ibid.*, p.140. Despite the relative state of peace, in the following summer, Lisbon sent an engineer to cross the border, while various military units were mustered in Lisbon, and a 700-man *terço* was formed with the funds allocated by the local traders.

Manuel Lobato Pinto.[62] These occasional changes sometimes make it difficult to accurately trace the history of the first infantry *terços*.

In addition to the *terços*, the Portuguese infantry also included independent companies, the aforementioned *companhias soltas*. These were especially useful to garrison less important locations. However, their maintenance and operational capacity were facilitated by their integration into temporary *terços*, as a result of which the free companies normally had a limited duration as independent units, as they were either dissolved after some time, or they became part of a regimental-sized *terço*. Though the free companies had a short life, their presence is often mentioned in the contemporary sources, confirming the flexibility of their employment also on campaign. Among the documented examples, there are several events involving these units in the Army of Alentejo army confirming their presence until 1664. The muster prepared by the *mestre de campo general* of Alentejo, Gil Vaz Lobo, reveals that these units were generally very small in strength, and that, according to Lobo, the best way to preserve the companies was to join them in a *terço*.[63] According to Lobo, there were five free companies of the garrison of Crato which were dispatched to Valença de Alcantara, numbering 290 soldiers and 20 officers; another company from Crato formed the garrison of Montalvão with 50 soldiers under four officers; two companies from the garrison of Avis with 40 soldiers and eight officers were in Monforte, 'where a third company has still to be raised'. Further free companies formed the garrison of Alter do Chão, one company with 30 soldiers and two officers: Fronteira had one company formed by 28 soldiers and three officers, which was assigned to Monforte as reinforcements, already garrisoned by a further three companies with 34 soldiers and nine officers; Alegrete had one company with 36 soldiers and four officers; Marvão, one company with 30 soldiers and four officers, Monsaraz, three companies with 108 soldiers and 17 officers. Overall, there were 18 companies with 71 officers and NCOs, and 567 soldiers, including 29 sick.

In 1642, Portugal had also raised a *terço* for the fleet, called *terço da Armada Real*. However, from 1658 this unit was deployed in Alentejo, in response to the border emergency. After this date, service as naval infantry was provided by a couple of free companies, formed by professional soldiers and by others raised on an ad hoc basis from the *Ordenanças*. The marines were also involved in major actions outside the Iberian Peninsula. The

---

62 *Ibid.*, 'Acerca dos terços pagos do período da Guerra da Restauração', in *Guerra da Restauração* (31 October 2013).

63 *Ibid.*, *Companhias 'soltas' de infantaria no exército da província do Alentejoem 1664* (18 December 2009). The Royal Decree dated 9 November ordered the War Council to give an opinion concerning the *terços* that, according to the *mestre de campo general* of Alentejo Gil Vaz Lobo, it would be necessary to formed by merging the free infantry companies still existing in the province. Lobo stated that the companies would be better preserved if joined in a *terço* and suggested the appointment António Tavares de Pina to the command of the unit. The War Council then asked for more detailed information about the companies and the places where they were located. In response, Gil Vaz Lobo wrote a letter from Estremoz on 22 December. He informed them that of the 15 companies (there should be 16, but one was not yet formed), the King should have a *terço* of 12 companies, adding the three companies serving at Monsaraz to the *terço* of the Mourão garrison. Attached to his letter, Lobo sent a detailed list, entitled 'Relation of the infantry companies in the province of Alentejo, and of the people they will be with'.

Franco-Portuguese alliance allowed Richelieu to request the Lisbon's aid to combat Spain at sea. In early 1646, Portuguese ships supported the French fleet in the Mediterranean, and then in August, a Portuguese squadron of seven ships under João de Menezes, with 1,500 marines, collaborated in the operation on the island of Elba, returning to Lisbon on 27 January 1647.[64]

After the war, the *Terço da Armada Real* resumed its original duties, but some independent companies were also raised when necessary. The most important action performed by the marine infantry occurred in September 1675 and involved the whole regular force. After rounding the Straits of Gibraltar, the Portuguese fleet landed 2,000 marine infantry and 1,600 sailors to assault Plaza de Sargel, a town 16 miles West of Algiers. At this action several volunteers of the richest Portuguese nobility also participated. According to a Portuguese source, 1,500 Algerian corsairs formed the garrison, and the town housed 8,000 inhabitants. Although the assault lasted a few hours, the fighting continued until the next morning and caused many casualties among the civilians. Then the city was plundered, and the fortifications demolished. The Portuguese captured a huge amount of booty and released 2,000 Christian prisoners.[65]

In the 1660s, the free companies became much less common in the professional army and usually only had a short existence, almost always being absorbed by one of the existing *terços*. Instead, the company was the basic organisational structure in the auxiliary infantry, since before 1660 just a few 'ad hoc' *terços* were formed by the militiamen, but only for a single campaign. The organisation of the auxiliaries passed through several phases and lasted a long time before reaching its final structure. Already, in 1641, the creation of a militia (the future *auxiliares*) was planned in order to support the regular infantry in guarding the borders, and one year later some companies had been formed in Alentejo and Minho. The Portuguese government dealt with the auxiliary infantry since the first months after the 'acclamation' of December 1640. Four month later, the newly appointed bailiff Braz Brandão agreed to raise a mobile force of '3,000 men or more' in the province of Entre-Douro-e-Minho. The king ordered that Brandão be granted commissions with blank spaces for the officers' names, who were to serve without pay, and he was assigned the financial means necessary to recruit and sustain this force.[66] However, the auxiliaries were the result of a compromise between the Estates and the Crown, because in 1642 the government removed all members of the privileged classes from their obligation to register in the *Ordenanças*. In addition to the nobility and the clergy, the traders, the business owners and also all the residents of Lisbon

---

64 Gastão de Melo de Matos, *Notícias do têrço da Armada Real (1618–1707)*, in 'Anais do Club Militar Naval' (Lisbon, 1932), p.19.
65 *Relación verdadera de la toma, y asalto de la Ciudad de Zargel, y su Presidio, por las Armas de Portugal, en Setiembre del año de 1675, Cádiz, 1676*. In this action, the Portuguese fleet was joined by one Genoese warship with its marine infantry.
66 Claudio de Chalby (ed.), *Synopse dos Decretos remettido sao extinto Conselho de Guerra* (Lisbon, 1869) Synopsis 88 – March 1641, vol. III, p.7.

and Porto were exempt from the military service in the *Ordenanças*.⁶⁷ But it was not just the economic and status concerns that caused the negative reaction from the Estates. The strongest objection arose from your typical civilian's aversion to the army and the fear of being enlisted by force, and even having to face the military courts. After 1643, all the civilians eligible to exemptions from military recruitment would receive a safe conduct letter that granted them exemption from service in the army. As a result, the *Auxiliares* were established in 1646, and mainly composed of peasants and members of the poorer classes. Alongside the latter, even felons convicted for ordinary crimes were sent to the *Auxiliares* to serve their sentences.⁶⁸ However, by the law already issued in 1645, all these troops were obliged to serve just for a single campaign. Since the war did not seem to have an end in sight, in March 1646, the King established that only the people enrolled in the lists of the *Ordenanças* of 1641 would not be obliged to serve under arms to defend the borders and fortresses to which they were called. Nevertheless, due to the continuing war, the regulation was not fully applied, and in practice, only the aged subjects were removed from the auxiliaries' lists.⁶⁹ The escalating military involvement forced the government to an even more focussed militarisation of the *Ordenanças* with the formation of semi-permanent corps similar to the *terços* of the regular infantry. The first Royal Order issued to join the companies of the *Ordenanças* in a regimental-sized unit dates back to March 1643, when 10 companies raised in Alentejo were assembled together to provide the garrison of Moura and later Mourão, where they remained in service until 1645. A further two temporary *terços* were raised in Estremadura in September 1643, included the one under the aforementioned David Caley, sent to the border fortresses of Alentejo until the end of the year. The career of this officer are useful to follow as it is possible to glean some details concerning composition and duties of these corps. At the beginning of 1644, Caley received the command of another *terço* raised in Estremadura, which was formed with a mixture of inexperienced and veteran militiamen under officers from disbanded units. The latter received a small fraction of the original pay, and could be enlisted again, even as simple soldiers. Caley's *terço* was destined for Alentejo, where it served for a period of three months, after which officers and soldiers were discharged.

---

67 The population of Lisbon would be recruited for active military service only from October 1807, with a first attempt made in 1661.

68 Rede de Bibliotecas de Defesa Nacional, *Ordenanças militares discutidas entre ossres. Joanne Mendes de Vasconcellos* (1643): 'And if the Report of this city (Lisbon) or Porto condemns someone to serve in the army or any border at his expense, he will not receive the salary, unless he is so poor that he has no way to support himself. And the *vedor geral* will ensure that these condemned men appear in the registers together with the other soldiers, and that they will be noted in the lists with a declaration of the form in which they serve, which will be the one of the sentence.'

69 The selection of the recruits destined to go to the companies was carried out on the lists of the *Ordenanças*, subsequently updated 'in order to be updated and find out if the people in the lists are still useful for the King's service.' The lists were transcribed into registers; in Alentejo 18 registers belonged to the province, four to the civil judges and one each to the villages of Vidigueira and Vila de Frades. See Chalby, *Synopse dos Decretos remettido sao extinto Conselho de Guerra*, vol I, p.16; decree of 3 March 1643.

In February 1644, he was still short of three companies to complete the *terço*, which also needed captains and one *sargento-mor*. It was with these men that, on 26 May, Caley fought at the Battle of Montijo. In autumn, the *mestre de campo* returned to Lisbon to take charge of one of three new auxiliary *terços*, quickly raised to cover the casualties suffered. With little military training and no weapons, the Scottish *mestre de campo* led 1,000 men to Estremoz, where they finally received weapons and ammunition captured from the Spaniards during the previous year's campaign. From there, the *terço* headed to Olivença, where it joined the local garrison.[70] The War Council planned to transfer the *terço* to the category of paid troops, but this optimistic provision was not confirmed. Many recruits did not adapt well to military life, and desertions increased after the soldiers got to know of the government's plan.[71] In March 1645 the *terço* of Caley was finally disbanded. Difficulties in recruiting troops continued to be a serious problem. On 7 January 1645, the Crown ordered the *sargento-mor* of the Santarém district to organise a corps by merging the local independent companies. The royal letter specified that 'It has been established, as a very important remedy, that a militia corps be formed in each district capable of handling this service that, with the title of auxiliary soldiers, and with the privilege enjoyed by paid soldiers … Two or three captains, chosen from among people of experience and value, will be enlisted, to whom patents will be issued with the signature of the King.'[72] The same letter was sent to the *sargento-mor* of Torres Vedras, on 12 February 1645. The response of the local Estates was not positive, nor was that of the other towns and cities of the province. For this reason, a new royal letter was issued on 26 January 1647. Since the auxiliaries had not yet been organised, the local council had insisted on maintaining the companies, forcing the King to engage in a real legal duel. Weeks later he restated the order, adding that:

> In accordance with chapter 18 of the Cortes … I was asked by all three Estates that the Regimento [regulation] of the Auxiliares be carried out in all the provinces and districts of the Kingdom, because it is a means so necessary for its defence and conservation … As a chapter for having done them mercy, I approved them, and already confirming what was ordered, I sent the statute of 13 March [1645], with which the militiamen of the Ordenanças are dispensed to march to the borders.

Despite problems and delays, the organisation of the auxiliaries developed well in Alentejo, albeit slowly. The royal letter sent to the recalcitrant district of Torres Vedras, in which the Crown explained what had been established in 1645, informed the local authorities that 'in matters of auxiliary soldiers, these have already settled in the towns and places of the counties of Tomar, Leiria, Vilaviçosa, and in others, [and therefore] I will be willing to serve my person with the same devotion, for the many and great comforts that this Militia can

---

70 Freitas, 'Um esco cêsao serviço de D. João IV – o mestre de campo David Caley (part II), in *Guerra da Restauração* (2 December 2008).
71 *Ibid*.
72 *Ibid*.

provide.' Regarding officers, the appointments proceeded fairly quickly. In a letter sent to the War Council dated 18 May 1647, the Governor of Alentejo was informed about the appointment of Diogo Fróis de Sande to the rank of captain of the company of auxiliary soldiers in the Portalegre district, 'which is currently under the captain of the *Ordinanças* of the same city'. The letter outlined that 'from the news sent to the Council, you will have understood that everything is being done with the utmost diligence for the safety of the kingdom and that the auxiliary military militias are generally respected by the population'. But again, the creation of auxiliary *terços* was not fully established. Only at the end of 1649 and the beginning of 1650, did the legislative activity on auxiliaries recommence. On 1 April 1650, João IV promulgated a more updated regulation for the *auxiliaries*, entitled *Regimento dos governadores das comarcas tocanteàs coisas dos auxiliaries*. The King returned to the question again on 17 December 1650, informing the courts of all the provinces, to grant the *auxiliares* some legal privileges.[73] Local authorities received a decrease in training days. Before 1650, the orders imposed exercises to be conducted every eight days, including Sundays and holidays, gathering the recruits by *esquadra*, and by company once a month. With the introduction of the new regulation, the training obligations became monthly for the *auxiliaries*. In this context, it is easy to guess the tacit agreement reached by the Crown with the *Estado dos Povos* and the acceptance by the King of the end of the military obligations of the *Ordenanças*, exchanging this with the creation of the paramilitary auxiliary troops. Although the Crown had to accept, at least provisionally, that the auxiliaries were not part of the military institution, the army could increase its strength.[74]

After the participation of the auxiliary *terços* in the campaigns of 1643–1645, new regimental-size units finally appeared between 1649 and 1650. It is from these dates that Luís de Meneses, in his famous work, begins to refer to these soldiers. The first time he mentions them is when he states that Jerónimo de Ataíde, Count of Atouguia, and newly appointed *governador das armas* of Trás-os-Montes, 'noticed that the province was devoid of paid people (regular soldiers) and then he tried to correct the lack of men with auxiliaries and other militia'. Then, Meneses states that in 1650 in Alentejo 'the auxiliary *terços* raised

---

73 It is not easy to clearly define the reason for the delay in the creation of auxiliary units by the government and the difficulties created by the local institutions. However, it is possible to glimpse, through the legislation issued subsequently, how the concerns of the privileged population of the municipalities had been decisive in slowing down the application of royal orders. Many of the objections put forward by the provincial Estates were aimed at not assimilating the auxiliaries within the regular army. In this regard, the royal letter of 30 November 1650 stated that the district courts were the only ones authorised to try individuals for crimes committed while serving as auxiliary soldiers. The letter confirmed chapter XXI of the regulations issued in the previous April. Probably, the local Estates thought that the privileges they had were not sufficient, since with the decree of 30 June 1651 further guarantees were added, which essentially reaffirmed how the population had to participate in the defence of the country, but without joining the army, demanding to remain under the ordinary jurisdiction, both civil and criminal, and not military. Due to the fragility of royal power, the Estates eventually succeeded. See also in Dores Costa, *Governadores das armas*, pp.201–202.

74 *Ibid*.: 'But the struggle between the *cortes* and the Crown continued, and as António Manuel Hespanha says: the animosity of the people slowed down the military organization of Portugal.'

in the counties of Campo de Ourique and Beja provided for the lack of paid soldiers'; finally, he writes that 'Sancho (Manoel, Count of Vila Flor) undertook in 1659 these measures with greater success' by sending on campaign the *mestre de campo* João Fialho, commander of the *terço* of Penamacor, with 500 regular infantry and auxiliaries with 200 horsemen, 'to run the countryside of Moraleja', the first major action performed by the *auxiliares* outside Portugal.[75] Over time, the auxiliaries proved to be a success, allowing for a substantial increase in the military forces available for a campaign at very low cost. Before 1661, the *auxiliares* participated in campaigns as companies integrated into the regular *terços* as reinforcements or by replacing regular in the garrisons so they could be released to serve with the field army. This is what is stated in a letter of Francisco de Saldanha in 1660. He wrote that 'due to the great lack of soldiers in the *terços* serving in the Alentejo army … it is very useful to fill them with more auxiliaries who are ready for this service, and with the number that appears necessary.'[76] The presence of the *auxiliares* continued in the following years. In 1662, for the campaign planned in Galicia, the army gathered in Entre-Douro-e-Minho under Francisco de Sousa Count of Prado fielded about 8,000 infantrymen, and half of these were *auxiliares*, gathered in five *terços* under their respective *mestre de campo*, one of whom was a Frenchman.[77]

Portuguese historians claim that the auxiliary troops had been decisive in the Portuguese military efforts, especially in the final phase of the Restoration War, being a sort of secret weapon of the Crown, but in the 'glorious history' of the *auxiliares* there are also several shadows. On 7 May 1663, barely a month before the victory won at Ameixal, the *governador de armas* of Alentejo informed the War Council that 'the *terços* of *auxiliares* coming from the province of Estremadura have so far not arrived, nor Beira have more than one [regular] *terço* in Portalegre, I also cannot fail to notice Your Majesty the dismay and impossibility with which this army finds itself by calling the [auxiliary] soldiers to leave their quarters to join the field army on campaign, without asking for help.'[78] In 1661, the auxiliary companies in each of the provinces began to be combined into semi-permanent *terços*. According to the intentions of the War Council there were to be no differences between the organisation and strength of a regular *terço* and one of *auxiliares*. Once again, it is not easy to reconstruct the process that led to the formation of these units, and to decipher the complex decisions resulting from the negotiations between the Monarchy and the *Cortes*. However, in the text of a letter sent to the War Council of 13 October 1661, which summarises a brief history of the auxiliary troops, it is stated that King João IV appointed Francisco de Faro, Count of Odemira, and Gaspar de Faria Severim, his secretary of *Mercês*, 'to introduce … the exercise of auxiliary soldiers who had not yet been established in some provinces, and so … to proceed in the joining of the companies and appointing the captains.'[79] Another clue

---

75 Meneses, *Historia do Portugal Restaurado*, vol. II, p.219.
76 ANTT, *Conselho de Guerra, Consultas,* 1660, M. 22, C. 12.
77 The *mestre de campo* Pierre de Sanpierre, Meneses, *Historia do Portugal Restaurado*, vol. II, p.431.
78 Dores Costa, *Formação da força militar durante a guerra de Restauração*, p.88.
79 *Ibid.*

to the final establishment concerning the formation of auxiliary *terços* is found in the text of another decree, dated 2 October 1665, in which António de Meneses, Marquis of Marialva, informs the War Council that the eight auxiliary terços of Alentejo had already been in existence four years earlier.[80] In 1661, Portugal was divided into 23 military districts, and each had to raise its own auxiliary *terços*. However, several scholars state that the auxiliary infantry formed 30 *terços* in all, while others quote a lower number, since not all the provinces formed regiment-sized units.[81] Characteristic of the *Ancien Régime*'s governments, and typical of Spain and Portugal, the promulgation of a law did not imply its immediate application, and even when it began to take effect, it did not always proceed until it was fully implemented. However, this matter remains difficult to solve because the various sources do not always agree.[82]

In the 1640s, the structure of the auxiliary companies followed the infantry organisation established in 1643, with the same number of rank and file as the professional infantry, which in turn reflected the existing pattern of the Spanish army. In general, the proportion between soldiers equipped with muskets or arquebuses was not far from the percentage established for the regular infantry. Obviously, the number of soldiers with firearms depended on the availability of weapons but even so, the differences were not very significant. Regular companies were equipped with arquebus and pikes in a ratio of 2 to 1. But it was possible to find companies fully equipped with firearms, since the auxiliaries were mustered to garrison the border fortress and intended for a static defence role, which made the pikes redundant it being more effective to use firearms. The musket being heavier than the arquebus, and with a greater effective range, was issued on a preferential basis to the regular troops of the *terços pagos*.[83] Furthermore, pikeman required specialist and longer training, a task that could be dispensed with for the second-line infantry.

Cavalry Organisation

The Portuguese cavalry during the first years of the Restoration War was essentially formed by light horsemen, comparable to the contemporary Spanish *jinetes*, and like them were made up of several kind of mounted soldiers. This variety was reflected in the various terms employed to identify

---

80   ANTT, *Conselho de Guerra, Consultas,* 1665, M. 28, C. 21.
81   General Gabriel Espírito Santo in his *A Grande Estratégia de Portugal na Restauração 1640–1668* (Lisbon: Caleidoscópio, 2009), states that in the 1660s the number of auxiliary *terços* was 25 from the provinces and another five from Lisbon, but this statement would seem incorrect, since Lisbon never recruited auxiliaries and also it is quite certain that not all districts had established auxiliary companies, not allowing the raising odd units with of regimental size.
82   In the contemporary work of Luís de Meneses, *Historia do Portugal Restaurado*, six auxiliary *terços* from Entre-Douro-e-Minhoare mentioned, assembled in 1662 for the campaign in Galicia. The *terços* are reduced to only two in the authoritative work of Melo de Matos, *Osterços de Entre-Douro-e-Minho*, published in 1940. Even if Meneses made some mistakes, it is not easy in this case to establish who is right in the absence of a thorough investigation of the sources preserved in the archives.
83   Freitas, 'Organização do exércitoportuguês (2) – Infantaria: o equipamento das companhias', in *Guerra da Restauração* (30 March 2008).

the Portuguese cavalry: *arcabuzeiros a cavalo, cavalos arcabuzeiros, clavinas* (carabiniers) or *cravinas* and also *carabinas*. In tactical terms, the Portuguese cavalry was similar to the light cavalry commonly found in Central and Western European army. In 1641, most of the companies in the paid (professional) army were *arcabuzeiros*. From September 1644, following the experience gained at the Battle of Montijo, another branch of cavalry was introduced: the *couraceiros* (armoured cavalrymen). These existed before that date only as an honorary designation on paper, since they were equipped with buff coat and breastplate, but without any tactical differences in relation to the rest of the cavalry, except for training in the use of the carbine. There were units wearing buff coat, and using carbine, in the regular (paid) cavalry, as they were considered elite troops, but this should not be confused with the actual concept, because more than the tactical use of the unit, it became above all seen as a commander's individual prestige, which gave his troops an elite distinction. The number of personnel in a professional cavalry company varied greatly over the course of the war. Between the beginning of 1641 and the end of 1648, the 100 men company establishment at the beginning of the conflict soon fell to 80, went back to 100, then 80 again, then 60, then 100 again, and finally back to 80. Schomberg's influence led to the establishment of 65 soldiers per company, introduced in November 1661. Obviously, the paper strength did not mean that it was the same as the parade strength present in the field. Several times during the war, there were even companies formed of just two dozen horsemen, as well as others, albeit rarer, with a strength above 100. The most common size, however, was between 30 and 60 horsemen per company. In a muster recorded in September 1661 concerning the cavalry of the Army of Alentejo, some companies had more horses than the number of men, while in others there were men dismounted due to a lack of mounts.[84] This drawback was the knock-on effect of the rights granted to cavalry captains in April 1647, the *Contrato com oscapitães de cavalos*. The 'contract' was still in force in 1661 and permitted to the officers to trade horses meant for their men. This was seen by Schomberg as a serious obstacle to the effective administration, organisation and discipline of the cavalry, and was a source of bitter debates with his Portuguese rivals.

Whatever the number of soldiers, each company consisted of a *primera plana* with *capitão, tenente, alferes, furriel*, chaplain, two trumpets, blacksmith and one page for each officer. Although the *alferes* did not officially exist in the mounted *arcabuzeiros*, many companies included them. The rank and file included a chaplain, farrier and blacksmith, all expected to be on horseback, but often it was difficult to provide these personnel in all the companies, and many had only a single trumpet. The company was divided into *esquadras* of

---

84 ANTT, Conselho de Guerra, Consultas, 1661, M. 21: Relação dos Officiais e Soldados de Infantaria e Cavalaria que se acharãoneste Exercito – ultima mostra (22–23 September 1661). The muster roll registers some officers whose biographies are known, like, for instance, Captain Jácome de Melo Pereira, a nobleman and member of the Order of Christ, a distinguished cavalry captain, with a long and brilliant service record, who would be arrested by the Inquisition in 1665, accused of Judaism, and later executed at Évora. See Freitas, 'Efectivos do exército da província do Alentejo em Setembro de 1661' (Part 2 – *a Cavalaria Portuguesa*) in *Guerra da Restauração* (12 February 2011).

Two units of Portuguese cavalry depicted in an *azulejo* preserved in the Palácio Fronteira in Lisbon. During the War of Restoration, Portuguese cavalry are randomly denominated as *cavalosar cabuzeiros, carabinas, cravinas* or *clavinas*. Campaigns typically consisted of *correrias* – cavalry raids – to burn fields, sack towns, and steal large herds of enemy cattle and sheep. Soldiers and officers, many of them mercenaries, were primarily interested in booty and were prone to desertion. Without men or money, neither Spain or Portugal mounted formal campaigns or long periods, and when actions were taken they were often driven as much by political considerations – such as Portugal's need to impress potential allies – as by clear military objectives. (Author's archive)

20 to 25 men, each commanded by a *cabo* (corporal). As granted by the royal decree issued with his commission, the captain could appoint the officers and the corporals. The *companhia* (company) constituted the administrative unit of the Portuguese cavalry throughout the War of Restoration. In 1661, the Count of Schomberg submitted a proposal for introducing the regimental system in the Portuguese cavalry. The proposal encountered strong resistance from the Portuguese commanders, who, among other reasons, admitted that this change would imply 'the loss of the social-military prerogatives of the captains, which were a well-established local tradition.'[85] The matter was discussed for three years, and in 1664 reform of the cavalry took place, but the most that was achieved was the introduction of more or less homogeneous *troços* under the command of a *comisáriogeral*. However, before 1664, there were already cavalry *troços*, since it was the name in use for any group of mounted companies, but only afterwards did they take on a formal organisation, which fixed the companies within the *troço* to eight, including the company of the *comisáriogeral*. However, these were not permanent units, since the *troços* were only formed for the duration of the campaign. Despite suggestions of the need to raise more dragoon units, none took shape. In March 1648, the dragoon company was transformed into *arcabuzeiro* horse.

---

85 Jorge Penim de Freitas, *A cavalariana Guerra da Restauração: reconstrução e evolução de umaforçamilitar, 1641–1668* (Lisbon: Prefácio, 2005), p.34.

THE BIRTH OF THE MODERN PORTUGUESE ARMY

Possibly a Portuguese cavalryman and trumpeter, late 1650s, depicted by Dirk Stoop (1610–1686), who was active in Portugal between 1656 and 1662. In the seventeenth century most armies employed two main varieties of mounted soldier; several included a third, depending on the horse's size. The two most common branches were 'the horse' and the dragoons. However, in Portugal only a single company of dragoons served between 1642 and 1648. According to some Portuguese commanders, the dragoons' tasks were also performed by the cavalry. (Author's archive)

As with the Spanish, Portuguese dragoons were barely represented in the mid-seventeenth century Portuguese army. Only one dragoon company served in the Restoration War, and it was formed at the beginning of 1642 for the Army of Alentejo. The first commander was António Teixeira Castanho, formerly a lieutenant of a company of mounted *arquabuzeiros*, an officer with previous military experience in the service of Spain. His lieutenant was António Banha, who is referred to in some battle records as the actual field commander. From 1646, the Portuguese dragoons always served under French officers. Unlike the other regular cavalry, the dragoon company had no ensign because it did not use a standard and further differences existed in the use of drums instead of trumpets. For the rest, it followed the structure of the normal company of horse, although it was still considered to be mounted infantry. However, the wages paid to the officers were identical to those in the cavalry and were therefore higher than in the infantry. Despite requests for more dragoon units, no other companies were raised. In March 1648, the dragoons were converted into mounted *arcabuzeiros*, namely carabiniers. In the opinion of the governor of arms of Alentejo, Martim Afonso de Melo, Count of São Lourenço, who ordered this conversion, dragoons were of little additional use because they performed the same duties as the cavalry. The brief history of the Portuguese dragoons came to an end. Curiously the company had normally been quartered in Olivença, a locality that later was again to be associated with dragoons.[86] However, a relatively common expedient throughout the war was to mount part of the infantry on mules, mainly the arquebusiers, but sometimes also pikemen and musketeers, to launch incursions into enemy territory or to assist the cavalry on the field on occasions of great need. Two soldiers per animal was the usual allocation. However, although some narratives confuse these troops, they should not be considered actual dragoons, as they did not perform the tactical roles of reconnaissance, ambushes, protection of the army train and other tasks usually performed by dragoons. In this case, the animals served only as a means of transport for the infantry.

In the early years of the war, the Portuguese cavalry already represented an essential component in the warfare along the border. The harshness of the terrain along the frontier and the consequent need for an elastic defence, which could be guaranteed by the mobility of the cavalry, gave a significant presence to the horsemen in the field. In the plan devised by the War Council in 1641, the cavalry strength was established at 2,800 horsemen out of 16,800 professional troops. In the Army of Alentejo, the percentage of horse compared to infantry was always higher than 20 percent of the total for the duration of the war, a percentage that reflected the large use of mounted troops made by the Spanish. The overall strength continued to increase through the raising of new companies by turning to every resource available. The cavalry were concentrated above all in the sectors most exposed to enemy incursions. In this regard, the letter dated January 1664 sent to the War Council, by the Count of São João da Pesqueira, *governador das armas* of Trás-os-Montes, was a very unusual document with a such a high level of detail.[87] Though within a provincial army it was necessarily common for this kind of request, it was not often that it involved the affairs of another province and even the War Council. In his letter, the Count of São João regrets the lack of cavalry in the province of Trás-os-Montes, due to the losses in the engagements sustained during the campaign of 1663, especially in the casualties sustained in Beira.[88] The Count attached the list of casualties as an argument to justify his urgent request for reinforcements. He also requested that Pedro César de Meneses, general of the cavalry of Entre-Douro-e-Minho, be ordered to raise soldiers to fill the weakened companies. The Count asked for money in order to buy 100 horses, even in Aveiro or Coimbra, although it was prohibited to trade with other provinces. Finally, he asked the King to authorise him to transfer the cavalry from Trás-os-Montes to winter quarters. This last request was a hazard, since military operations did not end with the cold season; on

---

86 Ibid., pp.67–68.
87 Freitas, *Rescaldo de umaoperaçãomilitar – as baixas detal hadas de umaforça de cavalaria no combate de 2 de Janeiro de 1664* in 'Guerra da Restauração' (16 April 2009). The attached list of casualties suffered in 1663 mentions the 'bitter loss' of the captain of the *coraças* João Correia Carneiro, who had served in the army for 23 years. The captain died of 'countless wounds' and notwithstanding 'the continuous praise deserved to him.' He left two sisters, his mother and father, with few financial resources. For this reason, the Count of São João asked the King to do even more than the expected mercy, 'because with the honour gained by the dead captain, the relatives are also rewarded'; excerpt from the letter of the Count of São João dated 10 January 1664.
88 *Ibid.* The listed casualties numbered 34 horsemen killed, 45 wounded, 61 horses dead and 18 wounded.

the contrary, it was more often the summer heat that hindered the campaign. However, the province of Trás-os-Montes was one that benefited most from the cold season, due to its altitude. The War Council issued a favourable response, to send as much money as possible, so that the cavalry could be reformed, consenting only to the buying of horses in Aveiro and Coimbra, as it was believed that this same lack of horses would be found in the province of Beira, and that the cavalry should be remounted with horses from both provinces, Trás-os-Montes and Beira. Regarding the request to go into winter quarters, the War Council added that the cavalry of Trás-os-Montes should not be sent to their barracks without first getting the views of the governors of Beira and Entre-Douro-e-Minho.[89] The presence of a significant cavalry body of cavalry and its importance in frontier warfare is also confirmed in the peripheral provinces. In 1663 of the 465 regular soldiers quartered in the district of Penamacor, in the province of Beira, 146 were horsemen.[90] Despite the difficulties of maintaining such a high percentage of cavalry, the Portuguese army increased its regular mounted force in a greater proportion than the infantry. In 1665, the Portuguese had more than 6,000 horse.[91] This figure quickly decreased one year later, and by the end of the war, the cavalry strength had dropped to 1,500 regular horsemen. During the 'cold war' against Spain, the cavalry again increased in strength. This had been approved by the *Cortes*, albeit to a much smaller number than originally planned. In 1673, just six new companies were recruited, by forcing the Lisbon merchants to collect the funds for raising 300 horsemen, attached to the cavalry *troço* quartered in Lisbon under the Duke of Cadaval.[92] In July 1676, the same number were raised, deducting the cost of doing so from the *asentistas*' credits.

Whatever tactical doctrine was adopted, and the one that favoured charging to contact and hand-to-hand combat fighting was the dominant one among the Portuguese as well the Spanish cavalry during the Restoration War, the basic formation was the *batalhão* (battalion). As in the Spanish cavalry, this term had different meanings and therefore it does not always correspond to a unit made up of two or more companies. The *batalhão* was similar to the more usual cavalry squadron of other European armies, although this term was more appropriately applied in the Portuguese and Spanish army to the infantry battle formations. Occasionally, a single company could be enough strong to form a *batalhão*, namely, to assemble a corps three lines deep, like those introduced by the Swedish cavalry commanders, or even four or more lines, with a front of at least 20 horsemen, or more. The tactical strength depended on the number of troops and the disposition on the field ordered by the cavalry commanders, like the *comisáriogeral*, *tenente general* or any other senior commanders. When a single company was not sufficient

---

89 *Ibid.*
90 ANTT, *Conselho de Guerra, Consultas*, 1663, M. 23–A, C.87, :*Efectivos detalhados que existiam no distrito militar de Penamacor, província da Beira.*
91 White, *Guerra y revolución militaren la Iberia del siglo XVII*, p.82.
92 Notes from the Abbot of Masserati, Lisbon, 25 May 1676, cited by Rodríguez in *Miedos de Guerra y Ecos de Frontera*, pp.136–138.

to form a battalion, it could be reinforced with horsemen from another, in order to give achieve numbers in the formation consistent with other battalions. The most experienced soldiers were always chosen for the first two ranks. The distance between ranks could vary from the length of two horses to a minimum that left almost no space between the lines in the front and rear ranks. The latter deployment was performed when the formation was ready to receive an enemy charge in order to open fire with two ranks. In 1662, with the arrival of the English cavalry, new tactics were introduced, turning to the experiences learned by the Cromwellian Ironsides and also from the French cavalry, which both used fire tactics and close combat. The English horsemen strongly influenced the Portuguese regular cavalry, which, from this date, assumed the typical structure of the Ironside and introduced their tactics.

In the 1650s, the *batalhão* had become the larger tactical unit of the Portuguese cavalry and was the formed by joining three or more companies in order to deploy units of 100–200 horsemen belonging to the same branch. In rare but documented cases, a large company with more than 100 troops could field two battalions, as happened in 1665 with the company of the cavalry General Dinis de Melo de Castro.[93] Cavalry battalions were usually deployed in the field in two lines, sometimes three, disposed in a chess formation. The lateral interval between each battalion was called *claro* (clear). This space served to leave enough free ground for the cavalry battalion to charge the enemy or to withdraw to rally in the rear: Meanwhile the enemy formation that pursued it would be counter-charged by a unit from the second line.

Organisation and tactics were identical for the cavalry belonging to the *Ordenanças*, introduced in 1650 as mounted auxiliaries. The province's *camara* appointed and selected the captains and other officers for these companies, but as in the regular cavalry, it was difficult to provide a chaplain and other posts like a blacksmith and a trumpeter. Furthermore, when the auxiliary companies were raised, the question soon arose as to who should serve in them. Auxiliary infantry companies had been created five years earlier, but the new legislation was now onerous, which should be maintained by enlisting anyone who could maintain a warhorse. It would be two years, however, before the War Council clarified the problem. In a letter from Francisco de Melo, *general da artilharia* of the Army of Alentejo, the matter is explained. The general expressed a doubt as to who would supply horses, since the regulation established in 1650 by the provinces for the auxiliary cavalry did not mention the matter. The ancient *Ordenanças* of King Sebastião, which were still consulted, obliged persons to have a horse who had an endowment of at least 600,000 *réis*, which in 1650 was not enough to support a single man, as Francisco de Melo said. The War Council then clarified that the people who were to be required to supply a war horse would be the ones with an endowment of 800,000 *réis* or more.[94]

---

93 Freitas, O batalhão, 'formação táctica da cavalaria', in *Guerra da Restauração* (13 June 2008).
94 *Ibidem*, 'Auxiliares a cavalo – quem deveria servir', in *Guerra da Restauração* (30 June 2020).

There were different kind of auxiliary and militia cavalry, at least as far as terminology is concerned. In contemporary documents, the *Auxiliares* were usually referred as *arcabuizeros*, or simply *cavalos auxiliaries*, while the companies raised as a defence force and considered as territorial militia were identified by the terms of, *pilhantes*, *moradores* and *amunicionados*. These cavalrymen had been already raised in 1647, before the creation of auxiliary cavalry but were contemporaries of the *Ordenanças* of cavalry. The difference between the mounted *auxiliares* and this type of cavalrymen was that the latter underwent training voluntarily. A further name was introduced in Algarve, where the traditional designation of the southernmost province of Portugal continued to identify the cavalry from this province. Here, the *ordenanças* cavalry continued the use of spear and shield for some time, as was still the case in the Portuguese outposts of North Africa. This equipment is recorded in a list of troops mustered in 1639. Auxiliary company officers usually came from the regular cavalry, but in this case, they were paid less. At least one company of *pilhantes* came to be commanded, in the early 1650s, by a French officer from the regular army. In 1650, the paper strength of auxiliary mounted companies was established at 50. The *ordenança* cavalry and the companies of *moradores* and *amunicionados* did not have a fixed number of troops, although they were expected to imitate the strength of the regular force.

Artillery Organisation

The birth of the artillery as an autonomous military body began in 1640 with the creation of the rank of *tenente general da artilharia* (lieutenant general of artillery), established with a special decree signed by the King on 28 December. The first lieutenant general, Rui Correia Lucas, was not a military professional but a civilian official, subordinate to the Council of Finance, and equivalent to other administrative charge like the *Provedor de Armazéns e Marina* (Provider of Warehouses and Ports). His function was to deal with everything related to war material in general and artillery in particular, and also included the production of weapons and gunpowder. His authority extended to the Lisbon factories like the *Tercenas* of Porta da Cruz (the modern-day quarter of Santa Apolónia) and Cata-que-farás (Cais do Sodré), later known as *Tenência*, and the gunpowder factory of Barcarena. The economic plan of the army, authorised in 1642, established an overall force of 300 professional artillerymen, with a command staff which remained under the supervision of the *tenente general da artilharia* for all the economy's matters. In the same years, a corps of *Engenheiros* (engineers) was also raised and comprising a directive staff with native and foreigner technicians.

The Portuguese artillery also included the venerable corps of the *Bombardeiros da Nómina*, a unit created in 1515 by King Manuel I and assigned to the artillery in charge of the defence of Lisbon. The *Bombardeiros da Nómina* retained this designation because they had received a royal appointment. In 1641, the corps still existed, but in the first year of the war they were below the expected strength of 100 artillerymen, not including the *conestável* who commanded them.

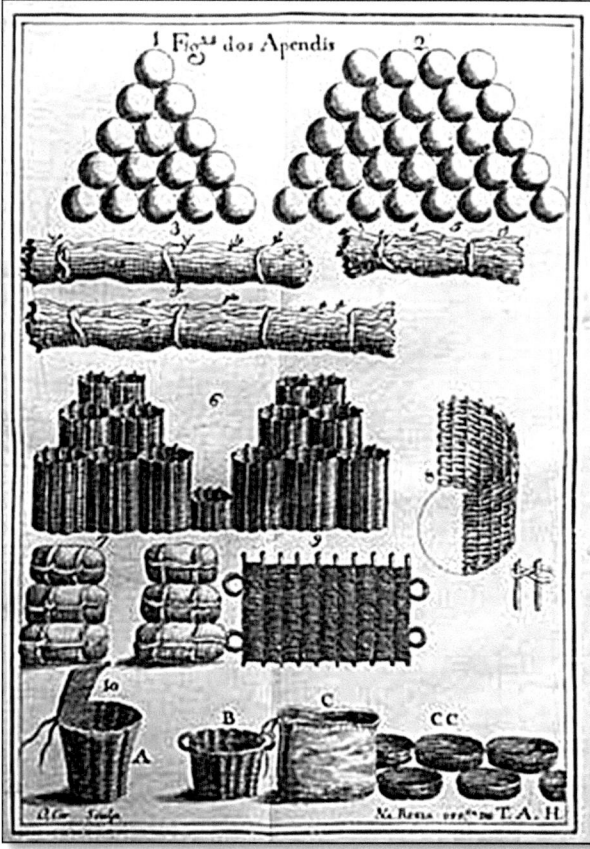

First page and illustration from the *Exame de Artilheros* of Jozé Fernandes Pinto Alpoym, artillery officer and theorist who served in Brazil in the last decades of the seventeenth century (author's collection). Portuguese artillery played an important role in the defence of the coastal forts and fortresses on the border with Spain and in the overseas domains. The government participated in the diffusion of the knowledge on these matters and commissioned treaties and other studies concerning the most up-to-date techniques for artillery. The work offers a detailed analysis on the main tasks of static as well as field artillery with a modern approach.

In the field, the artillery and its personnel operated under the army commander, who in turn could delegate the *general da artilheria* if one existed. The number of soldiers assigned to the provinces depended on the number of cannon present in the garrisons' arsenals. The command structure of the Portuguese artillery retained some late Renaissance features, which derived from its origin as a technical corps. The *gentil homem da artilharia* was responsible for a certain number of artillery pieces and of the train in the field army. He was also in charge of a static battery consisting of a variable number of pieces, when the artillery was present in a fortress or during a siege. Chapter 23 of the 1643 military ordinance refers that the gentleman of artillery was to be elected among the captain of *gastadores* (pioneers) or retired sergeants, 'with the necessary knowledge to use and move six cannons batteries, assisting it in the march, in encampment and in the deployment of the batteries, and making sure that the personnel and drivers have everything necessary for the service.'[95] With regard to the candidates for the rank of *gentil homem da artilharia*, Joane Mendes pointed out some reservations about the King's intention, or one of the individuals at court who privately advised him on this topic and the appointment of captains and sergeants, adding: 'if … they are capable to occupy the rank … they will be elected from them, if not practical officers and licensed sergeant, this being one of the posts that should be provided more by practice than by any other merit.' The six pieces mentioned above were not necessarily a fixed establishment since the composition of the artillery in the field army varied according to its intended purpose and availability. This is observed in a comment by Joane Mendes de Vasconcelos regarding another chapter of the Ordinances, number 47, which intended to regulate the distribution of artillery in proportion to the total number of infantry and cavalry. As the renowned general pointed out, artillery is regulated by factions, namely by the nature of operations, not by number, 'and so it is not a matter for Your Majesty to decide this matter on the Military Ordinances.'[96] The *gentil homem da artilharia* had under his orders a number

---

95 Aires, *Historia Organica e Politica do ExercitoPortuguês*, vol. IV, pp.83–84.
96 *Ibid.*, p.65.

of professional artillerymen, known as *condestável*, supported in turn by further personnel enlisted from the auxiliaries or by private *asentistas* in charge of conducting the artillery train. According to a French author, the Portuguese artillery resorted to pairs of oxen, mules or, more rarely, horses.[97]

On 2 April 1672, the artillery was organised in a single regiment, later designated *Troço de Artilharia do Mar* in 1677. This unit recruited in Lisbon, and in the towns and villages of Oeiras, Carcavelos, Sintra, Mafra, Torres Vedras, and environs, as well as in Coares, Ericeira e Cheleiros.

The Portuguese divided their artillery into the three usual categories according to their use: field artillery, siege artillery and naval artillery. The first category was in turn classified according to the weight of the projectile and was divided into large, medium and light pieces of different calibres. Examples of cannon of this class were *canhões, meioscanhões, colubrinas, sacres* (cannons, half-cannons, colubrines, sakers). Light artillery was made up of the smaller calibres; the *falconete* is the more usual cannon of this type. This type of cannon did not require the use of as many draught animals, and some weapons, like rampart muskets and falconets, could be moved by the efforts of one or more men.

Type:	Calibre	Gun weight	Projectile weight
falconete	51–55	95–98 kg	1 ¼ lb
sacre	89–93	1,134 kg	5 ¼ lb
meia colubrina	114	1,633 kg	8–9 lb
colubrina	127	1,814 kg	12 lb
meio canhão	152	2,722 kg	24 lb
canhão	178	3,175 kg	48 lb

These measures should not be taken as absolute since the variations within the same type of cannon were many. In Portuguese sources, in addition to the designation of the pieces, there are sometimes references to the weight of the projectile (in *livras*, pounds). Despite the variety of calibres and designations, the different categories are listed by the expert testimony of Luís de Meneses, who was General of Artillery in the Army of Alentejo and author of the *Historia do Portugal Restaurado*. He describes the composition of the artillery train at the Battle of Montes Claros, in 1665, listing the 20 pieces as follows: 15 of 4 lb, 6 lb and 7 lb bronze cannon; Three 12 lb cannon, and two 24 lb cannon. Very probably, the 6 lb and 7 lb cannon would be *sacros* or *meias colubrinas*, while the 12 lb guns were probably *colubrinas*. The two 24 lb cannon were certainly the *meioscanhões*, which also are mentioned in other pages of the Meneses' volumes, as for instance, in the artillery of the Spanish army of Don Juan de

---

97 Dumoriez, Charles François, *Campagnes du Maréchal de Schombergen Portugal depuisl'année 1662 jusqu'en 1668* (London, 1807), pp.XV–XVI. On this matter, the author emphatically stated: 'For example, of what utility are more than 4,000 mules for the use of the Court and its servants? Does this luxury expense add to the grandeur of dignity? By reforming 3,000 of these animals and distributing them for the train of the artillery and the crews of the army, Portugal would have enough left on this economy to train and maintain 2,000 men of cavalry.'

Portuguese guns on the first page of the treaty of Nicholas de Langres, printed about 1661. The Portuguese artillery retained some late Renaissance features, as recognisable in the denomination of ranks. For instance, the *gentil hom em da artilharia* was responsible for a certain number of artillery pieces and of the respective train in the field army and was comparable to a captain. (Author's archive)

Austria in the campaign of 1663 in Alentejo. These latter were the heaviest pieces of field artillery in the Portuguese and Spanish armies in the final decade of the conflict. If almost all the artillery was slow to move, the weight of these larger guns further slowed the movement of the army on campaign, with each cannon requiring many animals to pull it. However, it was also in the last decade of the conflict that pieces of smaller calibre were used, which supported cavalry and infantry at close range, being interspersed between squadrons and battalions. This was not exactly a novelty, because there are references to light-horse-trained artillery accompanying the cavalry in Alentejo in the 1640s, as well as experimentation with light cannons, similar to those introduced in the Swedish army, but this tactical employment became even more commonly used and effective over the following decades.

The siege artillery was made up of the large calibre pieces including those intended for firing explosive and incendiary projectiles, regulated by fuses, such as mortars. They were transported on carts and required several draught animals.

By a decree of 30 July 1644, João IV ordered the Council of War to give its opinion on the documentation prepared by the Council of Finance about artillerymen, war material and ammunition held in the fortresses of Lisbon, Setúbal and Peniche, as well as on the funds necessary to provide tools and spare parts. The detailed lists of weapons found in each fortress were attached to the findings of the War Council of 12 August 1644. From this document, is possible to get an idea about Portugal's costal defences with regard to artillery and arsenals. The monumental tower of Belem had 14 bronze cannon; one cannon of 24 lb, seven cannons of 16 lb, four colubrines of 12 lb, one *falconete* of 1 lb, and seven further cannons with calibres between 8 lb and 12 lb. In the arsenal there were two dozen hand grenades and 65 quintals of gunpowder. The local battery needed 600 projectiles and further 200 chainshot, as well as a further 35 quintals of gunpowder. In the arsenal, there were also 50 'muskets of Flanders', 28 harquebus and 50 pikes. The garrison was made up of 40 soldiers, but 'they are still more to 80, which will be there according to the order issued'.[98]

---

98 ANTT, Conselho de Guerra, Consultas, 1644, M. 4–B: Relação da gente paga, artelharia armas munições carretas mantimentos e maiscousas que ha nasfortalezas da barrades tacidade e nas de Setuval, e do que necessita cada huã dellas (12 de Agosto de 1644). In this document, the War

Militias

Since the Portuguese male population was almost all registered in the *Ordenanças*, the only corps of militia were formed in the cities of Lisbon and Porto, due to the commitment of the Crown with the *Cortes*, which accepted a tax increase, but obtained the privilege for these major centres of not being recruited for compulsory military service. In both cities, the *milicias* were created in 1643 raising a company of infantry with the same – theoretical – organisation and strength of the professional infantry. Subsequently, the government extended these obligation to other regions, and in 1646, after the full establishment of the *auxiliares,* each province received the order to organise its own militia. In order to alleviate the burden of the military commitment to the population of the kingdom, the Portuguese militia was another compromise between the King and the Estates since the war effort was seriously damaging the economy of the countryside. The *Cortes* of March 1646 dealt with this matter, as stated in the chapter 13:

> Since one of the greatest disturbances suffered by the Kingdom had been the call of people to the *Ordenanças* in all the encounters with the enemy … and in all the emergencies at the borders and fortresses the people have been called together with the (professional) troops to join them for guarding the trenches and bridges, sentries and more, causing serious harm to the farmers during the harvests … from now the people will exercise trades and jobs for the benefit of the common and private good. The King order that the people being not more called [to the *Ordenanças*] unless the enemy carries out an invasion so great making necessary to have recourse to all. In this regard, the King has added in these Cortes the necessary instructions to register the subject in the Camaras and the Governors will be ordered to keep the registers for themselves and for the captains of the districts.[99]

With this act, the *Ordenanças* ceased to have any kind of military obligation, both in time of war and peace, forcing the Crown to end their independence from the army. On the other hand, the government could maintain its selective draught system for the *auxiliares*, transferring a significant part of the male population to the militia, which continued to be designated *Ordenanças*. In order to differentiate the militiamen from the auxiliaries, the province's *camaras* obtained the right to appoint the officers for their own militia, in the face of the reaction of the military governors who claimed control of all the available troops. These decisions imposed a change

---

Council supported the opinion of the Finance Council so that the forts of Setúbal and Peniche, as they were more distant from Lisbon, had everything that was necessary within their walls, and for that purpose the Teniente General da Artilharia should visit the fortresses each month. As for the fortresses guarding Lisbon, 'these could be supplied with what was missing at any time, not requiring much urgency,' except for gunpowder and projectiles of different calibres, 'which should be provided immediately.' Finally, the War Council warned that the consignment of 1,000 cruzados (400,000 reis) already assigned to the lieutenant general was insufficient for the needs of the fortresses, so it would be convenient to assign more money.

99 Chalby, *Synopse dos Decretos remettido sao extinto Conselho de Guerra*, p.41; decree of 20 March 1646.

Lisbon's militia deployed in the *Terreiro do Paço*, 1650–55, by an unknown artist (City Museum of Lisbon). The function of the auxiliary troops and militiamen was well explained in a letter of 1650 of the War Council: 'The raising of these soldiers is to always keep them in arms, so that on the most important occasions, the commanders can use them for the defence of the kingdom, but what cannot be achieved, in any case, is that such soldiers are always happy to serve.'

in the legal status of the *Ordenanças*, and for this reason, the King agreed that the militiamen would never be tried in a military court.[100] The attempts of the monarchy to exert greater control over the *Ordenanças*, establishing the absolutist principle of centralisation, continued throughout the war and after, but was imposed only in 1808. The call to arms could be done in wartime, requiring captains and militiamen to muster for the defence of the fortresses, and guard the border in an emergency, but nobody would any longer be called to serve as 'mobilised auxiliaries'. This is the reason why, in 1678, in the regulation for the *governadores das armas*, it was again prevented from meddling 'in the election of the officers of the *Ordenanças*, because this corps belonged to the provinces, and their government.'[101] This decision reiterated that the militiamen did not form part of, nor were responsible to, the regular Portuguese army.

---

100 ANTT, *Conselho de Guerra, Consultas*, M. 20, C. 26 (December 1643); chapter 26: 'in order to know the guilt of the officers and soldiers of the Ordinance, it was decided that for the offenses committed by these soldiers of the Ordinance, any War Tribunal may take a decision contrary to the provisions of the ordinary courts, according to the response that the King gave an answer to this argument regarding the aforementioned soldiers, and the people of the Ordinance, who will therefore be free to present their cases before the ordinary courts.'

101 Chalby, *Synopse dos Decretos remettido sao extinto Conselho de Guerra*, p.456; decree of 24 May 1678.

Although the militia remained separate from the army, the militiamen had to carry out regular periods of training. The militia of Lisbon met every Sunday and on the other festive days, convening in the area before the Terreiro do Paço, and forming '*esquadrões* for Your Majesty to see them'.[102] In December 1650, following the new regulations issued to the *auxiliaries*, the militiamen modified their training duties, now reduced to only four times a year; the two annual reviews were maintained, and executed during the 'octaves of Easter and the day of São Miguel' (29 September, day dedicated to the Archangel Michael, patron saint of Portugal). According to a contemporary source, in 1658 Lisbon's foot militia deployed four *terços* with 1,390, 1,279, 1,817 and 2,645 men, under the command of *coronel* de Almeida, da Silva de Mello and Lima respectively.[103] Five years later, the *terços* were decreased to three, organised like the regular and auxiliary infantry, under the command of *mestre de campo* selected among the local nobility and men of substance.[104]

During the Restoration War, military engagements involved the militiamen in the early phase of the conflict, when they formed a static reserve of infantry assigned to the defence of the strategic strongholds. The militiamen did not engage in any large engagements, except for the militia of the most exposed border provinces, like Alentejo, and to some extent Entre-Douro-e-Minho, Beira and Trás-os-Montes. The militia of Alentejo was involved in several major sieges, like Olivença in 1657, Arronches in 1661, Juromenha in 1662, Évora and Estremoz in 1663, and Vilaviçosa in 1665. While at Évora the 3,000 militiamen performed very poorly,[105] in the latter action, the local militia formed by *espingarderos* supported the regular and auxiliary infantry in the defence of this key fortress.[106] This action proceeded the decisive field encounter of Montes Claros. After 1665, the obligations of the militia were limited to training and little else.

However, after the peace of 1668, the government did not completely disband the militia. In 1672 and even more in 1676, the rumours about a new war against Spain persuaded the King to call the militia to improve its training. This and other facts echoed widely in Spain and alarmed the Spanish ambassador, who immediately reported to the court every detail concerning the Portuguese rearmament. However, the reality did not correspond to the news circulating, which dramatically referred to the war preparations being made on the border, but the news had spread like wildfire causing great fear. According to Spanish sources, the regular *terços* were ready to march and the militia had intensified its musketry training. The news caused the formation of several auxiliary *terços*, and other news reported the zeal of some Portuguese commanders in preparing their contingents.[107]

---

102 Meneses, *Historia do Portugal Restaurado*, vol. II, p.215.
103 ANTT, manuscritos livraria 1658, *Terços de Lisboa*.
104 Santa Cruz, *Declaracion que por el Reyno de Portugal ofreceel doctor G. De Santa Cruz a todos los Reynos*, p.50.
105 The militia inside Évora was estimated by Hagner to be 3,000 men, in Dumoriez, *Campagnes du Maréchal de Schomberg*, p.36.
106 Espiritu Santo, *Montes Claros*, p.55.
107 Rodríguez, *Miedos de Guerra y Ecos de Frontera*, p.136.

Foreign Troops

Portuguese calls for assistance found answers from the countries involved in the war against Spain. After the acclamation of João IV in December 1640, the Dutch Republic signed an offensive and defensive treaty with Portugal on 12 July 1641. This alliance seemed a natural consequence of Spain being the common enemy. However political observers did not fail to see its uniqueness, as the United Provinces and Portugal were allies in Europe, but fought against each other in South America, Africa and Asia. But in the distress of the first months of the war, Portugal had a great need for soldiers with combat experience, and therefore just a few paid attention to the origin of these mercenaries, especially if they were veterans. The Dutch military help materialised in early 1642 with the arrival of a regiment of cavalry and one of dragoons. The Dutch corps served under Lambert Floris van Til, who was escorted by a Lifeguard company under his lieutenant Nathias Waremburg. Lieutenant Colonel Jan Willem van Til, brother of the commander-in-chief, held the command of the cavalry regiment formed of eight companies.[108] The dragoon regiment served under Lieutenant Colonel Estacius Pick, and also fielded eight companies.[109] Each company had a strength of 100 rank and file. These regiments were only as such administratively and contractually, because in the field they always served as independent companies. Six months later, the contingent was reorganised, and some dragoon captains transferred to the cavalry regiment, while other officers with their men returned home at the end of 1643. The dragon regiment is still mentioned in a 1644 document, but it is referred to as the cavalry unit, and the companies, now reduced to four, again operated independently. Lieutenant Colonel Estacius Pick, initially registered as a commander of the dragon regiment, received the rank of *mestre de campo* in the Army of Alentejo before the end of 1642 and commanded a *terço* of Portuguese infantry of 12 companies, which included several foreign personnel, including four Dutch and one French officers. Pick was eventually captured by the Spaniards in the Battle of Montijo, and he was not released until the end of 1646, when he returned home. The sources do not distinguish between Dutch cavalrymen and dragoons, and the official documents usually combine the cavalry and dragoons into a single regiment. In August 1644, a new agreement was signed to maintain the Dutch horsemen in service, and, effectively, the companies still serving formed a single four company strong cavalry regiment.[110] The contract

---

108 Freitas, 'Regimentos holandeses de 1641 aoserviço da Coroa portuguesa (cavalaria e infantaria – organiza çãoteórica)', in *Guerra da Restauração* (3 February 2009). The other captains were Conrad Piper, Jacob de Cleer, Jacob van Wagen, Alexandre Bery, Mauricius Lamair, Henrique Schilt, Gaspar van Berg.
109 *Ibid.*, the captains were Frederik van Plettemburg, Frederik Streecht, Johan Doecy, Peter Behan, Sigismundus Finkeltous, Roomfort, Johan de La Roche.
110 ANTT, *Conselho de Guerra, Consultas*, M. 4, C. 29, document attached to N. 75. According to Freitas, this document gives a new perspective on the matter. A letter from João da Costa, dated 28 December 1643, attached to a *consulta* of the War Council of January 1644, states that, unlike the French units, the Dutch had not yet been reformed (or reorganised or even disbanded, as the case may be), for the royal decree that ordered it had been lost. In afurther missive, the

Plate A

Portuguese Infantry, 1660s
1. Infantry *Mestre de Campo*, 1664–1668; 2. Musketeer, *Terço de Armada*, 1664; 3. Pikeman, Unknown Unit, 1665

(Illustration by Bruno Mugnai © Helion & Company 2021)

See Colour Plate Commentaries for further information.

Plate B

Infantry, 1670–1680
1. Fife, *Terço de Lisboa*, 1670s; 2. Officer, Early 1680s; 3. Marine Infantryman, 1680s
(Illustration by Bruno Mugnai © Helion & Company 2021)
See Colour Plate Commentaries for further information.

Plate C

Portuguese Cavalry, 1660s
1. Senior Officer, 1660s; 2. Cavalry Trooper, 1660s
(Illustration by Bruno Mugnai © Helion & Company 2021)
See Colour Plate Commentaries for further information.

Plate D

Trumpeter
Trumpeter, Portuguese Cavalry, late 1650s–early 1660s
(Illustration by Bruno Mugnai © Helion & Company 2021)
See Colour Plate Commentaries for further information.

English and French Soldiers in Portuguese Service, 1661–1680
1. English Musketeer, Portugal 1663; 2. English Infantry Officer, Portugal 1662; 3. French Musketeer, Regiment *Schomberg Allemand*, 1661–63

(Illustration by Bruno Mugnai © Helion & Company 2021)

See Colour Plate Commentaries for further information.

Plate F

Portuguese Infantry and Cavalry Ensigns
1. Infantry Ensign, 1640s; 2 and 3. Infantry Ensigns, 1660s
(Illustration by Bruno Mugnai © Helion & Company 2021)
See Colour Plate Commentaries for further information.

Plate G

Portuguese Infantry and Cavalry Ensigns
1. *Bandeira de aclamação*, 1650–1660; 2. Cavalry Standard, 1650–1660; 3. Cavalry Standard, 1662
(Illustration by Bruno Mugnai © Helion & Company 2021)
See Colour Plate Commentaries for further information.

Plate H

The arrival of the Apostolic Nuncio Giorgio Cornaro at Lisbon in 1693 (Museu Nacional dos Coches, Lisbon)

gives some details of the composition of the regiment, which comprised a Lieutenant Colonel, Alexander van Harten, one adjutant, one auditor, one provost, and a senior surgeon in the regimental staff, while each company had one captain, one lieutenant, one ensign, one farrier, three corporals and a trumpeter.[111] Overall strength was established 'from 60 to 80 troopers' per company, which had to increase back to 100 within two months.[112] In March 1645, the regiment was disbanded and the companies merged into the Portuguese cavalry. Until this date, for religious reasons, Dutch cavalry was prohibited from including Portuguese soldiers. With the dissolution of the regiment and the integration of Dutch officers and soldiers into the Portuguese army this discrimination ended.

More profitable help came from Spain's primary enemy, France. In accordance with the plan to open new fronts against Spain, Cardinal Richelieu supplied funds and military advisors to the Bragança cause. In September 1641, the first contingent was ready to sail to Portugal, formed of four infantry, five cavalry, one carabinier, and one dragoon regiments.[113] However, the designation 'regiment' was possibly exaggerated, considering that infantry regiments consisted of four companies or less, and those of the cavalry just four or three. Furthermore, the actual overall strength was very low; the infantry regiments were never completed due to a lack of soldiers, and already by 1642 rank and file were integrated into the Portuguese *terços*. Most cavalry regiments deployed companies of 25–30 horsemen, when they were supposed to have four companies of 40 to 50 each. Despite the different designations, the French cavalrymen and carabineers were equipped in an identical way with sword, carbine and a pair of pistols. Furthermore, the dragoon regiment was never constituted as such, although in 1644 one company was registered as dragoons, but without a single musket among the 20 horsemen that belonged to it, and presumably they fought with only sword and pistols.[114] Although small in numbers, the French presence in the Portuguese army continued until 1659, especially with technicians, advisors and field officers. Most of the cavalry captains were French nationals, but there were also Irish and Italians. Among the foreign officers, the French contingent in Portugal included the Genoese cavalry captain Francesco Fieschi, Count of Lavagna. Although he was not originally part of any

---

War Council points to the strength registered at the last review of the Dutch contingent. This numbered 369 cavalrymen in eight companies, later reduced to four, and 148 dragoons in four companies, which would be reduced to two. There were still 101 soldiers on foot. Costa suggests that one infantry company could be formed with these soldiers, so they can serve on foot, 'because there were no horses available for them.'
111 *Ibid.*, 1644, M. 4-B, (dated 2 August 1644).
112 *Ibid.*
113 The regiments were, Infantry: Viole d'Athis (four companies), O'Reilly (Irish, four companies), MacSuey (Scots, four companies), Tirelli (Italians, three companies); Cavalry: Boucquoy (four companies), Montjouant (four companies), Gravelins (three companies), Chantereine (four companies), Mahé de la Souche (four companies), Boisemont Carabiniers (four companies), Mazeros Dragons (four companies).
114 Freitas, 'Guerra da Restauração', *Regimentos franceses de 1641 ao serviço da Coroa portuguesa (cavalaria e infantaria – organização teórica)* (1 February 2009). The single dragoon company served under the Marquis of Gravelins.

regiment, his company was always included alongside the French cavalry in contemporary documents since the rank and file were ethnic Frenchmen. Fieschi was later captured by the Spaniards at the Battle of Montijo in 1644 and spent some years in prison.[115]

The Restoration War had become an ideal place for many adventurers in search of new opportunities, especially if their reputation at home had been ruined by some incident. In Portugal, however, their careers often remained uncertain. Since the foreign officers received their pay irregularly, sometimes waiting for months or a whole year, they were forced to turn to other sources of income. Unlike the Portuguese, who always found some more or less legal means of doing so, foreigners often resorted to illegal devices. In 1645, such a case involved two French officers who would later distinguish themselves in the Portuguese service. Achim Avaux de Tamericurt, who later held the rank of *tenente general da cavalaria* in Beira and would leave the army to return to France in October 1661, as a member of the escort of Catarina de Bragança on her journey to England was the first. With him in their illegal enterprise was Henri de La Morlaye, a cousin of another La Morlaye, a Knight of the Order of Malta, hence his nickname 'the Maltese', who had died in October 1642 while serving as a captain in the cavalry regiment Gravelins. This second La Morlaye would also fall in combat in May 1649, after he was appointed general commissioner of cavalry of Trás-os-Montes. The documents describing the *consulta* of the War Council say that the two officers had been accused by the Pagador General of the Army of Alentejo of allegedly selling some horses belonging to the army. La Morlay had sold five of them, and indeed horses bearing the military brand had been found in some farms and mills. Achim de Tamericurt had committed the same crime by selling two horses. Both officers had been also arrested while they were looking for buyers to sell more horses. Years before, La Morlay had been involved in other investigation, having pretended to be sick several times in order to avoid service, and for having tried to register as present some soldiers of his company who had already died and thus illegally receive their wages. The French ambassador in Lisbon intervened to prevent the two officers from being punished and his strong interference was outlined by the War Council. Eventually, the King himself intervened to order the punishment, but this was carried out in secret, to avoid further discrediting the officers.[116]

The need for more foreign mercenaries became urgent as the Peace of the Pyrenees approached conclusion. For this purpose, in 1659, the Portuguese regency sent Juan d'Acosta, Count of Soure, as ambassador to Paris to solicit the raising of a French corps of 4,000 foot and 1,000 horse to be transferred to Portugal. As soon as the Count of Soure landed at Le Havre, he received the overwhelming news of the suspension of hostilities between France and Spain. He was also informed that he could only come to Paris *incognito*, and that he would not be granted either generals or French troops. Nineteenth-century historians theatrically state that Cardinal Mazarin gave as an excuse

---

115 *Ibid.*
116 Freitas, 'Procedimentos irregulares de oficiaises trangeiros: o caso dos capitães La Morlaye e Tamericurt (1645)', *Guerra da Restauração* (21 July 2012).

that if peace was made, Portugal could not have even a single French soldier or commander, because the Spaniards would then have reason to doubt the Cardinal's good faith.[117] Nevertheless, Mazarin proposed to enlist a foreign general, and sent the Portuguese diplomat to Maréchal de Turenne, who had helped by choosing the most talented one.[118] At first, attention turned to General Murrough O'Brien, Earl of Inchiquin, an Irishmen who had served under four different governments.[119] In the autumn of 1659, the Irish lord sailed to Portugal, but he was captured alongside his son William, by Northern African Corsairs, who brought him to Algiers.[120] O'Brien's capture moved the Portuguese diplomat to request another foreign candidate, the German Friedrich Hermann von Schomberg. This Heidelberg-born general turned out to be the right choice for Portugal since he was a talented commander and a skilled organiser. Contemporary accounts describe him as a man of 'indefatigable zeal, imperturbability in the face of danger, moderate in victory, open nature and politeness'.[121] His mandate was to take command of the force in the field in Alentejo, as well as to reorganise and train the whole Portuguese army. As a foreigner who had taken the trouble to learn Portuguese, he was favoured by the common people and the King's ministers. However, during his eight years of service in Portugal, Schomberg had to face hostility from the Portuguese grandees, and more than once he was on the verge of resigning his post, threatening to return to France. Ultimately, he succeeded in transforming a crowd of inexperienced and disgruntled soldiers into an effective fighting force. Under his strategic direction, the Portuguese achieved a series of successes over the Spaniards that opened the way to the final victory.

Along with Schomberg, in 1660 a small contingent of 400 French cavalry,[122] including 80 officers and volunteer gentlemen and engineers sailed to Portugal.

---

117 Dumoriez, *Campagnes du Maréchal de Schombergen Portugal*, p.5.
118 *Ibid*.
119 Murrough O'Brien, 1st Earl of Inchiquin (1614–1674). After he served in Spain under Felipe III, O'Brien fought against the Confederate Catholics at the outbreak of the Irish rebellion during Charles I's reign. In 1642, O'Brien was made Governor of Munster and held command until the truce was brokered with the rebels. He was forced to submit unwillingly to Parliament in 1644, as the Parliamentarians controlled all aid to the Munster Protestant by sea. O'Brien gradually became master of the South of Ireland, and declared for Charles I in 1648, fortified the southern ports against Parliament and signed a truce with the Confederate Catholics; he himself converted to Catholicism in 1656. After Cromwell's landing in 1649, he retired to the west of the Shannon and then left Ireland for France in 1650, where he became a member of Charles II's royal council in exile and in 1654 was created Earl of Inchiquin. He entered French service and went to Catalonia during the autumn of 1657 to fight against the Spaniards. The Peace of the Pyrenees destroyed his chance of further employment and distinction in Catalonia, but Cardinal Mazarin connived to permit him going with Schomberg to Portugal (Author's note).
120 Riley, *The Last Ironsides*, p.55. The notice of his capture was reported in Paris in the following February, forcing the English Council to write on his behalf to the Algerian Bey, and by 23 August 1660, O'Brien was in England, but his son remained in Algiers as a hostage until ransomed. He later became the commander of the English contingent in Portugal. According to Dumoriez, *Campagnes du Maréchal de Schombergen Portugal*, p.6, before he came back to England, O'Brien landed to Lisbon.
121 Dumoriez, *Campagnes du Maréchal de Schomberg en Portugal*, p.6.
122 The colonelcy of this regiment was given to Murraigh O'Brien, but in 1661 the command passed to Schomberg, and later to his son Friedrich.

Murrough O'Brien, 1st Earl of Inchiquin (1617–1694), by John Michael Wright (Manchester Art Gallery). An Irishmen who had served under four different governments, he was the first designated commander of the English subsidiary contingent in Portugal.

In Lisbon, on 11 November, the cavalry was reviewed by the court 'and received the admiration of the Portuguese'[123] who hoped for further military aid, but until 1661 this was the only French contingent to serve in Portugal. The raising of French troops was impeded by the terms of the Peace of the Pyrenees, which prohibited the recruitment of soldiers for Portugal, and the King, 'learning that officers are raising soldiers on the borders of Picardy and in Hainaut for Portugal' reiterated the prohibition with an ordinance issued on 26 October 1660.[124] This order, issued to satisfy Spain, did not prevent Marshal Schomberg from forming foreign regiments, which sailed to Portugal in the following years. After the arrival of the 400 cavalrymen, in the summer of 166 a complete regiment of infantry landed to Lisbon. It was the German regiment raised on 20 December 1657 and commanded by Schomberg. Before departing France, the *Schomberg Allemand* deployed 10 companies with 100 men each, and immediately joined

---

123 Dumoriez, *Campagnes du Maréchal de Schombergen Portugal*, p.9.
124 Belmont, *Histoire de l'infanterieen France*, vol. II, p.92. The Ordinance forbid all the officers and others (King's) subjects 'to raise soldiers to pass them to Portugal or for any other cause; and forbids all King's subjects to take sides and enlist any troops, if they are for the service ofHis Majesty or raised through his commissions.'

THE BIRTH OF THE MODERN PORTUGUESE ARMY

Portuguese engineer depicted in the *Desenhos e plantas de todas aspraças do Reyno de Portugal Pello Tenente General Nicolao de Langres Francez que serviuna guerra da Acclamação* (Lisbon, ca. 1661). Nicholas de Langres (1610?–1665), was a French engineer and architect who entered Portuguese service in the 1650s. He restored and improved the Portuguese fortifications and supervised the production of artillery in Lisbon. In 1662 he suddenly left Portugal for Spain, where he entered the army as artillery general serving in the Army of Extremadura.

to the Army of Alentejo. Months later, another cavalry regiment under the Marquise of Monjorge sailed from France, but some ships of the convoy were intercepted by the Spaniards, who interned most of the soldiers. In September 1661, the regiment had 66 men and six officers, and just 18 horses.[125] French support for Portugal did not increase significantly in the following year but reinforcements sailed from France to maintain the regiments at an acceptable field strength. This task remained difficult, because in summer 1662 the French contingent numbered 750 men in all. This figure was probably the result, not of casualties in battle, but of the bad treatment received by the contingent, which resulted in many desertions and sickness. The soldiers must have been truly exasperated, at least judging from the description of their transit through a Portuguese village: 'the villagers had suffered the attention of the French soldiers

---

125 Source: ANTT, Conselho de Guerra, Consultas, 1661, M. 21, Relação dos Officiais, e Soldados da Infantaria e Cauallariadeste Ex(érci)to que se achaeffectiua, Conformeconsta dos roes de Lista da ultima m(ost)ra, que se lhespassounamaneiraseguinte.

who were exceptionally ill-behaved, stealing, plundering, looting, and not paying even the worth of an egg.'[126]

In winter 1662–1663, further French troops were secretly recruited for Portugal through the clandestine work of the French envoy Nicolas de Frémont d'Ablancourt, a fellow Huguenot, who landed to Lisbon in March 1663. The cavalry regiment Monjorge increased its strength to 300 horsemen, and the colonel replaced was with a new commander, Colonel Rougemont, since the former was still interned in Spain. As had been negotiated with England two years before, France had to meet the expense of recruiting the soldiers, transporting them to Portugal and the first three month's pay overseas. After that, their maintenance was entirely the concern of the Portuguese army. Between spring and summer, two cavalry regiments were raised, but their journey to Portugal was concealed by making them sail from Plymouth. The regiments mustered 300 cavalrymen each, under Colonels de Maret and Briquemaur, which brought the French cavalry in Portugal up to four regiments.[127] The French contingent fought in all the major battles from Ameixial to Montes Claros. In the latter, on 17 June 1665, the cavalry formed the left wing in the first line of the Portuguese deployment, while the infantry occupied the second line. The French involvement radically changed focus in May 1667, when Louis XIV declared war on Spain, at the beginning of the War of Devolution (1667–1668). Now, nothing could impede military aid to Portugal, but the war was going badly for Lisbon, and Portugal agreed to negotiate for peace under the mediation of England.

During the early 1660s Portugal had begun to engage the services of various foreign military support, trying to improve the army's performance in the field. Following the treaty of alliance agreed between Portugal and England in June 1661, the two monarchies agreed that England would send to Portugal two regiments of cavalry and two regiments of infantry.[128] The former would have a strength of 500 horsemen each, and the latter 1,000 foot: a contingent of 3,000 professional military personnel at full establishment. In order to avoid international involvement, the English troops in Portugal were to be considered 'auxiliary land forces' temporarily placed under the control of a friendly power. This was a frequent manoeuvre in this age, which allowed one state to actively support another without committing itself to a formal declaration of war. Charles II often resorted to this expedient, and unlike France, England could enact it also because they had not signed an agreement with Spain. Despite the good intentions, the number of personnel sent to Portugal was below the expectations. The cavalry was only one regiment, initially composed of eight companies, for 400 men overall. The raising of this regiment was particularly complicated.

---

126 Childs, John, *TheEnglish Brigade in Portugal*, in 'Journal of the Society for Army Historical Research' Vol. 53, N. 215 (Autumn 1975), p.137.

127 Riley, *The Last Ironsides*, p.119. Briquemaur, or Briquemault, was probably a Huguenot connection with Schomberg and a relative of the Protestant leader Franois de Beauvais, sieur de Briquemaut (1502–1572).

128 The treaty included the clause that committed Charles II to assist the Portuguese with a war fleet in the event of a Spanish siege of Lisbon. See also in Anthony R. Disney, *History of Portugal* (Cambridge, Cambridge University Press, 2009), vol. I, p.229.

The first core came from Flanders, where there were 150 troopers discharged from the French service, which included both Cromwellian and Royalist Irishmen.[129] They sailed from Dunkirk on 6 May 1662, and after losing their convoy after being intercepted by the Spanish fleet, finally made their way to Portugal. Further men were raised in England. One troop consisted of horsemen who had been enlisted in the New Model Army, and four additional troops were formed with new recruits.[130] The contingent was a very heterogeneous force, formed by veteran soldiers from Oliver Cromwell's former Commonwealth army and others who had fought for the opposite side during the English Civil Wars. Although the majority of the officers and men were veterans from the New Model Army, Charles II went to some lengths to make the higher command acceptable to the Roman Catholic Portuguese. The command of the expeditionary force was given to the aforementioned Murrough O'Brien, noted as 'a famous soldier of Ireland'.[131] He was seconded by Major General John Talbot, an old Royalist officer, coming from an ancient Catholic family of Cheshire. With them, another Catholic Irishmen, Christopher O'Brien, brother of the commander-in-chief, and Thomas Morgan, from Scotland, who had played a leading role in supporting George Monck and the Stuart Restoration, completed the command staff, each with the rank of major generals. Among the subordinate officers, there were also several Catholic Irishmen, like the first commander of the cavalry regiment, Colonel Michael Dongan (or Dugan), who until 1661 had served as *maestre de campo* in the army of Felipe IV. None of the officers was a fanatic Republican, unlike some of them who had been purged before departing England. With such an officer corps, the King was able to ensure a degree of control over the contingent, hoping to reduce the impact of a force composed by Protestants on a Catholic country. On the other hand, the two infantry regiments embarked for Portugal with a total number of 2,200 men, were all soldiers who had lost their job after the restoration of the monarchy in England, since Charles II disbanded most of the units created by Oliver Cromwell, maintaining just a few in the service of the monarchy. This was the case of three regiments garrisoned in Scotland, from which the infantry regiments which sailed to Portugal were formed. These soldiers were organised in two regiments under Colonels Henry Pearson and Francis Moore. The troops of cavalry were amalgamated with the ones of William Littleton William Salkeld and Michael Dongan. In May 1662, the contingent that left England numbered approximately 2,600 men. The infantry regiments deployed two thirds of the soldiers armed with matchlock musket and one third with pike. The cavalry were former Ironsides equipped and trained as 'typical' Parliamentarian horsemen. The contingent landed to Lisbon on 7 July 1662 and soon marched to join the field army quartered in Alentejo.

---

129 P.H. Hardacre, 'The English Contingent in Portugal, 1662–1668', in *Journal of the Society for Army Historical Research*, vol. XXXVIII (1960), p.115: 'This was Thomas Morgan's own troops of his regiment of Dragoons (later Horse), which had accompanied Monck from Scotland in 1660 under Morgan's captain-lieutenant Francis Kelly.'
130 *Ibid.*
131 Riley, *The Last Ironsides*, p.55.

Three months after their arrival in Portugal, problems arose with the payment of the wages. The clauses of the agreement stipulated in 1661 were evidently interpreted in a different way in Lisbon than was taken for granted in London. Although the Portuguese officials insisted that the English soldiers would be able to maintain themselves very well with the pay scales which were used in Portugal, the soldiers of the Portuguese army were only paid for seven or eight months in the year 'whereas the English were accustomed to payments all the year round.'[132] With some justification, the Portuguese government argued that paying the English troops at their usual rates would cause discontent between the foreign and the native soldiers. However, many of the troubles stemmed also from religious differences, forcing the Portuguese government to issue a proclamation in July 1662, forbidding the Catholic clergy from protecting anyone who wounded or murdered an Englishman.[133] English ambassador in Lisbon and other officials tried to remedy this as well as other troubles, but the delay of the pay continued to distress the English contingent for the rest of the year. In 1664, a colonel was sent to Lisbon with a group of commissioners to negotiate for the regular payment of the English troops, but no sooner had he departed than the Portuguese Secretary of State, the Count of Castelo Melhor, denounced the agreement and matters continued unchanged until 1668.[134] Desertion and war casualties made the numbers fluctuate greatly over the years, always tending to decrease, since replacements were scarce. Despite this humiliating treatment, the English contingent fought bravely, performing very well on many occasions. Their military experience proved to be very important in the achievements after 1662. At the battle of Ameixial-Estremoz, in June 1663, the English contingent consisted of two foot regiment with 1,600 men, and on horse regiment of six companies with 300 men. At the end of the campaign, the Portuguese government asked for the contingent to be brought back up to strength, and in January 1664, the Lord Lieutenant of Ireland, John Butler, 1st Duke of Ormond, was directed to provide 1,000 recruits from 'factious and dangerous' elements in the army of Ireland. When this news arrived in Lisbon, many objections were raised, since the Portuguese were so prejudiced against the Irish in general, who were thought to be partial to Spain, and therefore the project failed. After further troubles, 550 soldiers were shipped, arriving in Portugal in June and July 1664.[135] The campaign of 1664 would go down in history as the hardest for the British contingent. At the siege of Valença de Alcantara, the infantry lost 11 officers, nine NCOs and 158 soldiers killed, and more than 200 wounded. In the following campaign, the English contingent was attached to the French one, and together numbered more than 4,000 men, nearly 15 percent of the army and 20 percent of the cavalry.[136]

---

132 Childs, *TheEnglish Brigade in Portugal*, p.135.
133 *Ibid.*, p.137.
134 *Ibid.*, p.138.
135 According to Hardacre, *The English Contingent in Portugal*, p.120, the low repute of the Portuguese service soon became evident. 'In one district, a riot occurred and many of the recruits ran away after being incited by rumours that they were being arrested and sold for sugar.'
136 Riley, *The Last Ironsides*, p.135.

At the Battle of Montes Claros, the English infantry occupied the first line of the allied infantry, and according to contemporary reports, they performed formidably. The casualties were severe, but not catastrophic, and the English regiments suffered the loss of several officers and a great numbers of wounded. At the end of the campaign, just under 800 infantrymen remained available for the active service. By the end of 1666, the cavalry regiment had about 300 soldiers in the ranks thanks to a reinforcement from England, but the two infantry regiments were unable to deploy more than 700 soldiers between them. In 1667, the contingent had little more than a third of its initial strength, even after the companies had been filled with foreign deserters from the Spanish army, especially Germans.

The tormented history of the English contingent also affected the officer corps. In December 1662, Colonel Molesworth accused Murrough O'Brien of withholding pay from the soldiers and of plotting with his brother Christopher to lead the brigade to Spain. The accusations turned out to be a fabrication, and Molesworth was sentenced by court martial to be expelled from the army, but by then O'Brien had left the command to his brother, who in turn resigned in the January 1663. From this date, the command of the contingent was held by Friedrich Schomberg, who unified the direction of the foreign troops in Portuguese service. The unified command created a particular situation when, in 1665, England joined the war against the United Provinces of the Netherlands as an ally of France. For two years, Schomberg was simultaneously commander of troops belonging to two nations allied in Portugal, but enemies in the rest of the world. The situation, although paradoxical, did not cause any inconvenience, and French and English troops continued to serve together, but the Anglo-Dutch War involved a great deal of diplomatic cross-table negotiations.

After the last campaigns in Galicia and Minho in 1667, the English force numbered just 600 able men. The recovery of the soldiers from the hospitals and further reinforcements from England brought this expeditionary force up to about 1,000 men. These troops, always waiting for wages, returned to England between March and April 1668: 400 of them were shipped to Tangier to reinforce that garrison; the remaining reached Portsmouth in October. The English expedition to Portugal involved 6,330 men at all, and although not all losses were due to causes related to the fighting, the casualty rate was the highest suffered by the English army in the second half of the seventeenth century. Furthermore, England's engagement in the Peninsula was also their first intervention in European Continental policy since the Hundred Years War.

Contingent command: Murrough O'Brien, Count of Inchiquin (July–November 1662); Christopher O'Brien (November 1662–January 1663); Count of Schomberg (1663–1668).

Colonel James Apsley's Regiment of Foot. In 1665, the regiment passed to the personal command of the Count of Schomberg, but effective command was delegated to Lieutenant Colonel William Sheldon. This officer led the regiment at the Battle of Montes Claros in 1665, where he was killed in action.

Colonel Henry Pearson's Regiment of Foot. In 1663 the command was held by Lieutenant Colonel Thomas Hunt at the battle of Ameixial. Thomas

Detail from the *azulejo* illustrating the Battle of Ameixial, fought on 8 June 1663. Note the soldiers holding the muskets like clubs and qualified as *Angleses*. In the battle, the English contingent played a distinctive role and decisively contributed to the Portuguese victory. (Author's archive)

Hunt died in 1664 during the siege of Valença de Alcantara. The regiment passed to the command of Major John Rumpsey. This officer led the regiment in 1665 at the Battle of Montes Claros, as Pearson was still absent in England.

Murrough O'Brien, Count of Inchiquin's Regiment of Horse (July–November 1662); Count of Schomberg (honorary commander 1662–1668). Command in the field was held by Lieutenant Colonel Michael Dongan, until his death at the battle of Ameixial in 1663. The command was then held by Major Lawrence Dempsey, and when he died in 1664, to Meinhard Schomberg, the Count's oldest son, who led the regiment until the end of the war.

Alongside the Dutch, French and English troops, further foreigners entered the Portuguese army as volunteers or professional soldiers. Among the individuals enlisted as volunteers, there are several Catalans, who joined the Portuguese army after the failure of the uprising in 1652. In 1661, the Catalan cavalry captain Rafael de Aux still served in the Army of Alentejo after his arrival in Portugal eight years before.[137] Among the other foreigners who served as officers, there were also Swiss and Swedes.[138] As for the mercenary units enlisted as regular soldiers, the largest contingent is represented by

---

137 ANTT, *Conselho de Guerra, Consultas*, 1661, M. 21: *Relação dos Oficiais e Soldados de Infanteria e Cavalaria que se acharãonesteExercito – ultima mostra*(22–23 September 1661).

138 Rui Moura, *Presença militar estrangeira no Exército Português, do século XVII a Napoleão*, in 'Congresso Internacional de Arqueologia e História – CIAH,As Linhas Defensivas entre o Século XVII e Napoleão' (1–2 September 2017), p.4.

the Germans. After the infantry regiment recruited in Hamburg by the aforementioned Vannicelli in 1650, some free companies formed by German mercenaries are registered in the Army of Alentejo in 1652. Then, in 1663, in addition to the Schomberg's regiment in French service, the Portuguese army raised one *terço dos alemães* enlisting prisoners and deserters from the German *tercios* of the Spanish army. The 300 strong regiment was commanded by the Frenchman, Colonel Clairon (or Clairin) and received their baptism of the fire at the siege of Évora.[139] Two years later, the unit had lost half of its strength, but was still with the field army that fought at Montes Claros. Deserters from the Spanish army allowed for the formation of some Italian infantry companies in the last months of 1662. Louis de Meneses states in his *Historia do Portugal Restaurado* that in 1663 the Italians had been gathered in one *terço* under a French colonel, the same one who other sources assign to the German regiment.[140] However, in the following campaigns, the Army of Alentejo still included these units, which in 1665 were joined to the German regiment thus forming a tactical battalion deployed in the second line of the Portuguese order of battle at Montes Claros.

Colonial Army

The vast Portuguese overseas empire had been organised militarily as early as the end of the sixteenth century. It was based on the administrative regional divisions of the domains, which included a number of *capitanías* with their military personnel. In the next century, all the *capitanías* were involved in the colonial struggle and underwent a series of reforms due to changes in the regional structure. The presence of Portuguese regular forces overseas is a difficult matter to reconstruct. In the early seventeenth century, is estimated that 950 professional soldiers manned the garrisons of Brazil.[141] Possibly this number included the retired officers who trained the local militia and other personnel in charge to manage the artillery in the fortresses. The status of the latter was more properly one of semi-regular soldiers who served in the local 'military' for just a limited time and returned to their civilian job for the rest of the year. The war against the Dutch acted as a catalyst for the growth of the Portuguese military in Brazil and the development of a stable organisation. The introduction of the *Ordenanças* in Portugal also served as a model overseas, and in the province of Pernambuco and Bahia led to the creation of *terços* of militiamen formed by joining companies raised on an ethnic basis commanded by Portuguese officers. After the positive outcome of the war against the Dutch, these *terços* were disbanded, but the command structure remained as a cadre for future use. In the 1650s, in the major provinces the

---

139 Antonio José Rodríguez Hernández, *Financial and Military Cooperation between the Spanish Crown and the Emperor in the Seventeenth Century*, in Peter Rauscher (ed.), *Die Habsburger monarchie und das Heilige Römische Reich vom Dreissigjährigen Krieg bis zum Ende des habsburgischen Kaisertums* (Vienna: Aschendorff Verlag, 2010), p.278.
140 Meneses, *Historia do Portugal Restaurado*, vol. II, p.568.
141 Frederic Mauro, *Le Portugal, le Brésil et l'Atlantique au XVII siècle*, p.126.

staff officers favoured the formation of new auxiliary *terços*. Theoretically, each *capitanías* had to raise a company of foot militiamen regularly trained and led by a professional officer. In the 1650s, there were approximately 7,300 trained militiamen, including 800 on horseback and a field artillery company quartered in Bahia with eight cannons.[142] In 1654, Bahia deployed two *terços* of militia, known as *terçovelho* and *terço novo*, the first with 91 officers and NCOs and 823 men divided in 13 companies, and the second with 84 and 787 respectively in 12 companies.[143]

The actual military task of this force was limited to service in the costal fortresses, and to face the raids by hostile natives and former slaves who periodically threatened the Portuguese settlements. These latter became an increasing danger, because the escaped African slaves constituted an organised community in the interior of the province of Pernambuco known as the 'Kingdom of Palmares'. Between 1664 and 1665, this force was reorganised, and the officers' posts assigned to the most meritorious subjects, who had regularly trained the militiamen, now finally classified as *Ordenanças*.[144] The reform transformed these troops into actual paramilitary forces, composed of members who retained weapons and equipment in their home, with ranks and duties derived from the regular paid army. As in Portugal, *capitães-mores* and *vedores* held control and economic management of the troops. Taking advantage by a favourable economic upturn, in 1664 the province of Pernambuco gathered three *terços* of foot assigned to the major posts on the coast.[145] In the same year, provincial authorities gathered all the auxiliary cavalrymen into two corps of 600 and 500 horsemen divided in 10 companies.[146] The regular troops sent from Portugal were also garrisoned in Pernambuco, gathered in a *terço* of 610 men, which doubled its size in the 1670s. As in the homeland, the *auxiliaries* served as static garrison in the fortresses. The strength of the garrisons varied considerably; for instance, in 1664 the company under Captain António Gomes Roxo, assigned to the *Fortaleza do Morro de São Paulo*, had 49 men, including the officers.[147]

Whatever the troops were, all the field officers received the appointment from Lisbon and were credited by a Royal Patent. Documentary sources concerning the relations between Portugal and Brazil relates to the appointment of officers and officials, as well as the procurement of weapons and ammunition. Echoes of the pressing Portuguese involvement in the last phase of the Restoration War, resound in the correspondence between Lisbon and

---

142 Jozé de Mirales, *Historia Militar do Brazil, desde o anho 1549, em que teve principio a fundação de Cidade de S. Salvador de Bahia de Todos os Santos, até o anho de 1762* (Rio de Janeiro, 1900), p.65.
143 AHU, *Conselho Ultramarino, Consultas* (December 1654). The *terço velho* had been formed in 1626, the *novo* in 1631.
144 Mirales, *Historia Militar do Brazil*, p.67.
145 José Antônio Gonsalves de Mello, *João Fernandes Vieira, mestre-de-campo de terço de infantaria de Pernambuco* (Lisbon: Comissão Nacional para as Comemorações dos Descobrimentos Portugueses, 2000), p.385.
146 *Ibid*. The first corps was assigned to the district of Ytamaracá and Goyana, and the second to Alagoas, Porto Calvo and Sirinhaem.
147 *Ibid*., p.63.

THE BIRTH OF THE MODERN PORTUGUESE ARMY

Dinis de Mello de Castro, 1st Count of Galveas (1624–1709) was the third son of a *fidalgo* who served as governor of the Castle of São Filipe in Setúbal, and was a member of the *Conselho Ultramarino*. Immediately after the acclamation of João IV on 1 December 1640, he was dispatched, aged 16, to help secure the frontiers of the Alentejo under the Condé de Vimioso. During the prolonged wars of the Restauração he was almost constantly in combat, wounded 22 times, and received glowing reports from his superiors. He fought in the battles of Montijo, Forte de São Miguel, the Lines of Elvas, Ameixial and Montes Claros, where in 1665 he commanded the cavalry. He was several times governor of Alentejo.

Julio de Mello de Castro (1658–1721), the author of the book from which this image is taken, was born in Goa, the son of António de Mello de Castro, governor of India. He led a military life, serving under his uncle and in the company of his father, but for his literary talent was nominated by D. João V as a founding member of the Academia Real de História Portuguesa. (Print after *Historia panegyrica da vida de Dinis de Mello de Castro, Primeyro Conde das Galveas, do Conselho de Estado, & Guerra dos Serenissimos Reys Dom Pedro II & Dom João V*, by Julio de Mello de Castro, printed in Lisbon between 1704 and 1705. Author's archive)

its Brazilian colony. On 19 July 1663, the captaincy of Pernambuco sent a note to the Conselho Ultramarino about the sending of the artillery to Portugal.[148] In the following September, the captain of the *moradores* company of Recife, João Mendonça asked to be discharged, in order to serve in the *Sargenteria-mor* of the same locality as a chaplain. In the same month, Louis de Sousa, captain of an infantry company in Pernambuco, serving within the *terço* of *mestre de campo* António Dias Cardoso, opposed the dismissal from office due to age limits.[149] Apparently, military service in Brazil was less demanding than that in Europe, but it is important to focus on the unease deriving from the danger of foreign invasion. The War of Pernambuco had clearly shown how Brazil was largely unprotected and almost deprived of modern fortresses. Soon after the Dutch had been expelled from Brazil, the Spaniards replaced them as the major external threat. News of the presence of Spanish ships alarmed the Portuguese authorities, and in 1652, even the sighting of a Spanish squadron off Luanda was interpreted as the signal of an imminent invasion of Brazil.. In this regard, in 1654 Lisbon requested the famous *capitão* João Fernandes

---

148 Maria do Soccorro Ferraz Barbosa (Coordinator), *Documentos manuscritos avulsos da Capitanía de Pernambuco* (Recife: Ed. Universitária da UFPE, 2006), p.51.
149 *Ibid.*, p.53.

Vieira to carry out a detailed examination of the fortresses and garrisons in the north-eastern *capitanías*, in order to submit a defence plan including a project for the modernisation of their defences. This province had already received the attention of the *Conselho Ultramarino* in Lisbon. Two years before, Vieira had proposed to build a large, fortified settlement in the *sertão* of Pernambuco,[150] where the residents and soldiers could live; it would serve not only as a refuge in the event of an attack, but also as a storehouse for supplies.

In 1654 concerns increased because the possibility of a new enemy invasion of the newly liberated captaincies was feared. In March, Vieira had completed his plan, which represents a very informative document relating to Portuguese military strength in Brazil.[151] Vieira stated that in order to prevent a new attack by the *heregas* (heretics) or the Spaniards, it would be prudent and not inconvenient to fortify the captaincies, starting with Pernambuco, 'which is the head of the domain, and Recife is its main port'.[152] Here, the existing fortifications, and the ones left by the Dutch, were to be preserved. Among these, the *Forte do Mar* had a solid curtain wall made of stone and two batteries on each side, facing the sea and the river. In the same sector, the *Porta do Recife* guarding the entrance to the port needed a great deal of renovation. The *Forte do Brum*, on the isthmus before the town, although protected by just by a sand redoubt, could stand for many years with some restoration work. In the same way, it was necessary to conserve the *Forte de Buraco* located more to north 'because, as in the last siege, it could block the access to the area'.[153] He also pointed out that the village of Olinda should be fortified, given the distance from Recife and it had 'a very good port', with deep water and 'many fruits' and also for being 'the more cheerful and healthy harbour of all this coast'. If the enemy should seize it, Recife would not be able to hold out long, since from there they could occupy the interior and surround the town by land. Therefore, at Pau Amarelo beach, it was recommended that a fort be erected, as it was a good harbour, and from there the previous Dutch invasion had begun. To the west of Recife, it seemed convenient to Vieira to maintain the *Forte da Seca* or *das Três Pontas*, called *Waerdenburch* by the Dutch. To south, the *Forte das Cinco Pontas* had to be maintained and well manned, 'because for yet it is the only one in Recife'. Moreover, the report stated that a new modern fortress should be built, as soon as possible, being able to replace all the other existing ones in the interior, such as *Fort Erne*, and the ones at Altenar, and Arraial

---

150 This word refers to one of the four sub-regions of the north-east region of Brazil, similar to what might be termed the 'outback' with Australia in English. North East Brazil is largely covered in a scrubby upland forest called a *caatingas*. Its borders are not precise.

151 The original document has not been preserved, but a copy held in the archive of the *conselho ultramarino* contains the most important contents. Vieira introduced his plan writing that due to long experience matured in the Brazilian captaincies, he was not happy with what he saw in them, and that it was necessary 'to fortify the ports and harbours through which the Enemy entered 24 Years ago'. Vieira added that it would be worthwhile to gratify and reward the veterans of many battles by preserving the fortresses, 'not only for the strategic position they occupied, but also for the blood and the huge resources it cost' and asking the King to support him in the enterprise. See also Gonsalves de Mello, *João Fernandes Vieira*, pp.405–408.

152 *Ibid.*, p.406.

153 *Ibid.*

Novo. Further south, at Cape of Santo Agostinho, the recommendation was for a garrison of 200 men in the forts of *Castelo do Mar* and *Forte Negro*. To garrison all the fortifications in Pernambuco, Vieira estimated at least '2,000 well-trained men were needed.' As for the neighbouring area, in the captaincy of Itamaracá, Vieira proposed to maintain the *Fortaleza de Orange*, built on the island not only for the defence of the entrance of the anchorage, but for dominating a region rich of food, water, firewood and other useful stuff. In addition, it was necessary to build a network in Tejucupapo on the mainland bordering the island in the north. These forts required at least 500 soldiers to garrison them. In the captaincy of Paraíba, Vierira proposed to restore the forts of *Cabedelo*, *Restinga* and *Santo António*, building another one at *Cabo Branco*; 600 soldiers were needed to garrison them. In the Rio Grande do Norte River, he found it convenient to preserve the fortress on the border, namely, *Forte dos Reis Magos* 'built with stone', and making a redoubt on high ground that dominated the area, and another in Cunhaú, 'which is a good harbour'. Moreover, Vieria asked to build another fort at Bahia da Trayção, with a total garrison of 300 soldiers.[154]

Along with the regular and auxiliary force, the Portuguese colonial military also disposed of a varied number of mercenaries, or soldiers of fortune, who could be enlisted in case of need. According to some historians, Portuguese soldiers of fortune were most certainly a force to be reckoned with in the seventeenth-century Portuguese colonial empire. Many natives showed interest in signing on for military service but balked if they were not compensated accordingly. Indigenous foot soldiers were paid only one-third the wage received by Portuguese, and more often, their salaries were paid with a major delay compared to even their European comrades.[155] In Brazil, the typical soldier of fortune was labelled *bandeirante*. The name derived from *bandeiras*, 'flags', namely a large company of volunteers conscripted by colonists to penetrate the interior in search of slaves and gold. Generally, white European mercenaries could raise these companies, but some *bandeirantes* were usually known also as *mamelucos*, because of mixed indigenous and Portuguese ancestry. However, both terms identified people who went in search of profit and adventure as they penetrated the unmapped regions. Many *bandeiras* included Portuguese who saw the slave-hunting missions as less demanding than agricultural work. They formed bands of explorers, prospectors, and these also included natives, principally from the province of São Paulo. In this province, many Guaraní slaves worked in agriculture and as porters, and also assisted with trade and military tasks. The Portuguese colonists referred to these slaves as *forros* (freedmen), although they treated them as captives. However, there were the 'civilised' natives to fill the ranks of the *banderiras*. Indeed, a mid-seventeenth century *bandeira* included 900 *mamelucos*, 2,000 Natives and 69 white

---

154 *Ibid.*, p.407.
155 Hal Langfur, *Native Brazil beyond the convert and the cannibal, 1500–1900* (Albuquerque: University of New Mexico Press, 2014), p.181. According to some testimonies, it is reported that day labourers and soldiers often went six to ten months without receiving any pay, and unless the indigenous native employees were paid quarterly, they deserted.

Europeans, who usually held the senior ranks.[156] They were supplied by the Portuguese army with muskets, gunpowder, chains, collars, and a crude supply of provisions including manioc and some flour. Portuguese regular soldiers as well as auxiliaries did not join the *bandeiras*, but in some cases supported them with further facilities. The *bandeirantes* helped to establish Portugal's claim to the South American interior. In Brazilian historiography and national culture, *bandeirantes* occupy a very important and highly ambiguous position: praised for their endurance and discoveries and condemned for their brutality and cruelty that were visited upon the indigenous people scraping a living in the back-country.

As for the Indian and Far Eastern domains in the early seventeenth century, the mercenary forces were estimated to number at least 3,000 in Bengal, 1,500 in mainland Southeast Asia and 500 in Makassar, so totalling over 5,000 in these three areas alone.[157] Many of them were ethnic Europeans, but their cultural origins and social contexts were Colonial Portuguese. Moreover, if the numbers recorded are reliable, they indicate the *Estado da India* had an internal military problem of some magnitude. The report reckoned that all the official Portuguese forts and fleets east of the Cape of Good Hope contained just 4,500 professional soldiers, fewer than the soldiers of fortune.[158] Portuguese mercenaries generally enjoyed a good professional reputation, particularly as horsemen, gunners and musketeers, and often served as personal bodyguards. Their duties included a wide repertory of roles, including manual labour in dangerous areas. Clearing forest to open up roads was consistent with traditional male roles and might have been considered an acceptable means to acquire valuable trade items. By the end of the seventeenth century, Portuguese India as well as all the domains in Asia and East Africa were beset with military inadequacies and appeared to be living on borrowed time. Warnings about the vulnerability of these overseas possessions had often been expressed in the past and had long worried successive viceroys and secretaries of state. There were simply too many fortresses to defend, many of which were poorly maintained and equipped with substandard armaments. Garrisons were routinely undermanned, many of the troops were *degredados*, soldiers condemned to exile for various offences to remote, unattractive and unhealthy outposts of empire, and therefore desertions were common. Serving officers lacked genuine professional training, while even the headquarters staff at times seemed in chaotic disarray.[159] The potentially disastrous consequences of this disgraceful neglect were to be clearly demonstrated in the next century.

The backgrounds of informal settlers in the Portuguese African domains were diverse. The problem of insufficient local troops persisted in most Portuguese African territories during the seventeenth century, and it came to a head in Angola when the King of Congo joined in alliance with the Dutch. In this critical situation a significant force of 650 men sailed from Brazil in 1665, while other

---

156 *Ibid.*
157 Disney, *A History of Portugal*, vol. II, p.192.
158 *Ibid.*
159 *Ibid.*, p.319.

soldiers were sent from the separate Portuguese captaincy of Pernambuco. These Brazilians joined forces with the Portuguese garrison troops and militia, who were also supported by local African soldiers known as *empacaseiros* (from *mpakasa*, buffalo-hunter). One of the most successful leaders during this war was a mulatto named Luís Lopés de Sequeira, and within two decades the Portuguese king finally agreed that no distinction be made between 'whites, mulattos' and 'free negroes' serving in Angolan garrisons; henceforward, promotion would be on merit alone.

For many years, civil and military *degredados* were sent particularly to Cacheu, in Upper Guinea, where they are mentioned for the first time in the mid seventeenth century. However, most of the informal settlers were just freelancers seeking to make the best of life's opportunities that they could. Among them were people of various social backgrounds: royal officials, sailors, footloose adventurers, *forros* and slaves. Most of the inhabitants were of Cape Verdian rather than metropolitan Portuguese birth, while some were foreign Europeans. However, as a group they were usually referred to in contemporary documents as *lançados*, which roughly translates as 'outcasts'.[160] *Lançados* were expected to conform to the local laws and customs. Most settled down with their African women, whom they married in accordance with traditional tribal rites, although naturally such marriages were not recognised by the church and scandalised the Catholic clergy. Most *lançados* became in effect cultural hybrids, while their Afro-Portuguese descendants were inevitably from birth a people in-between.[161] They spoke a Portuguese creole that was also widely used as West Africa's language of trade, and their community evolved a form of Catholicism adapted to West African conditions. *Lançados* clung tenaciously to such symbols of European identity as musket, sword and broad-brimmed hat, but they spoke the local dialects fluently, and their food and everyday lifestyle was largely African.

Francisco de Távora, Count of Alvor (Collection of the Archaeological Survey of India, Goa). The Count was governor of Portuguese India from 1681 to 1686. During his mandate, he faced the Marathas' attempts to expel the Portuguese from their domains on the north-west coast.

---

160 Particularly during the early years, a clear distinction was made between *lançados* and those Cape Verdian settler-traders whose commercial activity on the Upper Guinea coast was considered legitimate. But in the longer run it is likely most *lancados* were at least in part of Cape Verdian origin. See also in Malyn Newhitt, *The Portuguese in West Africa, 1415–1670* (Cambridge: Cambridge University Press), pp.9–12.
161 Disney, *A History of Portugal*, vol. II, p.52.

Some of them became completely indigenised, underwent circumcision and had themselves symbolically tattooed. These were labelled *tangomaos* and little consideration was given to them as military force. During the sixteenth century, *lançado* numbers, particularly in the Guinean area, grew steadily. The largest concentration was at Cacheu and along the river with the same name, and from this area the local governors turned for assembling troops when necessary.

In East Africa, there had also been settlement of some areas beyond the control and protection of Portuguese coastal garrisons. These *sertanejo* backwoodsmen included *degredados*, escaped criminals, and even a few members of the aristocracy, all apparently unwilling to accept the discipline of fortress and garrison life. While the government had sufficient troops to control the coastal outposts, settlement and the establishment of trade deeper in the interior forced the authorities to rely on the armed followers of the most powerful settler leader, the *senhores*, each of whom had his *bandazio*. These local strongmen were indispensable, but less easy for the government to control. Indeed, powerful private armies were soon forcing land concessions from the local African chiefs. An armed retainer of an Afro-Portuguese leader was called a *chicunda*, literally 'slave', serving in an *ensaca* or company.

This mixed society was naturally involved in the slave trade. The right to trade in slaves was leased from the Crown by private contractors, who licensed or sublet this to traders. In the interior, slaves were purchased from African suppliers at slave *feiras*, markets. Particularly in the mid to late seventeenth century, slaves were also bought from Portuguese or Afro-Portuguese soldiers who had taken them captive in raids and military engagements. Finally, some slaves were extracted as tribute from subject African chiefs. Neither the major slave exporters nor the importers of trade goods from overseas normally ventured far into the interior, preferring to remain in or near the major centres. Usually the governor himself figured prominently among both groups, especially in Luanda, the Portuguese capital of Angola at least until the eighteenth century.[162]

---

162 Disney, *A History of Portugal*, vol. II, p.77: 'Slaves acquired in the interior were brought down to the coast by small traders, traders' agents and caravan masters. Often called pombeiros, these backwoodsmen were almost always Afro-Portuguese, indeed, some were themselves trusted slaves. Losses on the journey to the coast were high, probably averaging about 25 percent.'

3

Portuguese Wars

Portugal's theatre of war had a specific conformation which offered three natural ways of approach to an enemy coming from east. Alentejo was always considered the 'Gate to Portugal' since the main routes crossed the border in more location between Alcántara–Montalvao and Alconchel–Mourão. This gate extends for 110 km from north to south, and apart for some high ground in the northern sector, has little in the way of natural obstacles and sufficient usable roads. There were also two locations from where it was possible enter the country. In the north, some routes cross the border from La Guardia in Spanish Galicia and Monção in Portuguese Entre-Douro-e-Minho. Another invasion route is located between Ciudad Rodrigo in Spain and Alfaiates in Portugal, comprising the Portuguese provinces of Trás-os-Montes and Rib-Coa, and Spanish Castile. This latter area had best routes, but the countryside here had scarce resources for sustaining a field army. However, both these sectors were far from the main strategic objective for an invasion, namely Lisbon, which was the principal seaport and vital trade centre of Portugal. Therefore, in Alentejo occurred mostly of the engagements of the war started with the Acclamation of December 1640.[1]

However, an invasion coming from the east encounters further problems when wanted to advance into the interior. Portugal is relatively flat, arid, thinly populated and difficult to cross, especially in the seventeenth century, when the countryside offered few resources and the inhabitants' welfare was in average very low. In the north-east of Portugal, the highlands of Beira Alta and Trás-os-Montes rise above 2,000 metres and the mountains are a continuation of the Castilian Plateau. Further south, the regions of Beira Baixa and Alentejo have a conformation similar to Spanish Estremadura. The two principal rivers, the Tagus and the Duero-Douro, are natural obstacles that offer some advantage for a defence, but as both the rivers flow to the west, these could be useful to transport supplies and men for an invasion from the east. Minor rivers and streams, usually deeply incised, ran in torrents that

---

1 There was a fourth, southern front, where the Portuguese Algarve abuts Spanish Andalusia. The Spanish province was a logical target for Portugal, but it was never the focus of an attack, probably because the Portuguese queen, Luisa de Guzmán, was the sister of the Duke of Medina Sidonia, the leading noble of Andalusia.

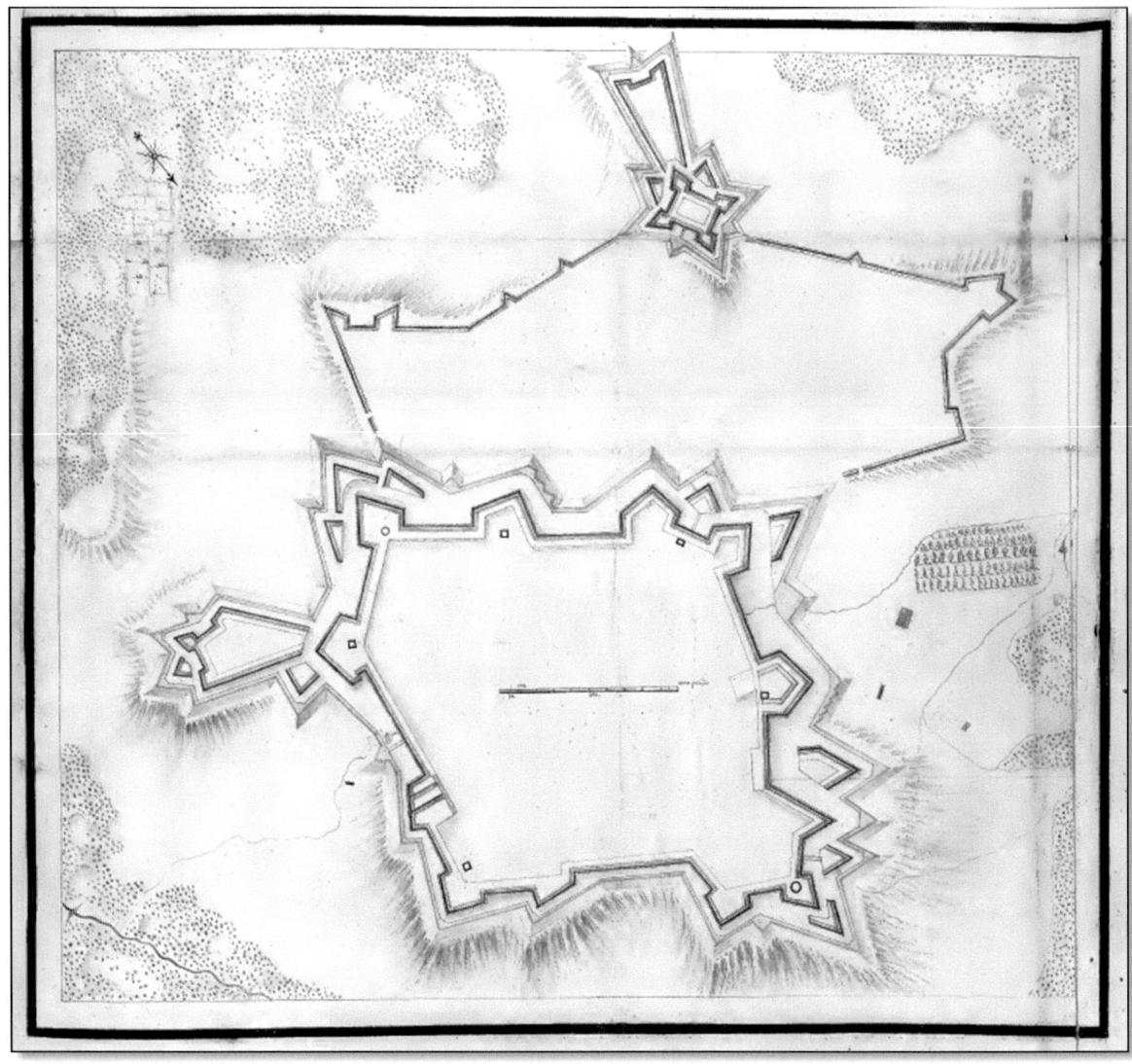

The fortification of Elvas after the *Desenhos e plantas de todas as praças do Reyno de Portugal* by Nicholas de Langres. From the beginning of the war, the town's defensive works were constantly improved and formed the strategic centre of gravity for the Portuguese defence in the Alentejo region. Throughout the entire war, every Spanish attempt to seize the town failed.

obstructed movements for a few months of the year, and then they dried up during the heat of summer, leaving deep channels that had to be traversed, without the benefit of anything to drink for an army which had to cross the region. Roads were rare in seventeenth-century Portugal, and they were generally poor even by the standards of the rest of Europe at that time.

The central mountainous region, the Sierra de Estrela, is a continuation of the Spanish mountains of Guadarrama, and divides Portugal diagonally into two parts. Consequently, Portugal has two climate zones. The Atlantic and Northern regions are characterised by ocean air currents with a moderately hot temperature, while the smaller southern zone has a typical Mediterranean climate with hot, dry summers and mild, wet, winters. From mid November, rain, cold and sometimes snow in the interior restricted the movement of troops as well as being outside the growing seasons; it was because of this that rivers and streams became impassable except on the very few bridges at this time of year, so that the campaigning stopped. It could take a whole day for even a well-equipped army to cross a river, even if the river was low. Traversing the country only became possible from mid April but even in spring, heavy rain could turn roads into swamps. In summer, high temperatures and the lack of food and water obliged the armies to cease the operations again. These features and restrictions produced the two short campaign seasons of spring and autumn, which remained a constant feature through the war against Spain.

Although the mountainous and meteorological conditions favoured the defence, the fortresses played a decisive role in the course of the war. Border towns such as Elvas in Alentejo and Badajoz in Extremadura became the principal logistics centres of the war and were updated with additional strong defences. In the 1640s and 1650s, Portugal directed considerable resources to improve the major fortresses. As well as Elvas, Juromenha, Vilaviçosa, Valença do Minho, Mourão, Estremoz, and all the forts protecting Lisbon were updated with modern works and devices. For this task, engineers were enlisted from France and Italy. However, lack of adequate resources did not allow the completion of the improvements to the defences, leaving some towns exposed to the enemy threat.

All these characteristics are fundamental for understanding the development of the campaigns and the events that followed. However, many episodes remain contradictory or difficult to understand if placed under the gaze of the reports from the two opposing sides. Several questions remain inexplicably unanswered, and their influence on events is not always recognisable: for instance, the Portuguese intrigues against Schomberg and the struggle at the court of Lisbon between the Francophile and Anglophile parties in the last years of the war. There are many recent studies on the Restoration War, mostly published in Portugal, but despite some excellent contributions, this remains a mysterious conflict, especially concerning the strategic and tactical errors committed by both sides in the key moments of the campaigns after 1659.[2] No less surprisingly, some contemporary works also state as factual judgements that are surprising at least, such as questioning that Portugal would even have had an army just after the War of Restoration.[3]

Inevitably, conflicts generally are remembered and recorded differently by eyewitnesses, and the Restoration War is no exception. Whilst Spanish sources attribute their failures to the economic shortages in the army, the harshness of the environment and, not as an afterthought, their bad luck, it is equally true that the Portuguese too had to face an economic situation

---

2   Among the most recent and interesting studies concerning the Restoration War, see Jorge Penim de Freitas, *A cavalaria na Guerra da Restauração: reconstrução e evolução de uma força militar, 1641–1668* (Lisbon: Prefácio, 2005), and Emilia Borges Salvado, *A Guerra da Restauraçáo no Baixo Alentejo (1640–1668)* (Lisbon: Colibri, 2015). Among the non-Portuguese works, worthy of being mentioned is Jonathon Riley, *The Last Ironsides. The Portuguese Expedition to Portugal, 1662–1668* (Solihull: Helion & Company, 2014).

3   'Although armed force has been a major factor in the development of the Portuguese nation-state, a standing army did not exist until after the War of Restoration.' This statement appears in Douglas L. Wheeler and Walter C. Opello Jr., *Historical Dictionary of Portugal* (Lanham, Toronto, Plymouth UK: The Scarecrow Press, 2010), p.47.

no less serious, and that they too suffered from the same environmental harshness. Most of the testimonies are certainly reliable, and among these many are certainly made in good faith, but as always happens, they remained conditioned by subjective evaluations and in a few cases, it is possible to understand the ideas and motivations regarding the choices of those who had a wider vision and a more detailed view of the conflict, such as Don Juan de Austria. Unfortunately, he left only a few and somewhat thin explanations regarding the decisions he took during the crucial campaigns between 1661 and 1663. Similarly, also one of the major sources relating to the Restoration War presents us with several problems around reliability. The *Historia do Portugal Restaurado* by Dom Luís de Meneses, Count of Ericeria, offers a very detailed account of the events from the Portuguese side, and therefore it is partisan in some parts. However, this not a problem since spreading propaganda is normal in this kind of work. The Count supplies a large amount of information about troops and commanders involved in the events of the war, but his statements are not always confirmed from other contemporary sources. Meneses relied only on his memory when writing of the chronicle, and, above all, he often alluded to references to the quarrels between the Portuguese commanders and the foreigner, General Friedrich von Schomberg. Once again, therefore, scholars are faced with a contemporary and fascinating but not reliable source.

Historians of the nineteenth century, and even those who in recent times wrote about the Restoration War focused on the determination of the Portuguese soldiers to defend their country against the Spaniards, instead of mentioning that they mostly relied on contingents formed by foreign mercenaries. This situation would explain the reasons for the Portuguese victory, and the Spanish historians agreed on this perspective. Portuguese had surely more motivation compared to their enemies for defending their homes, but this is a statement clearly influenced by the Nationalist view of the past.[4] On the other hand, the presence of French and English contingents alongside the Portuguese appears to be in contrast with this statement. In turn, British and French historians claimed that it was thanks to the presence of these soldiers, hardened by the conflicts Europe, that Portugal was able to prevail over the Spaniards. For this and other reasons, little attention has been paid to the characteristics of Portuguese warfare or to the organisation of the army. With these considerations, historians of all nationalities have little investigated the social impact of the war and the effort of the Portuguese economy to sustain the army on campaign. The numerous skirmishes, encounters and battles fought in the neighbourhood of the military zone caused considerable economic loss among smallholders, farmers and peasants.[5] The war drained resources, either directly, through taxation, by

---

[4] Among the works most oriented to a Nationalist view, see Chistovam Ayres de Magalhães Sepulveda, *Historia Orgánica e Politica do Exercito Portugués*, vols I–V (Lisbon, 1908) and Serafin Estébanez Calderón, *De la conquista y pérdida de Portugal*, vols I–II (Madrid, 1885).

[5] Teresa Fonseca, *The Municipal Administration in Elvas During the Portuguese Restoration War (1640–1668)*, e-JPH, Vol. 6, number 2, Winter 2008, p.6. 'During the most critical years, the profits of the municipality of Elvas fell quite dramatically, as there were municipal rents which

the damage suffered by the areas marched through by the armies, and for the effects of the imposition of a war economy on the border areas. The arrival of thousands of national and foreign soldiers increased local economic activity, mainly commerce and craftsmanship, but the rise in demand meant a general increase of prices and a decrease in the quality of products. Furthermore, it also favoured the proliferation of monopolists, smugglers and profiteers. The army's suppliers were a huge problem for Portuguese towns and villages involved in the war. Based on the greater ease and lower cost of transport, which was quite dangerous in such times, rich merchants acquired large quantities of wheat, rye, barley, meat and vegetables in order to supply the troops. As this practice affected the supply to the population and led to a rise in prices, the Town Council of Elvas, the main logistic centre of the army of Alentejo, introduced new and more coercive measures to prevent such abuses, even though ultimately, they proved to be less effective.[6]

The quartering of troops was another burden imposed on the population and represented a serious problem for the Portuguese authorities, as described in the contemporary reports. Already in the 1640s, most families lodged two, four or even six soldiers, with the consequent 'risks to the family honour', 'theft and extortion' and even the possibility of 'danger for life', the latter due to the conflicts frequently arising between 'guests' and owners. Although such duties normally fell upon the poorer population, the billeting also affected wealthier ones, as proved by the fact that 'the best houses in town' were occupied by 'captains and noble soldiers'. In order to minimise the effects of such onerous obligations, which the continuation of the war transformed into an actual calamity, some towns decided to build barracks for the troops.[7] The local authorities had to improvise new barracks, as well as to control and repress the thefts and illicit economic activities perpetrated by the soldiers. Obviously, this produced new costs, and in 1666, the Council of Elvas was forced to suspend the cleaning of the town, as the money originally allocated for this activity was needed to build new barracks to accommodate a regiment of English troops.[8]

---

were not paid or that were charged at a lower price. Due to this, of the twelve years for which municipal accounting ledgers have been found, seven showed negative balances. However, the percentage must certainly have been higher, as we do not know the accounting balance for some of the most difficult war years, namely 1658 and 1659. At the beginning of January 1659, the Town Council, contrary to what had previously been the norm, did not receive any municipal rent, as there was no one interested, because the town had been under siege for more than 40 days.'

6   Ibid., p.9. There was also frequent friction between the army officers and the magistrates of the town: 'The military governors often complained about the condescending tone with which the royal ministers, used to a less severe practice of civil justice, administered military justice in the army as auditors.'
7   In 1660, in Elvas there were 101 houses built in which the infantry was lodged. In December of that same year, the Town Council asked the officials responsible for the supply of beds to the army to buy 393 blankets, 305 straw mattresses, 306 pillows and 252 rugs to accommodate the troops in the public quarters. See in Emilia Borges Salvado, *A Guerra da Restauração no Baixo Alentejo (1640–1668)* (Lisbon: Colibri, 2015), p.224.
8   Ibid., p.366.

Generally, the Portuguese had the reputation of being skilled sailors and even soldiers, as everyone could assume considering the size of their empire. Some contemporary accounts give interesting details on the reputation of the Portuguese soldiers:

> The Portuguese are shrewd, well-disposed and skilled, but due to the little military exercise, they become uncontrollable and act as they please, until they no longer obey their senior officers.[9]

Another commentator stated:

> Soldiers of Portugal, without having spent years in the school of Flanders, nor camped on the borders of Africa, no matter how much they are ordered to carry weapons and exercise them, because they regard as an affront to avoid the [military] service and idleness as an offence.[10]

These judgements seem to confirm the authoritative statement of Friedrich von Schomberg, who often wrote that the Portuguese soldiery and their officers performed well on campaign and earned his admiration but insisted on the need for improving the discipline within the army. However, Schomberg had not much admiration for their high command, which had consistently led down their own men. Of his fellow generals, he wrote that:

> They understand nothing about war. The soldiers are brave enough, but the chiefs carefully avoid all risks, and as to him who could have led us, no one saw him during the battle at all … the cowardice with which the commanders have acted in beyond anything I ever saw in any war … they ought to be hanged.[11]

Obviously, this statement was subjective, and it cannot take into account the entire Portuguese generalship. During the war, several Portuguese commanders demonstrated their boldness in action, like the valorous Francisco Barreto de Meneses, who received 20 combat wounds during his service as a field officer. Schomberg's analysis adds further details about the Portuguese army, especially when he outlines the role of the English and French troops in providing an example in matters of tactics. In this aspect Portuguese infantry adopted a thinner battle formation compared to the Spanish, following the model introduced in the Dutch Republic and in

---

9   João de Carriam (1595), quoted in Ricardo Rui Moura, *Presença militar estrangeira no Exército Português, do seculo XVII a Napoleão*, in 'As Linhas Defensivas entre o Século XVII e Napoleão' (Congresso Internacional de Arquelogia e História, 1–2 September 2017), p.4.
10 *Ibid.*, quote of Padre António Vieira.
11 Riley, *The Last Ironsides*, p.114. According to Charles François Dumouriez, *Campagnes du Maréchal de Schomberg en Portugal depuis l'année 1662 jusqu'en 1668* (London, 1807), pp.29–30, Schomberg's 'representations of ignorance, irresolution, and the stubbornness of the Portuguese generals, procured him, of course, many enemies who rallied against him to the party of the Lisbon court. One of the French officers of his staff, who Schonberg had appointed Lieutenant-Colonel of his own regiment, and treated with great friendship, planned against him to hold the command of the foreign troops in Portugal if he could keep his General away.'

England. Combat reports and contemporary images show that the infantry *esquadrões* were deployed in five or even four ranks, and the fire occurred without musketeers and arquebusiers exchanging their positions, since the first two ranks were with kneeling, and the others fired through the intervals.

However, in 1656, the French diplomat Monsieur d'Ablancourt, noted that the Portuguese infantry still retained the Spanish habit of deploying on the wings two pickets of arquebusiers, in a few files, on each side of the block of pikes and muskets.[12] As for the army in overall, d'Ablancourt wrote that:

> All the cavalry in this country are cuirassiers and chevaux legers, which differ only in dignity and provenance. The King gives them the bread all year, and barley and straw to the horses, except in the spring when he gives fodder in money in order to put the horses in the countryside, which restored them perfectly. They have few infantry regiments maintained all year; some auxiliary regiments are raised when necessary, who are given the bread all the time they serve, and are very prone to disband; the details of the infantry is beautiful but too long. I would just say that the bread given to them is bigger and better than in other countries; there are shops maintained for each regiment, that carry the water to be distributed to soldiers on campaign and in the encampment; without it they could not withstand the hot climate in a country where people walk all day without finding water. Although all these soldiers (the auxiliaries) go on campaign by force, they fight very well; on the wings of their battalions there are usually four or five rows of musketeers, whose muskets resemble small arquebuses, and use of cartridge of twelve to the pound; with time, good sergeants, alferez, majors and assistants majors, who are taken from these militias.

Portugal was able to exploit the auxiliary infantrymen, who generally performed better than those of the *tercios provinciales* of the Spanish side. Although they served mainly in garrison duties, the *auxiliaries* represented a useful strategic reserve for the regular army. Furthermore, the regional structure of the defence ultimately proved to be effective for keeping the enemy beyond the borders. The Portuguese could move the troops along internal lines, while the Spaniards had to transfer soldiers from locations hundreds of miles away, but the cooperation among the Portuguese governors was more effective compared to the Spaniards. In this regard, troops coming from different provinces fought together without any animosity, which by contrast was a frequent issue among the Spanish soldiers from different regions. In 1663, contingents from Estremadura and Beira joined the army of Alentejo under Sancho Manuel de Vilhena, Count of Vila Flor, and performed positively during that crucial campaign. The Count left the encampment on 1 June, having incorporated the troops sent from Lisbon under the command of the general commissioner Gonçalo da Costa de Meneses and those from Beira commanded by the cavalry general Manuel Freire de Andrade. On 2 June, he learned about the presence and number of cavalry and infantry

---

12 *Memoires de Monsieur d´Ablancourt. Envoye De Sa Majeste Tres-Chretienne Louis XIV en Portugal* (Paris, 1701), p.89.

sent by Don Juan de Austria to approach Évora. The Count decided to move against the enemy trying to surprise the Spaniards while they were on the march. According to a contemporary account, since the plains around Évora were very vast, the army marched in 'a perfect battle formation'.[13]

It is interesting to note that the Portuguese had been able to turn their weaknesses into advantages. In this regard, the numerical inferiority of their cavalry could be counterbalanced on the tactical level, as stated by João de Mascarenhas:

> It should be noted that the cavalry at our disposal is always fewer in number than the one of our enemies. Therefore, it is not convenient to form large corps of horse, because we will never be able to fill the gap and we will always be outnumbered. So, it seems to me that we can adjust our batalhões [squadrons] to 80 men each, because even if the Castilians are more numerous, as seen this year [1663], even only 60 troopers well-disciplined and trained will offer sufficient resistance, and the cavalry can always be adapted to the form of the battle.[14]

The War in Four Phases

Fighting between Spain and Portugal broke out periodically between 1641 and 1668. During these 28 years, only five major battles were fought, with a slightly higher number of sieges, and therefore the bulk of the hostilities took the form of border skirmishes and the sacking of nearby towns. Scholars usually divide the war in three or, more precisely, in four phases. The first phase began after the proclamation of João IV as new King of Portugal and lasted until 1644. In this period, the Spanish response was slow and uncoordinated since there were too few troops to conduct a strong offensive. Portugal, for its part, felt no need to take Spanish territory in order to win, and it too was willing to make the war a defensive contest. In the early months of 1641, siege operations affected Elvas and Olivenza and culminated in field encounters with Spanish victories, but the shortage of troops did not permit them to exploit their advantage. This permitted Portugal to muster its forces, and to receive reinforcements from the enemies of Spain: Sweden, England, Denmark and obviously, France. In 1642, the indolence and the weakness of the Spanish forces on the borders permitted Lisbon to launch an offensive into Galicia, where the Portuguese troops of Entre-Douro-e-Minho seized Salvaterra de Miño. The next year, the Portuguese seized Valverde in Extremadura, aided by the fact that the garrison was without pay and delivered the fortress to the besiegers without a fight.

Apart from some minor encounters that involved infantry, most of the fighting was in the form of cavalry skirmishes, which mainly occurred on the border between Alentejo and Extremadura. In early 1644, rumours

---

13   António Álvares da Cunha, *Campanha de Portugal da província do Alentejo, na primavera do ano de 1663* (Lisbon, 1663), p.33.
14   João de Mascarenhas, Conde de Sabugal, *Maneio da Cavallaria* (Lisbon, 1665), p.15. Thanks to Jorge Freitas for this notice.

suggested that Spain was gathering a field army in Extremadura under Geronimo Maria Caracciolo, Marquis of Torrecusa. On the Portuguese side, 6,000 foot and 1,100 horse with six guns under Matias de Albuquerque were camped near Campo Maior, ready to face the enemy. Since the Spaniards were still assembling their forces, Albuquerque decided to cross the frontier in early May, attacking, pillaging and burning the countryside near Badajoz until reaching the town of Montijo, which surrendered without a fight. Not having encountered the Spanish army, the Portuguese returned to Alentejo. While on the march, the Portuguese were confronted by a Spanish force dispatched from Badajoz led by the Baron of Mollingen consisting of 4,000 infantry and 1,700 cavalry with two field guns. On 26 May 1644, the two armies met not far from Montijo. The battle was indecisive and cost many casualties on both sides, but for the Portuguese this action represented confirmation that their efforts had been enough to raise an army capable of facing the Spaniards in the open field. This major encounter led to the second phase of the war. Apart from the siege of Elvas, the Spaniards did not go on the offensive since the war in central Europe required all their resources to face France and its allies. From 1645 to 1659, the campaigns assumed the characteristics of frontier warfare with raids and ambushes that produced little in the way of strategic results. These fights, often between local forces, involved neighbours who often knew each other well, but this familiarity did not moderate the destructive and bloodthirsty impulses of either side. Due to the shortage of resources and soldiers, neither side mounted actual full-blown campaigns, engaging instead in small-scale encounters and raids to burn fields, sack towns, and steal herds of cattle and sheep from enemy territory, as had happened during the *Reconquista*. Mercenaries and foreign conscripts exacerbated the struggle and episodes of singular cruelty were also reported on both sides.[15] The Portuguese settled old animosities that had festered during 60 years of Spanish rule, and the Spaniards often took the view that their enemies were traitorous and rebellious subjects, not an opposing army entitled to respectful treatment under the rules of war.

Only when the war in Europe was finishing did hostilities resume, with actions in the field performed by corps of cavalry and infantry in a more 'regular' pattern. The first clash occurred on 8 November 1653 at Arronches, in Alentejo, where the Portuguese achieved the victory. However, the battle was actually a very small affair that engaged 950 Portuguese cavalry and 100 infantry of the army of Alentejo, against about 1,300 Spaniards of the army of Extremadura.[16] Spanish sources are quite laconic about the actions that occurred in the 1650s, which are usually described as episodic and very limited. On the contrary, Count Luís de Meneses stated that the war 'vigorously' resumed in 1655. The Portuguese author refers about a

---

15 Riley, *The Last Ironsides*, p.30. In November 1645, 800 Portuguese soldiers took on a Spanish force and came off worst: 17 escaped, 143 were taken prisoner, and 640 were killed. In 1650 it was reported that the Portuguese tortured Spanish captives through burning, castration, and cutting off their ears.
16 Emanuel de Faria, *The History of Portugal ... Translated and Continued down to this present Year, 1698. By Capt. John Stevens* (London, 1698), p.474.

The battle of Montjio, fought on 22 May 1644 (Museu Militar, Lisbon). The battle was the first major field episode of the Restoration War and resulted in an indecisive outcome, though both sides claimed it as a victory.

cavalry raid planned by the *general de la cavalaria* André de Albuquerque at the beginning of the year, which prevailed against enemy mounted force under captain Francisco Guzmán in the environ of Mourão. The action was performed by a regular force of 60 cavalrymen, against the same number from the other side.[17] Further encounters engaged the opponents in the following days. In March, the Portuguese launched an incursion against Alcantara, which continued into Castile, destroyed enemy facilities and stole cattle. These actions started not only from Alentejo, but the cavalry of Trás-os-Montes also performed incursions into enemy territory. From this province, 250 cavalry and 200 infantry under the *mestre de campo* António Jaquez de Pavya crossed the border and fired the countryside in the Duero valley; their orders were clear: 'cause as much damage as possible'.[18] In early April, the brave Pavya gathered a further 500 foot and 150 horse and ambushed an enemy column coming from Zamora, and finally returned to Miranda do Douro with a huge amount loot and was acclaimed as a hero by people.[19] The Portuguese strategy was aimed to delay the enemy preparations depriving them of resources, and for this task the Portuguese even resorted to draining the wells and flooding of the countryside.

---

17 Luís de Meneses, Conde de Ericeira, *Historia de Portugal Restaurado* (Lisbon, 1679), vol. I, p.849.
18 *Ibid.*, p.850.
19 *Ibid.*, p.851.

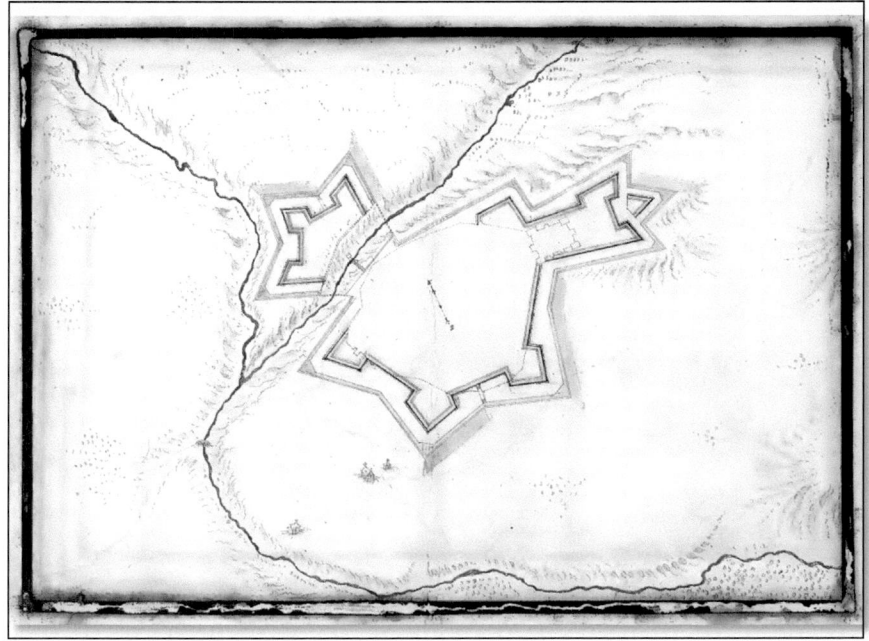

The fortification of Arronches, after Nicholas de Langres. The town was conquered by the Spaniards in 1661. but returned to Portugal following the Peace of Lisbon in 1668. (Author's archive)

In the following year, the intensity of the struggle increased further. In 1656, in order to divert the Portuguese forces from Alentejo, Felipe IV and the War Council of Madrid planned an offensive from the north. The Spanish governor of Galicia, Vincenzo Gonzaga-Doria, crossed the Minho River with 6,000 infantry and 900 cavalry with the aim of seizing Salvatierra de Miño, occupied by Portugal since 1642, but the lack of forces forced him to abandon the siege.[20] Gonzaga-Doria ordered a fort to be built atop the hill of San Pedro de la Torre, near the Portuguese side of the Minho River, named San Luís de Gonzaga, and located a few kilometres from Valença do Minho. The next year, a Portuguese army under João Rodrigues de Vasconcelos, Count of Castelo Melho, besieged the fort, obtaining its surrender. In 1657, Portuguese operations planned against Galicia were frustrated because of the Spanish conquest of Olivensa and Mourão in Alentejo. The next year, the Portuguese planned an offensive to take possession of Badajoz, in order to deprive the enemies of their major logistics centre in Extremadura. The army of Alentejo gathered 14,000 infantry, and 3,000 cavalry with a siege train comprising 20 guns under Joane Mendes de Vasconcelos. The campaign began in July 1658 and lasted until October, but it cost the Portuguese heavily as during the four months' blockade of Badajoz, most of the Portuguese troops had either died, mainly from the plague which had broken out in their camp or deserted. In October, the arrival of a relief army of 14,000 infantry, 5,000 cavalry with 19 field guns and three mortars, under King Felipe IV of Spain's favourite Don Luís de Haro, broke the Portuguese siege. Mendes de Vasconcelos, the Portuguese commander, was stripped of his

---

20   Emilio González López, *El águila caída: Galicia en los reinados de Felipe IV y Carlos II* (Madrid: Galaxia, 1973), p.160.

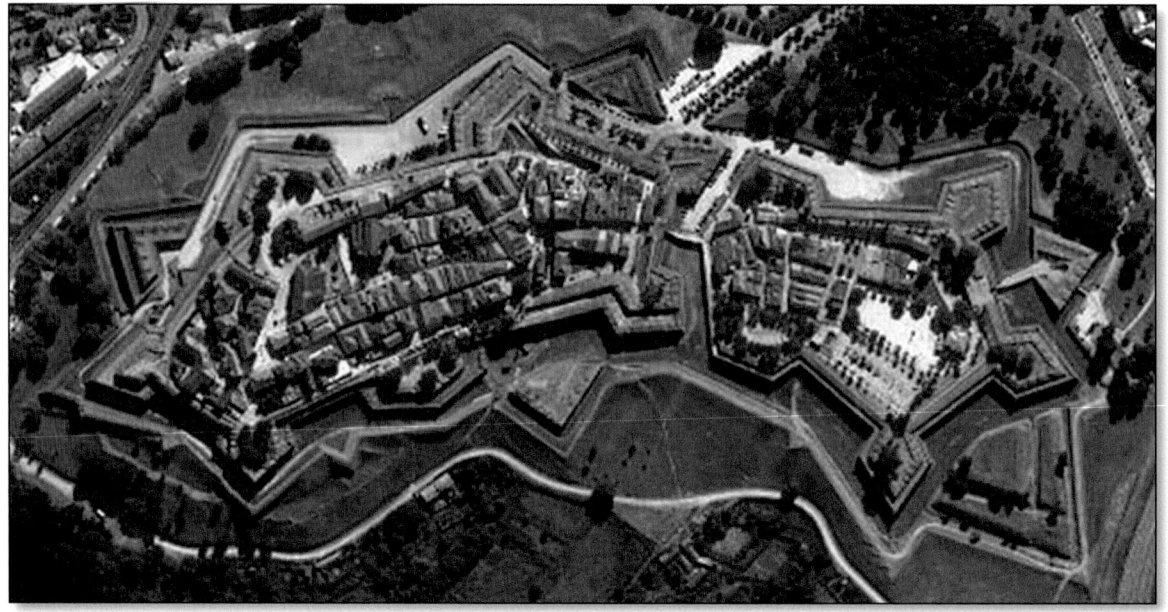

A bird's eye view of Valença do Minho. The town's defences are a well-preserved example of the great work of fortification of the Portuguese towns in the Alentejo region. (Author's archive)

rank, and imprisoned for this failure. Taking advantage of the Portuguese retreat, de Haro, invaded Portugal and besieged Elvas, the main supply centre of Portugal's defence, where the army that had besieged Badajoz took refuge and suffered a second catastrophic plague. A Portuguese relief force of 8,000 infantry, 2,500 cavalry and seven field guns was improvised in Alentejo under António Luís de Meneses. Despite great difficulties, the Portuguese gathered recruits from every corner of Portugal, included Cabo Verde and the island of Madeira, and with regular soldiers from the garrisons of Borba, Juromenha, Campo Maior, Vilaviçosa, Monforte and Arronches, marched to relieve Elvas. Meneses and his second in command, Sancho Manoel, decided to move heading towards Murtais, in order to approach the enemy unseen. The Portuguese plan succeeded and on 19 January 1659 the troops occupied the hills between Murtais and Elvas, from where the besieged city and the enemy siege lines could be seen, giving them a considerable advantage. Although the Spaniards occupied some redoubts and the entrenched line of circumvallation, the troops were scattered for several kilometres around Elvas. This contributed to the ineffective Spanish response. Luís de Haro, even after the arrival of the Portuguese army, probably did not believe that it would attack his troops. Thus, the Spanish commander did not immediately order a concentration of forces to face the enemy approaching from Murtais. The assault started before midday, but the battle remained undecided for some time, as the Spaniards put up a strong defence. However, after a half hour of fierce fighting, the Portuguese managed to break through the trench lines. Panic spread and the communication between the troops collapsed.[21]

---

21   Estébanez Calderón, Serafín, *De la conquista y pérdida de Portugal*, vol.I (Madrid, 1885), p.193. The Spanish historian attributed the defeat to the Duke of Osuna, the cavalry commander, who performed very poor during the battle. According to him, Osuna failed to protect the besieging army against the Portuguese assault. Haro's army suffered more than 5,000 casualties, 2,000

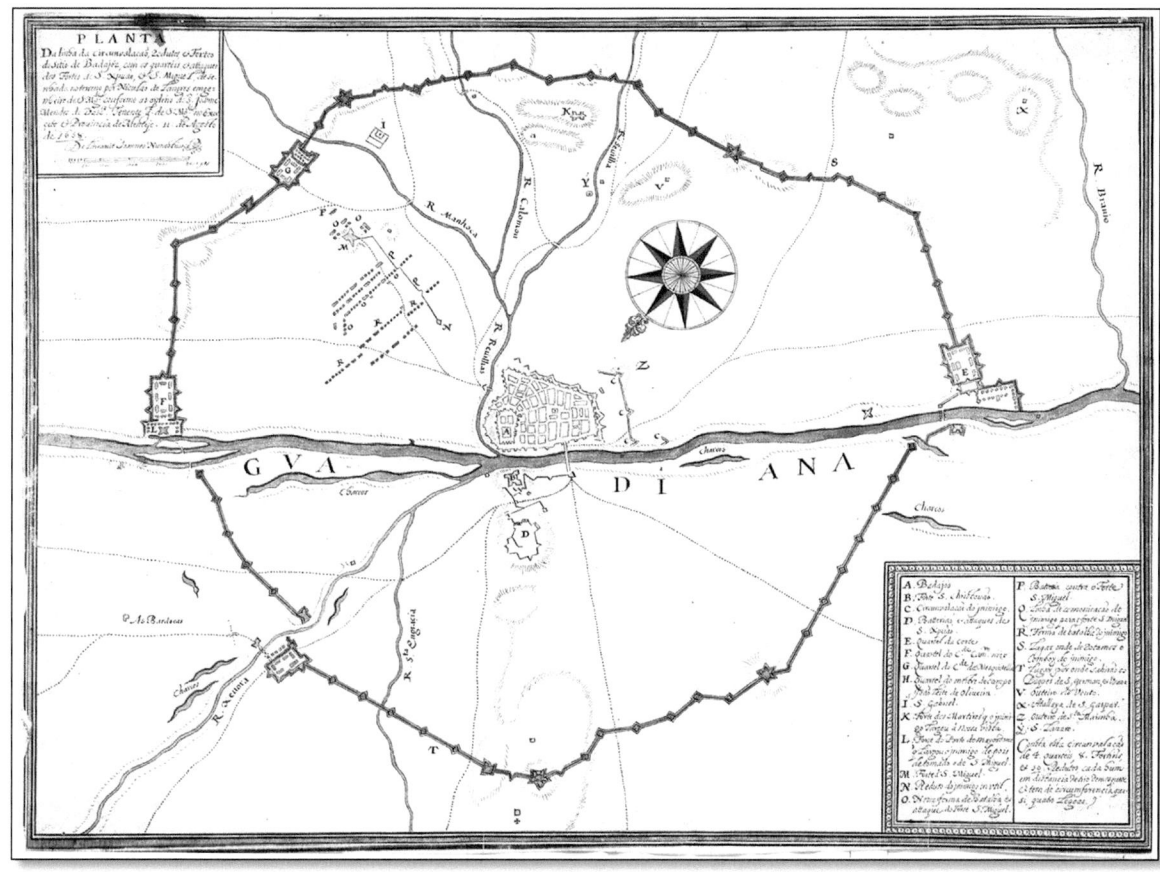

Plan of the Portuguese siege of Badajoz in 1658. The city was the logistics centre of the Spanish Army of Extremadura, and its fall should have placed the Portuguese in a favourable position, anticipating the expected and feared enemy offensive after the end of the war against France. However the campaign turned into a dramatic struggle, and a plague epidemic weakened the Portuguese army. A large, fortified line of circumvallation was also built, but Badajoz resisted, valiantly led by the Duke of Dan Germano, until the arrival of the relief Spanish army under Luís de Haro. (Author's archive)

Meneses and Manoel inflicted a crushing defeat on the Spaniards, but the Battle of the Lines of Elvas was not decisive, because they were not able to exploit their victory because of a lack of manpower.

On the secondary front of Galicia, the Spaniards were ahead of the enemy and entered the Entre-Douro-e-Minho, where they found the Portuguese defenders unprepared to face them. The army of Galicia numbered 10,000 men and included sappers and militiamen under Rodrigo Pimentel, Marquis of Viana. The Portuguese gathered barely half of this force under João Rodrigues de Vasconcelos, Count of Castelo Melhor, and on 17 September 1658 met the enemy near Vilanova.[22] The battle was little more than a skirmish and resulted in a Spanish victory, since the Portuguese infantry fled after their

---

prisoners and thousands more deserted after the battle. Only 5,000 infantry and 300 cavalry took refuge in Badajoz. The Portuguese claimed the loss of just 200 men.

22 Fernando Fulgosio, *Crónica de la provincia de Pontevedra* (Lisbon, 1867), p.71.

A depiction of the Battle of the Lines of Elvas in a seventeenth-century *azulejo*, a Portuguese ceramic tile. Note the Portuguese infantry (auxiliaries?) wearing short jackets, breeches and possibly barefoot. (Author's archive)

cavalry was routed.[23] Viana exploited this success and soon seized Nogueira and other enemy-held villages and forts in the area. On 30 September, having reorganised his army, the Spanish commander laid the siege to the fortress of Lapela, which surrendered on 6 October. Monção was also besieged, falling into Spanish hands on 7 January 1659, after a costly and bloody fight for both sides. The Count of Castelo Melhor died of illness during the winter and the fall of town could not be prevented. The main Spanish objective, the recapture of Salvatierra de Miño, was achieved on 17 February. The campaign of 1659 did not include any further significant episodes and brought the second phase of the war to a close. Meanwhile, the Peace of the Pyrenees had been agreed, and some articles of the treaty worried the Portuguese court considerably. In exchange for Spanish territorial losses in Flanders, France pledged to end its support for Portugal, withdrew all the troops from the Iberian Peninsula, and renounced the claims to the county of Barcelona, which the French Crown had claimed since the Catalan revolt. The Portuguese could also no longer receive any other form of support from France, although Mazzarino continued covertly to provide a financial subsidy and a force of 600 'volunteers'. However, Lisbon's major complaint was the clause by which France recognised Felipe IV of Spain as the legitimate king of Portugal.

The third phase of the war began in 1660, and it coincided with the preparations of Madrid to gather forces to wage war against the Portuguese,

---

23 The commander of the Spanish cavalry was the Portuguese loyalist don Bernardino de Meneses, Marquis de Peñalba, Count of Tarouca and Grandee of Portugal.

since the Peace of the Pyrenees permitted them to concentrate troops in Extremadura and Galicia, moved from the theatres of the war that had just ended. The conflict became an all-out war, in which every expedient was used to defeat the opponent, including the destruction of resources, the draining of wells and retaliation against civilians. This phase of the war was decisive for the final outcome of hostilities. Most of the battles and sieges occurred between 1660–1665 and were the major actions of the whole war. Spain waited two years before starting the offensive. Portugal exploited this pause by strengthening their defences while diplomacy achieved more help from France and England, allowing them to deploy a core of experienced troops and officers: a move that proved to be most effective. In May 1660, Felipe IV authorised the formation of four armies against the rebel kingdom. Extremadura and Galicia were the depots for the two major armies, which were supported by another small army in Castile and a fourth in Andalusia. In this period, the only significant action was the Portuguese attempt to size Valença de Alcantara, between May and June.

The news concerning the gathering of troops near the border alarmed Lisbon, where frenetic Portuguese diplomacy and ministers negotiated aid from foreign powers. The prospect of the royal wedding between the Stuarts and the House of Bragança in London was seen as a gift from heaven, and despite the marriage of a Catholic Portuguese princess with a Protestant monarch which was very unpopular in Lisbon, every effort was made to ensure the wedding went ahead. King Charles II was eager for the commercial and colonial advantage promised by a Portuguese alliance, and for the great dowry offered, but the risk of provoking a war with Spain by providing military assistance to Portugal represented a serious obstacle which long delayed any decision. The Spanish ambassador to the English court openly protested against the King's approach to taking the Portuguese side, reminding him that Spain had once offered asylum to the King, and that 'he was now repaying that favour by helping the rebel enemies of the Monarchy.'[24] A betrothal in Portugal would have provided further obstructions from Spain, since a Papal dispensation would have been required, difficult since the Pope sided with Madrid. The religious implication reverberated in England. The contemporary chronicler Gilbert Burnet, Bishop of Salisbury, reported the phases proceeding the King's wedding and the alliance with Portugal, describing the strong contrast between the Catholic and Protestant parties at court. After Charles' decision to declare Catharina as his wife, a street battle erupted between the two factions on 30 September 1660. Supported by French and Spanish ambassadors, the parties engaged a bitter encounter near Tower Hill. The garrison had received order not to interfere with the factions, and therefore there was no obstacle to prevent the wild encounter. The pro-Spanish party had the best of the skirmish, since five opponents were killed, and another 30 wounded, but in the end, the Protestant side prevailed since the support of France in the marriage's settlement was ultimately decisive. To facilitate Charles II in his decision, Louis XIV sent

---

[24] Burnet, Gilbert, *History of His Own Time* (London, 1906), p.64. The Spanish ambassador tried remonstrating with Charles and then deprecating the Portuguese *Infanta* Catarina, declaring that she was deformed, sickly and barren.

letters of credits amounting to 500,000 *livres* to relieve the English king of any pressing temporary financial embarrassment. In the following two years, the French subsidy to Charles II totalled 2,000,000 *livres*.[25]

In early 1661, the army of Extremadura, totalling 16,800 infantry and 4,500 cavalry, was ready to operate under Don Juan José de Austria. Before then, the Hispanic armies that were used against Portugal had never been in such good order, and this, with the well-known bravery of Don Juan, persuaded Madrid that the double advantage was the seal for a safe victory. Don Juan's plan was simple. He would advance along the route from Badajoz to Lisbon after secured the flanks seizing, Évora, Vilaviçosa and other strategic Portuguese strongholds in Alentejo. In Don Juan's plan, this goal could be achieved in two or three short campaigns. With great expectations, the Spaniards entered Alentejo and seized the fortress of Ouguela, and after this achievement, they headed against Arronches. This town had obsolete defences and a weak garrison, which tried to hold off the enemy besiegers as long as possible. Don Juan avoided a regular siege and tried to persuade the enemy commander to surrender by opening up with artillery fire. After seven hours of bombardment, Arronches opened its gates to Don Juan, who agreed to the free evacuation of soldiers and inhabitants 'since much of these were irreducible enemy of Spain.'[26]

Meanwhile, all that Portugal could do was to assemble troops in Alentejo, numbering about 13,000 men at all. The command in the field was held by Friedrich Herman von Schomberg, who had arrived in Portugal the previous year. He used this time to familiarise himself with Portugal and to instruct Portuguese officers in the practical matters like drill, discipline, musketry, and in seeing to necessary improvements to the field fortifications in Alentejo. He also reformed the method of arranging marches, quarters and billeting, introducing simple and useful changes, like one to ensure that the army would be formed on the march in regular columns and when at rest in battle order. Furthermore, Schomberg ensured that marches were not made during the worst heat of the day, and finally insisted on efficient arrangements for the reception of units at the end of their day's march were in hand.[27] All these reforms were 'a mighty advantage to the newly-levied troops and auxiliaries'.[28] Finally, he attempted to reorganise the Portuguese cavalry, which was the arm which was considered as indispensable in the strategic scenario, and also because their standard of effectiveness was most markedly inferior to that of the enemy. However, the proposal to form cavalry and dragoons in regiment-sized corps met with so much opposition from the Portuguese commanders that no progress was made for the next two years.

Schomberg assembled the army at Estremoz, in order to prevent enemy encroachments and subsequently pursue the Spaniards back to their bridgehead

---

25 Riley, *The Last Ironsides*, p.39.
26 Estébanez Calderón, *De la conquista y pérdida de Portugal*, vol.I, p.199.
27 Charles François Dumouriez, *Campagnes du Maréchal de Schomberg en Portugal depuis l'année 1662 jusqu'en 1668* (London, 1807), pp.11–12. 'The previous, haphazard, practice had been that every quartermaster, according to seniority, chose a billeting place for his unit. The next morning, the whole army would have to be re-assembled, given orders and sorted out according to precedence, so that it was seldom before noon that the columns began to march.'
28 Riley, *The Last Ironsides*, p.70.

as they retired. Reconnaissance and intelligence informed Don Juan that the enemy troops were dispersed among various towns with orders to fortify them. Portuguese intensified their guerrilla warfare, cutting the supply lines behind the advancing enemy. Notwithstanding the Portuguese being outnumbered, these actions caused a delay to the Spanish offensive, forcing Don Juan to face the destructive incursions of the enemy within Spanish territory. Of particular resonance was a raid led by the Portuguese with a cavalry corps of 17 companies, which attacked the enemy troops guarding a bridge near to Badajoz. Friedrich von Schomberg, who succeeded in encircling the enemy after isolating them with a daring manoeuvre, led the action. The Spaniards lost all their soldiers, included the *teniente general de la caballeria* don Pacheco, one of the favourite officers of Don Juan. Further problems affected the Hispanic army, when a bitter dispute involved the Spanish and Italian infantry in matter of privileges and position in the order of battle. The quarrel became serious, since the Italian officers threatened to resign the service if their prerogatives were ignored, and the soldiers would follow them.[29] However, before the end of 1661, the Spaniards managed to besiege Alconchel. A cavalry corps under Diego Caballero blockaded the town, which represented a double strategic goal, since it secured the crossing of the Táliga River and had been one of the first Portuguese conquests at the beginning of the war. Don Juan knew that inside the town there were still inhabitants loyal to Spain and therefore limited the siege to a blockade. His patience was rewarded since the Portuguese governor opened negotiations and finally surrendered on 12 December.

Don Juan resumed the offensive in the spring of 1662, with the conquest of the Portuguese fortress of Villa Boim, which surrendered without resistance. The Spanish goal was to seize Estremoz, but the *generalissimo* was informed about the presence of the Portuguese army within the city, and he realised the enterprise as much too difficult. While the Spaniards were marching to Villa Viçosa, intercepted enemy letters stated that the Portuguese army in Alentejo numbered 8,000 infantry and 4,000 cavalry, and further troops were gathering in Lisbon to join the campaign. The offensive then turned against the town of Borba, which fell on 7 April after a fierce defence by the garrison that comprised regular soldiers and militiamen.[30] The Spaniards entered the city after a costly assault, but the siege continued after the Portuguese retired into the citadel and resisted for three more days. After the surrender of the citadel, Don Juan executed the Portuguese governor with eight captains, 'because they had violated the laws of war', while the town was burned and razed to the ground.[31]

Rather than lapse into idleness, in early April Schomberg had taken the army of Alentejo into the field and with the cavalry surprised a major Spanish

---

29 Estébanez Calderón, *De la conquista y pérdida de Portugal*, vol.I, p.203. It was necessary for royal intervention to accommodate the dispute. Felipe IV ordered Italians and Spaniards to alternate in the position of honour in the order of battle.
30 *Ibid.*, p.218. The Portuguese governor refused to surrender after Don Juan offered the free evacuation of the garrison and citizens, and the 'insolent reply' of the governor much irritated Don Juan.
31 *Ibid.*

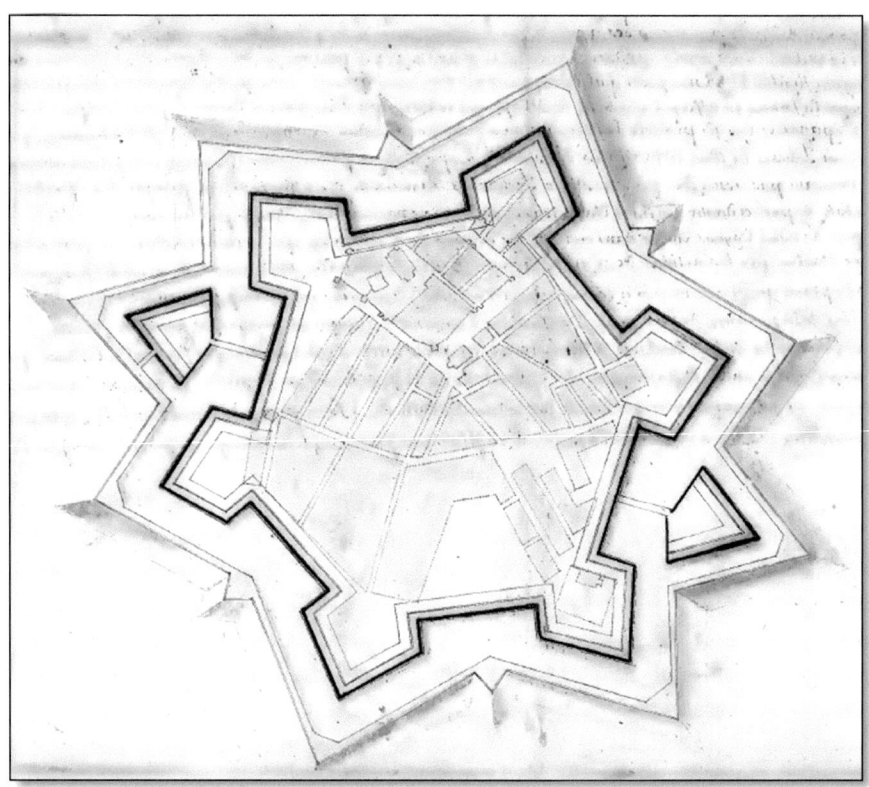

The town of Olivença, after de Langres. (Author's archive)

convoy of 150 wagons escorted by six squadrons of cavalry and some infantry. The Portuguese dispersed the escort, plundered the convoy and burned the wagons. In May, a succession of governors changed the status quo and caused the first serious rift between the Portuguese commanders and Schomberg. With the arrival of António Luís de Meneses, Marquis of Marialva, who had replaced Jerónimo de Ataíde, Count of Atouguia, as governor of Alentejo, Schomberg was suspended of his position of commander-in-chief, but maintained the command of the French troops. The new governor radically modified the strategy without listening to the contrary opinion of his allied general, and he advanced on Badajoz, believing he would find the Spaniards unprepared. Marialva had 6,400 foot and 2,500 horse under his command, but after reconnaissance and information gathering, he learned that the Spaniards had approximately 9,000 foot and 5,000 horse. The disparity between forces was not unbridgeable, but when the Portuguese reached Badajoz, the enemy strength had risen to nearly 20,000 men after the arrival of the troops with Don Juan de Austria. The war council was in favour of a retreat, but the order was carried out with too much haste, and chaos overwhelmed the troops, who returned in disorder to Elvas. Some historians argue that Don Juan missed a great opportunity to deal a heavy blow to his opponents.[32]

After this failure, Marialva moved the army to Vilaviçosa, against Schomberg's advice, which was to protect Estremoz, where the army had stores

---

32 Dumoriez, *Campagnes du Maréchal de Schomberg*, p.22.

and supplies, and which he considered the actual key to Lisbon. This time Schomberg's opinion prevailed and Estremoz was put into a state of defence. In the Spanish camp, Don Juan now had a considerable number of soldiers at his disposal. He was supported by experienced commanders, such as the veterans San Germano and Diego Caballero, and was anxious to resume his march on Lisbon. For the coming campaign, the Spanish commander planned to seize Elvas in order to deprive the enemy of the major stronghold in Alentejo. His second in command San Germano instead suggested a move against Juromenha since the loss of this fortress would have isolated Elvas made its future conquest possible with less effort. On 16 May, the Spaniards crossed the border and advanced, burning villages and farms that lay in their path.[33] Juromenha had a garrison of 2,200 infantry and 60 cavalry under the skilled and loyal Manoel Lobato Pinto. The curtain walls were solid and had been improved with additional defences, therefore the Portuguese generals thought the place in no immediate danger since the town was provided with all that was needed to withstand a long siege.[34] Schomberg proposed that the army should attempt the seizure of Albuquerque from the Spaniards, but his suggestion was rejected by Marialva, the Portuguese governor preferring to relieve the besieged Juromenha. Meanwhile the brave Lorenço Sousa de Meneses tried to send some reinforcements into the town, but the Portuguese attempts to enter Juromenha by exploiting the course of the Guadiana River was successfully repulsed by the Spaniards. The Portuguese succeeded in delivering a letter that informed the defenders of the arrival of the relief army. Between April and May, the army of Alentejo had grown to 15,000 men and in the mind of Marialva it would be large enough to persuade the enemy to raise the siege. Don Juan was not however distracted and after four days of fruitless waiting, the Portuguese withdrew back to Vilaviçosa.[35] The retreat was not an easy

André de Albuquerque Ribafria (1621–1659), governor of Alentejo for three times between 1647 and 1659, portrayed by Feliciano de Almeida (Uffizi Museum, Florence). Orphaned at a young age, Ribafria won fame as a commander during the Restoration War, fighting in several encounters before being killed in action at Elvas after the failure before Badajoz.

---

33 *Ibid.*, p.23. According to the author, the Spaniards hanged all the Portuguese officers captured during the offensive, since Don Juan treated them like rebels and not as regular soldiers.

34 Estébanez Calderón, *De la conquista y pérdida de Portugal*, vol.I, pp.223–224. The garrison comprised 900 men from the *terço* Mesquita-Pimentel (PI–17), 12 auxiliary companies from the *terço* Monroa (PA–17) with 600 soldiers, four companies of the *auxiliares* of Serpa, and seven militia companies with 350 men. The cavalry company was under Captain Ambrosio Pereira de Barredo. The artillery comprised 12 bronze and one iron gun. Among the Portuguese, there was the Castilian born captain Tomás de Estrada y Zúñiga, while in the opposite side, the French engineers Nicholas de Langres, commanded the siege artillery. He had previously served Portugal.

35 *Ibid.*, p.240: 'The Portuguese, to gain knowledge of the besiegers' progress, sent messengers under the pretext of conferring with the 'quality people' inside Juromenha, and also spies who

The fortified town of Juromenha in the drawing of Nicholas de Langres. (Author's archive)

operation, since the Spaniards engaged the Portuguese rearguard and routed the cavalry. The garrison of Juromenha continued to offer fierce resistance, forcing the Spaniards to open a third approach against the curtain. However, the failure of Meneses' expedition had doomed the city, which surrendered on 9 June.[36]

Cavalry skirmishes resumed during the next few weeks, while the Spaniards took the minor forts of Monforte, Crato, Alter Pedroso and Assumar. After these actions, in July the armies took up their summer quarters, and the Portuguese troops dispersed to the border garrisons of Alentejo. The pause coincided with great changes at court. Afonso VI had come of age, and the powerful Luís de Vasconcelos e Sousa, Count of Castelo Melhor, saw an opportunity to gain power at court by befriending the young King and removing the regency.[37] Alongside with Castelho Melhor, Atouguia was among the supporters of the revolution at court and immediately he acted against Marialva when the Count

intruded among the prisoners in the Spanish camp, but Don Juan, guessing the subterfuge, had them transferred to Seville.'

36 *Ibid.*, p.263. The Portuguese governor of Juromenha obtained the free evacuation of the garrison with the honour of war to Vilaviçosa alongside with the civilians who did not want to return under the Spanish rule.

37 Castelo Melhor managed to convince Afonso that his mother was out to steal his throne and exile her in Portugal. As a result, Afonso sent his mother to a convent.

became one of the King's chief ministers in the new government. However, the position of Schomberg was also shaken because months before he expressed his opinion of Atouguia, questioning lack of resolution and intellect, as well damning the uselessness of Portuguese commanders.[38] Schomberg then had to face ruthless hostility and even the betrayal of one of his lieutenants, who, as in a novel move, offered to replace him as commander of the French troops in Portugal. Schomberg therefore seriously considered the idea of resigning the post and returning to France, but Louis XIV and the Council of Tradesman in Lisbon convinced him to remain in Portugal and maintain his office of field commander.[39] News spread of the arrival of a French delegation to negotiate the arrival of 20,000 soldiers, but dependent on accepting peace with Spain, an event that was openly at odds with the terms of the treaty signed with Charles II of England.[40]

The army of Alentejo needed money for the next campaign in autumn, but the Portuguese treasury could not supply further resources. As commander of all the foreign troops in Portugal, Schomberg at least managed to get the English troops paid, as they had not received their wages for months. In August 1662, the Portuguese were bolstered by the arrival of further foreign soldiers, including reinforcements for the English brigade. They were veterans of the English Civil War, and for Charles II, this was a convenient way of getting rid of the demobilised soldiers of Cromwell's New Model Army and removing them from England.

However, the Spaniards were also suffering from shortages of supplies and desertions. In the second half of 1662, the small but disciplined Portuguese army of Alentejo performed better than the larger but poorly supplied Spanish troops under Don Juan. The autumn campaign did not see any significant episodes, as a direct consequence of the Spanish difficulties in resuming the offensive due to their shortage of resources. Don Juan was forced to wait until the spring of 1663 to resume the offensive. The army of Extremadura had been strongly reinforced, transferring troops from the garrisons of Aragon and Castile; many units had been amalgamated to form *tercios* and *trozos* worthy of the name, and further troops arrived from Naples and Milan. This produced a force of about 14,000 infantry and 6,000 cavalry which mustered at Badajoz in mid April 1663. Their Achilles' heel, however, was the supply situation, considering that at the beginning of the operations, on 24 April, the army had enough provisions for only six weeks, and fodder for just two. Reading the correspondence between Madrid and Badajoz, historians have concluded that the original plan provided a sea blockade of Lisbon, or alternatively a landing at Porto, to support the offensive in Alentejo, but the presence of the English fleet in the east Atlantic Ocean put paid to the plan.[41] Furthermore, Don Juan

---

38 Dumoriez, *Campagnes du Maréchal de Schomberg*, p.22.
39 Riley, *The Last Ironsides*, p.72. The superintendent of La Rochelle, Charles Colbert du Terron, Marquis de Bourbonne, delivered the letter of Louis XIV to Schomberg. The French king asked him to be patient and that the services would be recognised and rewarded.
40 From the summer 1662, Schomberg simultaneously served as field commanders of three kings: Portugal, France and England.
41 Estébanez Calderón, *De la conquista y pérdida de Portugal*, vol.II, p.8.

not had moved his headquarters onto Portuguese territory and had failed to make the best use of the short campaigning seasons, or the Portuguese food supplies, so shifting the economic burden of the war from the Spanish border provinces to the enemy.

The Portuguese had reinforced the garrisons of Évora and Vilaviçosa, considering these towns likely to be the next targets of the enemy offensive. However, Schomberg considered both garrisons unable to guarantee a reasonable defence and after his insistence, only Évora was reinforced with some artillery. On 26 April, the Spanish vanguard was sighted advancing to Campo Major. Days after, news reached the Portuguese that the enemy had razed to the ground several forts that they had erected in key sectors. On 30 April, the Spaniards seized the fort of Ouguela, close to Campo Major, and then invested Évora. The Portuguese army of Alentejo, under Sancho Manuel de Vilhena, Count of Vila Flor, launched a series of cavalry raids; in one of these, the Portuguese engaged the Spanish rearguard and succeeded in destroying some enemy supplies. However, the siege progressed and on 5 May, the Spaniards opened the fire with the siege artillery. Évora surrendered tree days, having lost any hope of a relief. Don Juan and Lobato negotiated the agreement for the free evacuation of the garrison, and 1,950 infantry and 573 cavalry[42] marched out of the town. In Don Juan's plan, Évora would be the base of the future Spanish operations in Portugal. The news of the fall of the city caused great concern in Lisbon and consternation throughout Portugal. There was rioting and the people sacked the houses belonging to ministers, since there was now no major obstacle to arrest a Spanish advance on Lisbon.

However, the conquest of Évora was the last major achievement of the army of Extremadura and marked the beginning of the Portuguese counter-offensive. The beginning of the Spanish crisis occurred when the Portuguese were ready to face the enemy with a strong field army reorganised and trained by Schomberg. The army of Alentejo had been reinforced with troops from the northern provinces of Beira and auxiliary infantry, and now numbered 12,000 foot including 2,000 English and 1,600 French, together with 3,000 horse, and 15 artillery pieces. The army was mustered at Estremoz on 10 May, and immediately a reconnaissance party of 200 horsemen moved forward to locate the enemy. Further cavalry was sent to the villages around Évora to dissuade the Portuguese peasants from supplying food and fodder to the Spaniards. Schomberg soon realised that the enemy had insufficient troops and not enough ammunition, food and money for an offensive campaign. Schomberg persuaded Vila Flor that Don Juan would not be able to maintain Évora and then extend his lines of communication without first capturing another town to secure his rear. In the opinion of the Schomberg, the Spaniards were forced to pause and resupply the army because a further advance would have exposed them to a Portuguese incursion from Estremoz. This situation now left the strategic initiative with the Portuguese. The gruelling council of war took place before the unprecedented events in Lisbon could evolve into a pro-Spain coup, as reported by Simão de Vasconcelos e Sousa, *mestre de campo*

---

42   *Ibid.*, p.25.

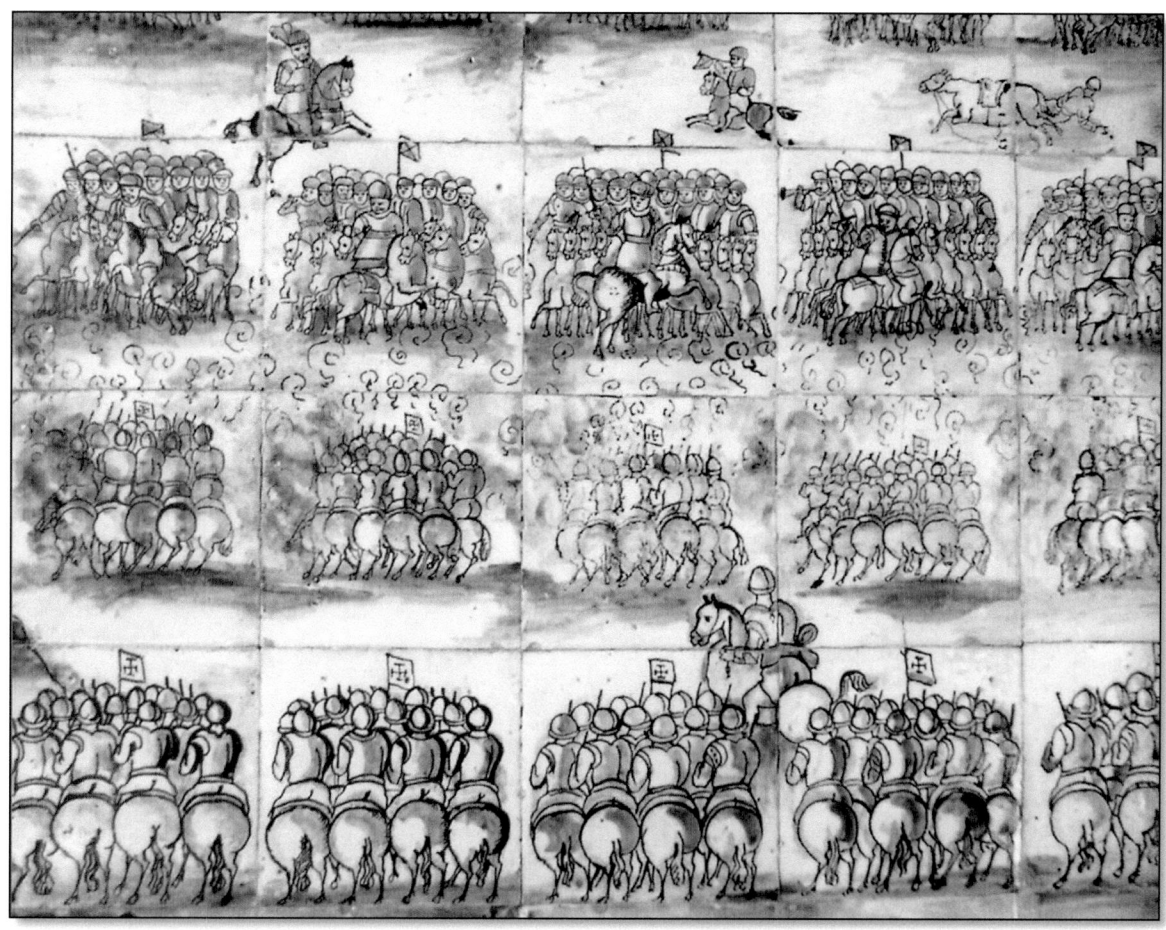

Portuguese cavalry deployed in two lines engages the enemy in an *azulejo* ceramic tile, preserved in the Palácio Fronteira in Lisbon. During the war there were little differences in dress and equipment between the Portuguese and the Spanish cavalry. This could either be a problem for the identification of the nationalities or on the other hand exploited. In 1660 a coeval chronicle mentions that a whole Portuguese cavalry company of the army of Alentejo deserted to the Spanish side. To achieve this, the captain planned to avoid the suspicions of the Portuguese troops while marching to the front. With the excuse of attending a party with his family near Campo Maior, he led his company to escort the convoy in which his family and other people travelled. Before arriving at the destination, the officer encountered a Spanish cavalry troop with whom he feigned combat, and eventually along with his company, 40 other people changed sides, including the captain's wife, his brother, several cousins and other members of his family and supporters.

of the *terço de Armada* (PI–01), but Vila Flor continued to wait for more information before moving the army. As had been planned by Schomberg the army of Extremadura was facing a compelling problem, since during the march from Badajoz to Évora and during the nine days of the siege, the cavalry had consumed all the sown fields for up to 14 kilometres around. The enemy was now in a precarious situation, since the army was divided in two parts, and by late May, the temperature had begun to burn off the pasture, further dispersing the forces. On 20 May, the fodder was so reduced that they were forced to send out a large corps of 2,000 cavalry and infantry deep into Portugal, to bring in as much corn and meal as they could gather. During this action, the 'flying corps' burned the villages of Alcaçovas and Alcacer de Sal, but without gathering enough provisions for the army. When the news of the expedition arrived in Estremoz, Schomberg proposed moving as rapidly as possible to interpose the army between the separate enemy corps and thus be in a position to deal with each part in turn, on favourable ground. After two further days of talking at the war council, finally, the Portuguese army headed against the enemy, but the slow pace of the supply train did not allow them to intercept the enemy for a few hours. On 23 May, the Portuguese arrived in sight of Évora from north-east, and their approach had been spotted by the Spaniards. Schomberg personally led the reconnaissance and observed the enemy deployed in battle formation on the western side of the Degebe River, about five kilometres east of Évora. Don Juan was slowed down by the baggage, the Portuguese prisoners, and above all by the siege artillery, and therefore his main concern was to move the army as quickly as possible to the shortest route to obtain supplies. However, he was forced to leave a garrison inside Évora, of 3,000 infantry and 500 cavalry. However, to reach safety, the Spanish army had first to defeat the Portuguese army which lay in his direct path. The Degebe River represented a modest obstacle, but it had steep deeply incised banks, was thickly lined with trees and thorn bushes, and muddy, passable for infantry and cavalry but not by wagons and artillery without a bridge or ford. Don Juan ordered a bombardment the enemy camp during the night. On 24 May, the Spaniards attempted to force a passage of the river at a ford near Redondo, in order to clear their escape route. The Spanish vanguard advanced with three infantry battalions and three cavalry squadrons but the attempt was repulsed by the two English regiments deployed in the first line.[43] The fight lasted no more than an hour, and the Spaniards, personally led by Don Juan, made another attempt to cross the river with the main army, but the Portuguese artillery, well deployed and directed by the French *colonel* Desfontaines, and the arrival of Portuguese infantry to support the English regiments made Don Juan change his plan. On 25 May, the Spanish troops received half rations, and marched to the left, following the river and approached Évora. The Portuguese manoeuvred to follow the enemy like a shadow on the other side of the Degebe. This retreat allowed the Spaniards to finally be able to cross the river on the main road to Estremoz and from there to march toward Arronches. Don Juan allowed only three days to cover the 70 kilometres from Évora to Arronches, but the march proceeded slowly, and the Portuguese spotted the enemy on open ground. Schomberg and Vila Flor believed that the enemy would have given battle taking advantage of their cavalry superiority, as well as being able to bring up the garrison of Évora in support. Therefore, during the night, the Portuguese and their allies dug entrenchments and rested the infantry, but instead of attacking them, Don Juan spent the whole of 25 May in bringing up his baggage train to Évora and putting the garrison in a state of defence. Don Juan was trying to gain time and the next day, after moving the baggage and the prisoners in the night, he directed the army along the main road through Évora, followed 12 hours later by Vila Flor and Schomberg from west. The Portuguese made a forced march that caused the death of many soldiers

---

43   Riley, *The Last Ironsides*, p.97.

from exhaustion and the high temperatures, but on the night of 26 May, the two armies made contact and camped four kilometres apart on either side of the River Tera. The next day, both armies resumed their march and skirted around Estremoz on the southern side before turning north. After a march of 15 kilometres the Spanish and Portuguese halted that night near the village of Ameixial. The battle that followed was known in Spain and Portugal by the names of these localities. Schomberg remarked that this broken ground was the least favourable battlefield to engage the enemy for the Spanish would not benefit from their cavalry superiority.[44] If that opportunity had not been exploited, in the following days the Portuguese would have had to face two problems: to fight an enemy superior in numbers and to recover Évora. But if they lost no obstacles would stand in the way between the enemy and Lisbon.

On 28 May Don Juan realised that he could not outrun his pursuers any longer and must therefore stand and fight.[45] The Spaniards were deployed with half of their foot, in two lines, on each of the two hills that flanked the main road to Badajoz. The veteran Spanish and Italian *tercios* occupied the right side, while on the left sector stood the provincial *tercios* and the German infantry in support. On the top of each hill Don Juan deployed a four-gun battery of field artillery. The cavalry, the strongest and most feared component of the army, was placed in two corps below the hills: the right corps covering the exposed flank, under Juan Jácome Mazacán, and the left corps securing the road and the gap between the hills, under the *comisario general de la caballeria* Diego Caballero. Overall, Don Juan could manage to field 11,122 foot and 6,154 horse. According to contemporary Portuguese and allied reports, the enemy held a formidable position.[46]

The army of Alentejo was drawn up with the bulk of the Portuguese infantry on the right, and the foreign regiments on the extreme left, again in two lines. The artillery was deployed between the two so to be able to support the infantry with direct fire. The first line was under Afonso Turtoda de Mendoza, and the second line by the Count de la Torre. The artillery operated under the nominal command of Dom Luís de Meneses, but the skilled Desfontaines was responsible for the actual direction of the guns. The cavalry formed two lines: the first one as a vanguard of 800 horsemen, included the English and French horse. Behind them stood the 2,000 Portuguese cavalry under Denis de Mello, reinforced by 'squadrons' of musketeers drawn from Portuguese *terços*.[47] The Portuguese and their allies approximately numbered 13,900 infantry and 2,800 cavalry.

Vila Flor and his senior officers met in the war council and yet again behaved irresolutely, but everyone was also conscious of the King's order to give battle.

44　Dumoriez, *Campagnes du Maréchal de Schomberg*, p.31.
45　The Hispanic war council agreed to stand and fight, except San Germano, who instead proposed entrenching the army and exploiting their cavalry superiority to gathering resources in enemy territory. See in Estébanez Calderón, *De la conquista y pérdida de Portugal*, vol. II, p.30.
46　Riley, *The Last Ironsides*, p.103.
47　The deployment of both armies can be seen in the contemporary print of the battle, entitled *Entrada do Exercito del rey de Castella, Governado pr D. Juan de Austria*. This picture is more about propaganda than an exact representation of the battle, but the whole sequence of the action through its various phase within the same canvas, and so must be carefully interpreted.

The strong enemy position and its considerable advantage in cavalry worried the council, but Schomberg decided to take a risk and ordered Mello move his cavalry on the left bank, using the ground to conceal the move and to engage the enemy cavalry with the infantry between the spaces. Meanwhile, the rest of infantry were to assault the enemy on the high ground. For this move, the cavalry could exploit the low slopes of the terrain for concealment. The move took longer than Schomberg expected, and the deployment was observed by the Spaniards. They in turn redeployed their cavalry on the same flank. One hour before the dusk, Schomberg ordered the French and English cavalry forward in the centre. The charge succeeded in defeating the enemy horsemen, which included the life guard of Don Juan. The charge also engaged the second line of the enemy cavalry, after which the French and English horsemen rallied out and took cover using the ground, waiting for the support of the Portuguese cavalry. There are several accounts of the battle, and these agreed on this first phase of the battle, but after the first assault performed by the English and French cavalry, the sources do not agree on several details.[48] The decisive episode occurred when the allied infantry contacted their enemy counterparts. The discipline and the good order of the Portuguese and their allies gave them the advantage. The fire of Spanish artillery placed on the hills was ineffective, while the Portuguese and allied musketry, deployed in three ranks, emerged from the smoke of the artillery and targeted at close range and with deadly effect the deep enemy infantry formations. The action proceeded perfectly and surprised even the Portuguese commander, since the English infantry had advanced without firing from long range, as was the Portuguese custom, and Vila Flor believed they meant to throw their weapons down and surrender to the Spaniards.[49] Chaos and poor communication led to the disintegration of the Hispanic army despite the sacrifice of several veteran units. The defeat doomed the garrison of Évora, which surrendered on 13 June after a short siege. In the campaign of 1663, the Portuguese strategic moves had prevailed over the Spaniards and after Ameixial-Estremoz, where the army of Extremadura suffered so many losses, it was impossible for Spain to continue the campaign, since almost all the infantry had been lost.[50]

The war stopped in the summer, as always, but in the following autumn, there were a few noteworthy events. In 1664, the Spaniards tried to seize Elvas by surprise with a bold cavalry action under by Diego Caballero but suffered another failure. The problems for the Spaniards were not over, because in early March a fire destroyed the gunpowder depot at Arronches

---

48 According to the Portuguese and allied sources, the Hispanic horsemen also rallied and engaged the Portuguese infantry placed between the cavalry. The foot soldiers, without the protection of the pikes, and poorly supported by their cavalry, withdrew in disorder. The French and English cavalry intervened again to remedy the situation, while the Portuguese and allied infantry advanced against the enemy. See also in Riley, *The Last Ironsides*, p.106.
49 *Ibid.*, p.109.
50 English sources give 4,000 Spanish casualties, including those who fell into the hands of the Portuguese peasants and who received no mercy. The Spanish sources move the actual figure between 5,000 and 7,000 killed, wounded and missing. Among the prisoners were eight general officers and 50 other officers. The Portuguese also captured the artillery and the enemy train with thousands of mules and oxen. The Portuguese and the allies claimed the loss of 1,000 killed and 500 wounded.

PORTUGUESE WARS

Print depicting the initial phase of the Battle of Montes Claros, fought on 17 June 1665 between the Portuguese Army of Alentejo with approximately 22,000 men under António Luís de Meneses, Marquis of Marialva, and the Spanish Army of Extremadura, under Luís de Benavides, Count of Caracena, with about 23,000. Thousands of Hispanic soldiers were captured and made prisoners, with eight generals being among the captured. A large quantity of arms and war materials was captured by the Portuguese. The total Spanish casualties amounted to 4,000 killed on the battlefield. Almost 1,500 fugitives died in the immediate weeks after the battle and eventually 6,000 prisoners and 4,000 wounded were taken. The Portuguese and allies suffered some 700 killed and more than 2,000 wounded. (Author's archive)

and killed or wounded nearly 2,000 people. Although Don Juan had managed to demonstrate that the responsibility for the disastrous defeat suffered the previous year could not be attributed to him, important changes took place in the command of the army of Extremadura. The hope of being able to reverse the unfavourable course of events was placed in Prince Alessandro Farnese and then in Luis de Benavides Carrillo, Marquis of Caracena, a veteran of campaigns in Italy and the Low Countries. In Portugal too, the command in Alentejo passed again to Marialva. Before the end of the spring campaign, the Portuguese were successful at Valencia de Alcantara, which surrendered notwithstanding the heroic resistance of the Spanish–Italian garrison under Fabrizio Rossi.[51] The small Portuguese army under Pedro Jacques de Magalhães also prevailed in Entre-Douro-e-Minho, pursuing their enemies

---
51 Estébanez Calderón, *De la conquista y pérdida de Portugal*, vol.II, p.75.

Valencia de Alcantara, in Spanish Extremadura, was one of the favourite targets of the Portuguese raids, due to its strategic position close the border. (Author's collection)

into Galicia after the unsuccessful attempt of the Duke of Osuna to seize Castelho Rodrigo. In the second half of 1664, the Portuguese intensified their incursions into Spanish territory with large corps of cavalry. The fortresses of Serpa and Moura became the logistics centres of these actions performed against Extremadura in order to destroy all the resources for the Spanish army. The third phase of the war ended on June 1665 at Vilaviçosa and Montes Claros with the sensational Portuguese battlefield victory over Spain. These events would obligate Spain to open for a peace agreement: the main goal for Portugal.

When Luís de Benavides Carrillo, Marquis of Caracena, was appointed commander in Extremadura, to lead the new invasion of Portugal, he planned to end the war by capturing the Portuguese capital of Lisbon. To achieve this result, Caracena proposed a variant of the plan designed by Don Juan de Austria in 1661. In order to secure the flank of the army during the offensive, his army had first to take Vilaviçosa, followed immediately after by Setúbal. Carrillo had a long career as a field commander and as a military governor, and his organisational skills were lauded, but his plan was unrealistic, since the Portuguese could cut his lines of communication in several places during their advance. However, Caracena believed that the army could have sustained itself in enemy territory with requisitions and captured provisions. Once he was in command, Caracena wanted to gather his army's strength to ensure that he outnumbered whatever Portuguese army was to engage him. However, the worsening illness of Felipe IV caused the court to order him to proceed with the invasion, as the ministers feared that the death of the King would strengthen foreign support for the Portuguese. The Spanish Crown was also facing financial difficulties, and there was a legitimate fear that the army would have to be disbanded for lack of funds if the war continued. Furthermore, in 1665, the Portuguese seemed to be better prepared than three years before, and their high command had foreseen such an attack. In April, 3,500 men were moved from Trás-os-Montes in the north to Alentejo in the south. A further 7,800 men came from Lisbon, bringing the field strength of the army to 22,000 men, a figure that the intelligence gathered in Lisbon suggested was enough to face Caracena. The Portuguese were aware that the Spaniards had any number of ways to invade the country. As such, Marialva reinforced the border garrisons of Elvas and Campo Maior, hoping to toughen the frontier defences and in doing so influence the route Caracena would take. Having been present during the Portuguese victory at Ameixial, Meneses and Schomberg were well aware that the Spanish faced logistical challenges when invading Portugal, and as such they planned to keep the enemy army trapped in the border hinterlands as long as possible to wear down their numbers. The Portuguese commanders were also conscious of the failing health of the Spanish King Filipe IV, and they suspected that this would force them to attack before his health turn another turn for the worse. The Hispanic army moved into Portugal on 25 May. Caracena first took Borba without any resistance after it was abandoned by the Portuguese garrison. He then laid siege to Vilaviçosa, taking the city but failing to capture the citadel, which he was forced to besiege. The Portuguese commanders decided to exchange land for time, as it was hoped that the rough terrain of the hinterlands would degrade the enemy army's ability to fight. Despite this strategy, Meneses was determined to engage the Spanish army on a battlefield of his choosing. The main corps of the Portuguese army set itself in motion towards the Spanish force surrounding Vilaviçosa, but it stopped in Montes Claros, halfway between Vilaviçosa and Estremoz. Caracena, who was at that time leading the siege of Vilaviçosa, was fast losing men to enemy action, desertion and disease. By June, attacks by Portuguese intruders were taking a heavy toll on his lines of supply, Vilaviçosa continued to offer an unexpectedly fierce defence, and the Spanish court was demanding action. In spite of these setbacks, Caracena continued to rely on his previous plans for the capture of Lisbon. However, on 17 June, when informed that Meneses was advancing on him from Estremoz, Carrillo decided to engage in battle with the enemy.

 The Portuguese commanders deployed their troops in a defensive formation adjacent to a long ridge. A dense wood and hills lay further to the south of the Portuguese positions. By defending the space between these two features, Meneses and Schomberg posted the infantry, composed of seasoned veterans and foreign mercenaries, in two lines and positioned the artillery to support them. The rest of the Portuguese army was held in a reserve line and ordered to prevent the Spanish from ascending the ridge. Caracena was well aware of the Portuguese defences and massed his cavalry and artillery for an all-out attack on the area between the ridge and the wood. The first Hispanic assaults failed and a second was also repulsed. Caracena then ordered a massive third assault, incorporating both cavalry and infantry. The battle raged on and

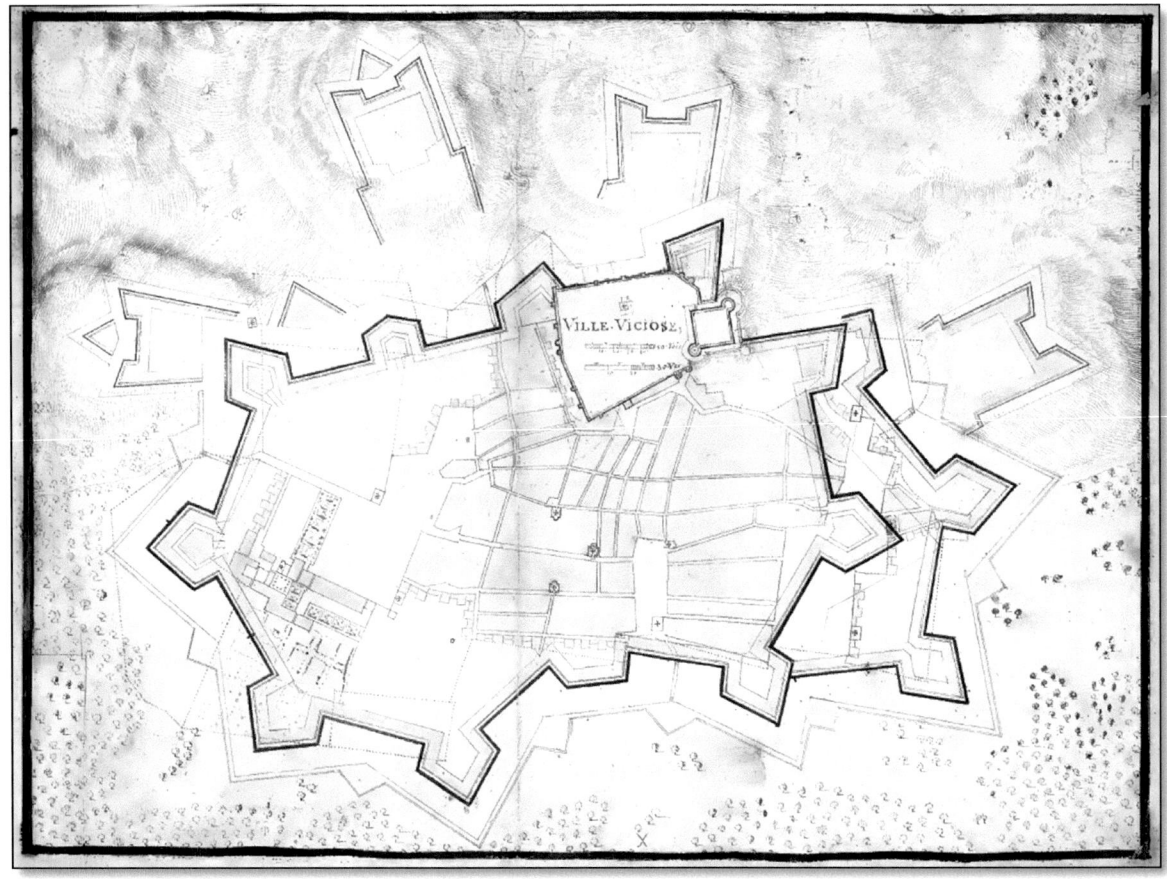

Vilaviçosa in 1659, after de Langres' *Desenhos e plantas de todas aspraças do Reyno de Portugal*. (Author's archive)

Schomberg had his horse shot from underneath him and was almost captured. The Portuguese artillery was devastating as shot after shot was fired into the advancing mass of the enemy troops, while the Hispanic artillerymen were soon forced to cease in their firing for fear of hitting their own troops. The assault collapsed, and Hispanic infantry and cavalry were soon pressed tightly together, becoming easy targets for the Portuguese. The Spanish cavalry alone suffered over 1,200 casualties in the third charge against the Portuguese line. The Portuguese forces remained mostly intact, while the already diminished Hispanic army began to lose all cohesion. Having failed to crush Meneses's defences, Caracena began to withdraw to the north. After seven hours of hard fighting, the Portuguese launched a counter-attack with the cavalry led by Luís Melo e Castro, which had until this point played only a limited role. The charge overran the weakened left flank of the enemy and the Hispanic troops fled in disorder towards the East, leaving behind all their artillery and many dead and wounded. Thousands of soldiers were made prisoners, with eight generals being among the captured. A large quantity of arms and war materials was also captured by the Portuguese. The total Hispanic casualties amounted to 4,000 killed on the battlefield and 4,000 wounded. Almost 1,500 fugitives died in the immediate weeks after the battle and in all there were 6,000 prisoners. The Portuguese suffered some 700 killed and more than 2,000 wounded.

PORTUGUESE WARS

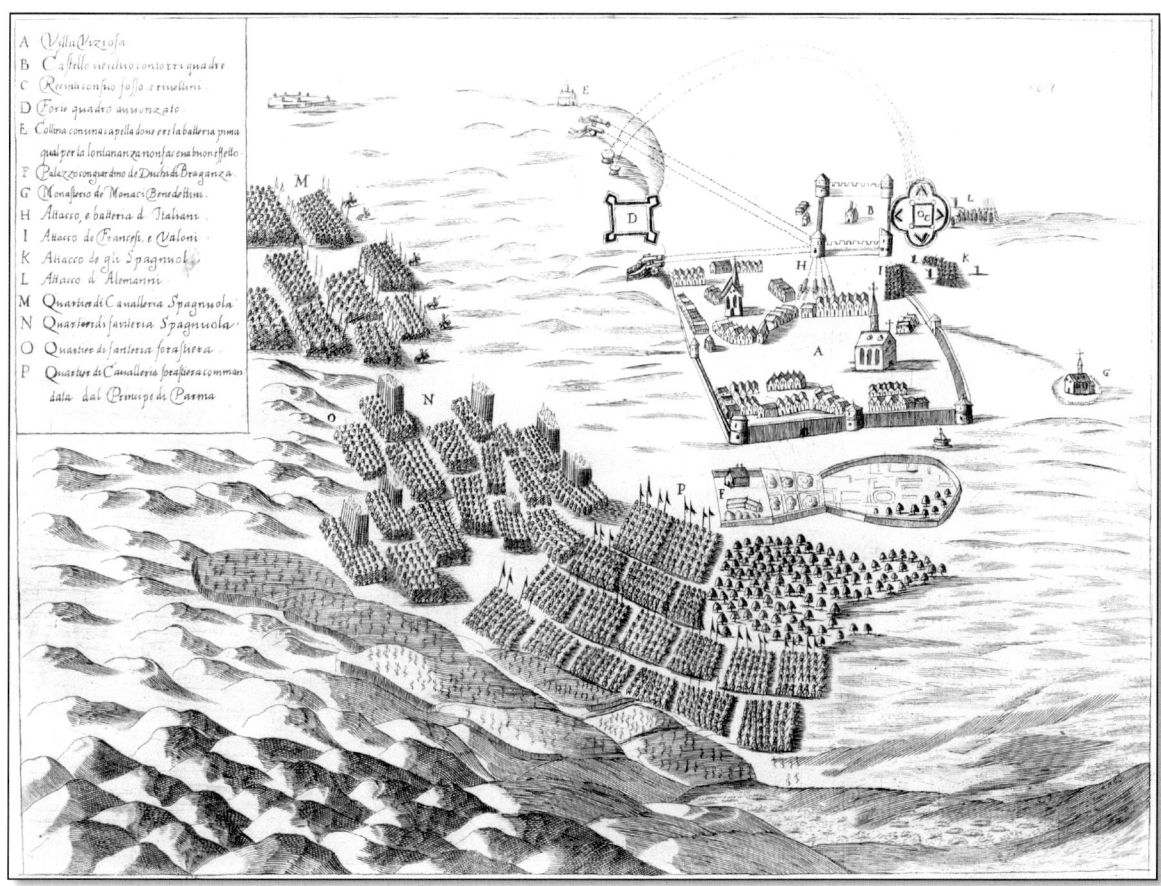

The fourth and last phase lasted until February 1668, when the war finally ended with the Peace of Lisbon. In this period, the war turned once again into one of skirmishes and small border actions, because the Portuguese were also running out of resources. Military action by both Portuguese and Spaniards became small scale. Villages were raided, crops and olive groves were requisitioned, and cattle seized on either side of the border.[52] Isolated and with a few resources, the Spanish garrisons gave only sporadic resistance to the Portuguese. In 1666, the *Mercurio Portuguez* relates that the soldiers who manned some outposts before Ciudad Rodrigo surrendered to the Portuguese cavalry, but they questioned the right to be treated as prisoners, because it was said throughout Castile that peace had already been signed between the two kingdoms.[53] The only significant field event occurred in 1667, with the Portuguese offensive into Galicia, devised as prize of reparation to Portugal. However, the campaign failed after the valiant resistance at La Guardia by the German–Spanish–Irish garrison.

The siege of Vilaviçosa opened the campaigns of 1665 in Alentejo. Between 27 May and 15 June, the Hispanic attempt to seize the Portuguese fortress failed and cost 1,500 dead and wounded. (Engraving by Gaspar Bouttats)

---

52 In autumn 1666, Pedro Jacques de Magalhães, governor of Riba Côa, entered Castile with 500 horses and 1,000 foot soldiers. The troops looted more than 600 head of cattle, more than 2,000 sheep, 100 horses and many pigs, reaching three leagues from Ciudad Rodrigo. *Mercurio Portuguez*, 1666.
53 *Ibid.*

WARS AND SOLDIERS IN THE EARLY REIGN OF LOUIS XIV - VOLUME 5

Portuguese infantry. During the Restoration War, the Portuguese commanders exploited every expedient for gathering troops in the extensive theatre of operations. The Count of Ericeria records that on many occasions the infantry moved on mules in order to increase the speed, rushing to the threatened sectors. (Author's reconstruction)

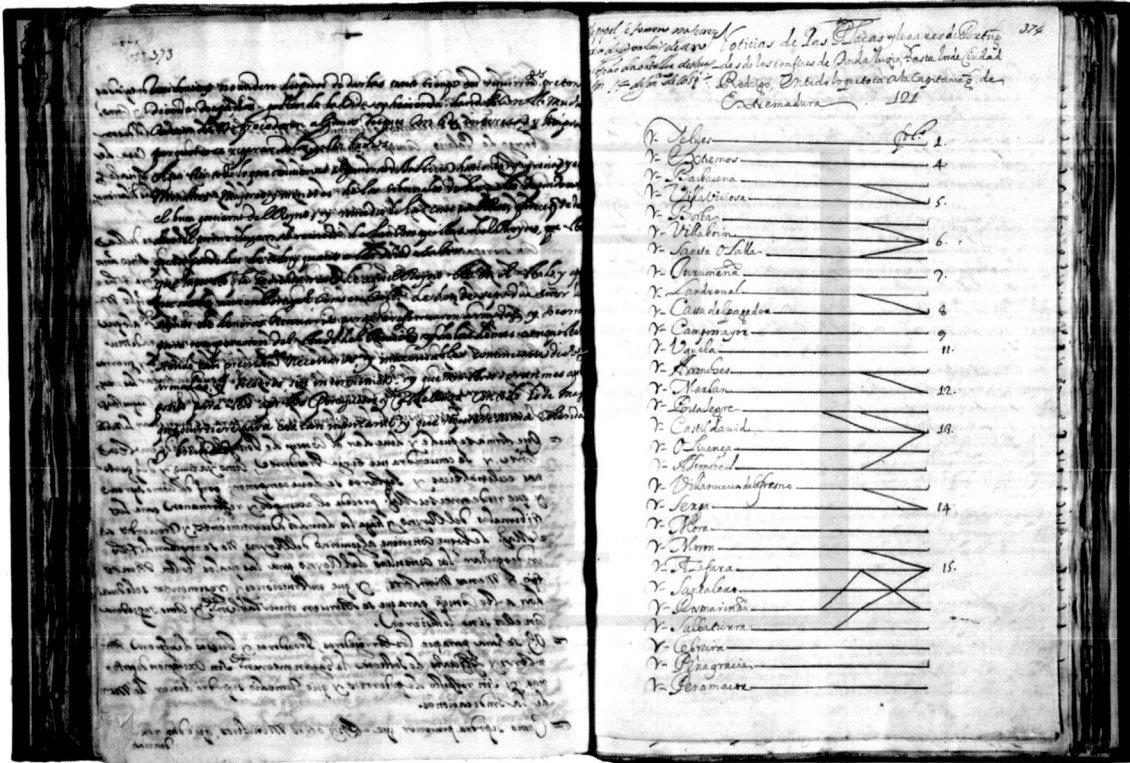

List of Portuguese fortresses on the borders of Extremadura, in a page of a Spanish report dated 4 November 1658. The document is now preserved in the Portuguese Archives, and was a probable war prey in the battle of the Linhas de Elvas in 1659. The Spaniards were well informed on the conditions of the enemy fortresses and the conquest of Évora in 1663 had not been accidental. In Portugal the loss of this town was even greater, because Évora had huge symbolic importance. It was a royal city and had also been the home of the Jesuit University since 1558. The Jesuits represented a progressive contrast to the Inquisition and in 1663, in the seize of Évora the Spaniards had made a religious point as well as a statement about sovereignty, since Inquisition on both sides of the border was a firm supporter of Iberian unification. (Arquivo Torre di Tombo, manuscritos Livraria)

Portugal's Global Warfare

Despite their involvement in the war against Spain, Portuguese aristocracy continued to plan for colonial expansion, which would bring them gains in the forms of both honour in battle and windfall riches. Those who went on to serve in the garrisons hoped for the same benefits by participating in the perennial 'little wars' in America, Asia and Africa with raids and ambushes in which stout deeds were done and prisoners, cattle and other prizes taken. The overseas expeditions provided opportunities for young noblemen to build up their service records so they could then claim some reward from the King. However, under the Habsburgs the idea of neo-Reconquest in Morocco was finally abandoned. Instead, the Crown pursued a policy of watchful pragmatism, designed to ensure both the Ottomans and the Moroccans were effectively contained. Ceuta, Tangier and Mazagão, along with the Spanish *presidios* further east, formed part of a broad defensive ring of North African fortresses. Their role was to guard against corsairs

First page of the *Methodo Lusitanico*, written in the 1670s by Luis Serrão Pimentel (1613–1679). The work dealt with the construction of fortifications and other defences according to the most up-to-date techniques. Portugal experienced several sieges during the war against Spain, and for improving tactics and the quality of her engineers favoured the development of schools of practice. The government turned also to foreign personnel, but some of these experts did not perform adequately or were even revealed to be completely without knowledge: for example in 1663 during the reconquest of Évora, when the Duke of Schomberg realised that the Italian engineer sent from Lisbon was completely unable to plan the siege.

or surprise attack and pass on intelligence. They also allowed military recruits to gain experience in a setting that was exotic, yet not far from the peninsula. Nevertheless, from a Portuguese viewpoint, whether their retention was really justified given the heavy costs involved is highly doubtful. The Portuguese interest in Morocco continued after the loss of Ceuta and the secession of Tangier to England, since Mazagão lingered on as a Portuguese possession much longer, an all but useless and irritatingly expensive anomaly.[54]

The major involvement of Portugal in their overseas domains took place in Brazil. After the positive end of the war against the Dutch, the attention of the Brazilian captaincy turned to the interior. Although enslaving the indigenous Indian population was not practiced everywhere in Brazil, at least on a very large scale, it was widespread in the state of São Paulo in the South and in Maranhão in the north. The colonists originally planned to use coerced or willing labour of the local Indians, following the pattern that was becoming well established in Spanish America. However, by the previous century, the Tupi natives along the Atlantic coast had begun to die out and to retreat from the Portuguese settlers, who were proving less than willing to share the land equally with their native hosts.

The Portuguese then sought to capture Indians from the interior. In Bahia, Portuguese settlers initiated a widespread campaign to capture natives as slaves but ran into opposition from the Jesuit priests who condemned the abusive enslavement of the indigenous peoples. The virtual war between the missionaries on one side, and the colonial army and settlers on the other, spread throughout the colony. In the seventeenth century the Jesuits, who had settled the Guaraní indigenous tribes in missions on the border with Paraguay, became a particular target of the *bandeirantes*.[55]

---

54 Anthony R. Disney, *History of Portugal*, vol. II (Cambridge, Cambridge University Press, 2009), p.21.
55 In 1628, the explorer and *bandeirante* António Rapôso Tavares led the most successful attack against a cluster of several Jesuit missions in the interior of São Paulo. Attacking with a force of 3,000 men, Tavares burned the missions to the ground, captured the inhabitants and marched them back in chains to his base at São Vicente.

PORTUGUESE WARS

Portuguese *bandeirante*, 1675–80. The Europeans in Brazil retained old-fashioned clothing, and usually the leaders wore breastplates or gorgets. In combat the officers preferably used sword and buckler. The broad-brimmed hat was the main distinctive item of the *bandeirantes*. (Author's reconstruction)

These soldiers of fortune often allied themselves with one native tribe against another, and end by enslaving both weakened all belligerents. The loss of men who were captured as prisoners-of-war or who were killed in battle also weakened the ability of these groups to survive. The mission villages established by the Jesuits for the natives were prime targets for slave raids. The first *bandeira*, organised by António Rapôso Tavares in 1628, raided 21 such villages in the upper Paraná valley and captured about 2,500 native people. By around 1650, there was a broad shift among *bandeiras* from slave raiding to searching for precious metals. By this time, African slaves were fulfilling the colony's servile labour requirements, while the Jesuit missions had fortified their defences, making the enslavement of the locals more difficult. The *bandeirantes* were also involved in the wars against the *quilombos*, formed by runaway African slaves who managed to organise themselves into defensive communities. The most famous *quilombo* was the one of Palmares, an independent, self-sustaining community near Recife,

Brazilian-Portuguese militiaman (above) and Tupi-Guaraní native (facing page), portrayed by Albert Eckhout in the 1640s (National Museum of Denmark, Copenhagen). Troops of the infamous *bandeiras* comprised Europeans as well as free mulattos known as *mamelucos* and native freedmen.

was established in early 1600. Palmares was massive and consisted of several settlements with a combined population of over 30,000 citizens, mostly of African heritage, ruled by a skilled leader who took the name Ganga Zumba. This was the only *quilombo* to survive almost an entire century. In 1675, Pedro Almeida, organised a strong corps to destroy Palmares, but Ganga Zumba succeeded in averting the threat moving warriors and non-combatants into the interior. Here, the Palmaristas took advantage of the thick tangled bush to prevail against the Portuguese. In 1678, the governor of Pernambuco and the Afro-American leader negotiated a peace agreement, which was soon broken by a group of dissident Palmaristas, who killed Ganga Zumba and resumed the struggle against the Portuguese. Six expeditions tried to conquer Palmares between 1680 and 1686 but all failed. Finally, the governor of Pernambuco joined his force with the troops of the *bandeirantes* Domingos Jorge Velho and Bernardo Vieira de Melo and defeated the Palmarista force, putting an end to the Afro-American 'republic' in 1694.[56]

While the Portuguese Crown remained superficially committed to the protection and Christianisation of the Indians, they were willing to exploit the *bandeirantes* for their own ends. When the *bandeirante* Pedro Teixeira led the first expedition into the Amazon in 1630, his force numbered over 1,000 native allies and some 120 Portuguese. Such occurrences were to become all too familiar in the history of the occupation of the Amazon. Teixeira's brother, the Vicar General of Maranhão, claimed that 'almost two million' natives had been killed in the course of the Portuguese occupation of Pará region during the 1630s and 1640s, a pattern that was to continue unimpeded as Portuguese control was extended along the whole of the river and up its major tributaries over the next century.[57]

---

56 José de Mirales, *Historia Militar do Brazil (1549–1762)* (Rio de Janeiro, 1900), p.51.
57 Neil L. Whitehead, 'Colonial Intrusions and the Transformation of Native Society in the Amazon Valley, 1500–1800', in H. Langfur (ed.) *Native Brazil beyond the convert and the cannibal, 1500–1900* (Albuquerque: University of New Mexico Press, 2014), pp.91–92.

In 1647, António Rapôso Tavares led a *bandeira* across South America in an attempt to find another route to Peru. The expedition explored much of the interior of Brazil and effectively extended Portuguese dominion into territory previously claimed by Spain. As a makeshift group of disaffected whites, mixed race, and indigenous native recruits, the *bandeirantes* never established political sovereignty over the territories they explored. They did, however, lead the way for subsequent bands of settlers, prospectors, and traders who effectively established Portuguese control over much of the Brazilian interior. Despite the *bandeirantes*' expeditions, the loss of indigenous lives from disease precluded their use as slaves, and even their very survival, in anywhere but the more distant reaches of the Amazon. In general, the demise of the indigenous population was overwhelming. The natives died by the thousands from disease, overwork and depression resulting from the complete destruction of their habitats.

The Portuguese expansion in Brazil sporadically encountered organised native groups, but cases of successful indigenous resistance to Portuguese military occupation, and religious and civilian settlements were few. The only exception in late seventeenth century came from 'the abominable Mura'. They formed a group of communities that resisted for so long and managed through cunning and bravery to maintain their autonomy. The Portuguese feared these warlike natives, as noted in military records from the late 1600s, which remarked on the need for naval cannon and artillery at distant outposts in Pará to guard the settlements against Mura's attacks. The Mura successfully resisted the Jesuits' missionary efforts, and for more than 30 years beat back slaving parties, enticements from the priests, and retaliatory attacks. They were one of the few groups that saw all whites as the same and chose to have nothing to do with any of them. Their tactics were effective against the regular soldiers as well as the *bandeirantes*, however, the Mura rarely burned colonial settlements to the ground nor annihilate the encroachers; rather they attacked and swiftly drew back in guerrilla warfare tactics. As some historians commented, 'the Portuguese were simply kept on the defensive, and prevented thereby from ever fulfilling the colonial government's production quotas.'[58] The Mura resistance lasted until the late eighteenth century.

---

58 *Ibid.*, p.94.

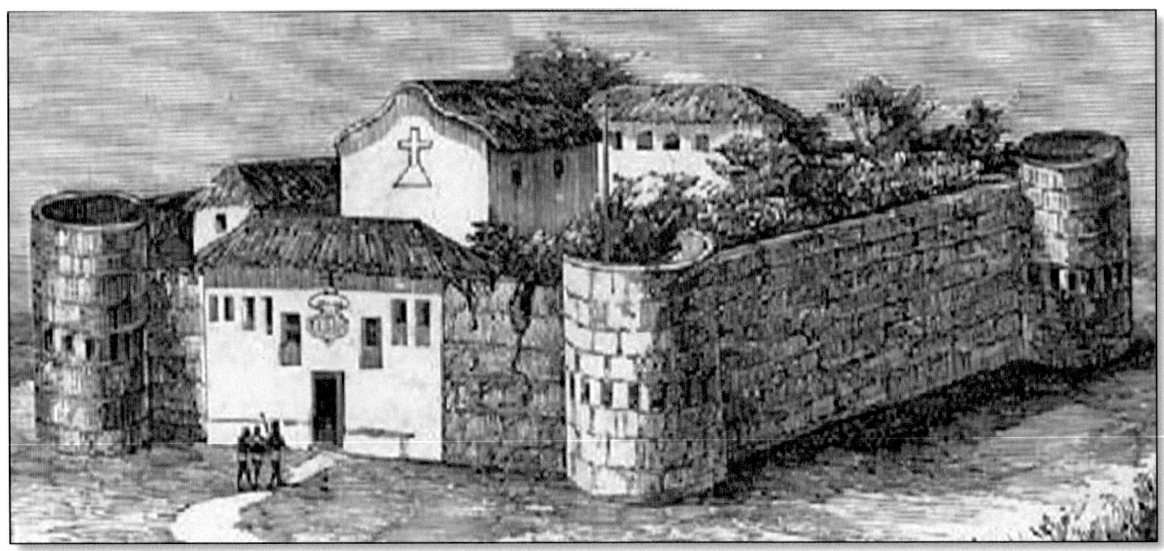

The fort of São João Baptista de Ajudá in Benin, in an eighteenth-century print. This was the typical look of most Portuguese settlements in Africa. (Author's archive)

The Portuguese encountered greater resistance in Africa. In Angola in particular, the formidable founder of Matamba, Queen Nzinga (of Mbundu) (approximately 1620–1663), leader of the African tribes unwilling to accept Portugal's yoke, successfully resisted through the 1620s and 1630s both the Portuguese and their client *ngola*, Ari.[59] The Portuguese in Angola were about to launch a new campaign to deal with Nzinga as well as with the Kasanje kingdom, which was refusing to admit missionaries, when they were suddenly confronted with a major challenge from the Dutch that almost ended their presence in west-central Africa altogether. Under the command of Salvador Correia de Sá e Benavides (1602–1686), a leading citizen, prominent *senhor de engenho* and former governor of Rio de Janeiro, a counter expedition was launched from Brazil in 1648. With remarkable ease, it successfully retook first Luanda, then the rest of Dutch-occupied Angola. The failure of the Dutch was a serious setback for Queen Nzinga who had welcomed them as allies against the Portuguese. After the expulsion of the Dutch, she withdrew for a while to Matamba, but continued to obstruct the supply of slaves to Luanda. The Portuguese themselves, after initially renewing the war against Matamba, agreed to peace in 1656, hoping to revive the slave flow. Portuguese resident captains were then appointed to both Matamba and Kasanje, mainly to facilitate this flow. Meanwhile, in Ndongo Ngola Ari, Portugal's client ruler, was trying to re-establish his autonomy. This led first to disagreement then war with the governor of Luanda. Ari was attacked, defeated and killed by the Portuguese troops and their allies, and another great haul of Ndongo prisoners was taken and enslaved. After this success, the Portuguese decided that trying to control Ndongo indirectly through a malleable *ngola* was a failed strategy, so in 1672 they annexed the region. Portuguese hostilities with Matamba were renewed in the early 1680s, but the Mbundu here were better placed to resist than in Ndongo, and Matamba proved too difficult for the

---

59 *Ngola* was the title for rulers of the Ndongo kingdom which existed from the sixteenth to the seventeenth century in what is now north-west Angola.

Portuguese to crush. Both sides now had reason to compromise so negotiations were re-opened, and a new peace between Luanda and Matamba was finally signed in 1683, effectively bringing to an end the Portuguese–Angolan wars.[60]

Descriptions of warfare in Angola show the realities of these military encounters between Africa and Europe. To increase their numbers, the Portuguese relied on their occasional allies, on their own clients known as *guerra preta*, and on the soldiers provided by vassal *Sobas*, but there were also contingents of Portuguese infantry and frequently small units of cavalry and artillery. These might consist of soldiers sent from Portugal and Brazil, but more often, they were irregular contingents raised from the local Portuguese community. It was the muskets, artillery and cavalry that, when they could be deployed, gave the Portuguese an advantage, but in the press of a battle or a rout, Portuguese troops would easily be outnumbered and overwhelmed. Moreover, many Afro-Portuguese were to be found fighting for the African kings, and at the Battle of Mbwila, the Congo King even had in his army a contingent of Portuguese under their captain to confront the official Portuguese soldiers from Luanda.[61]

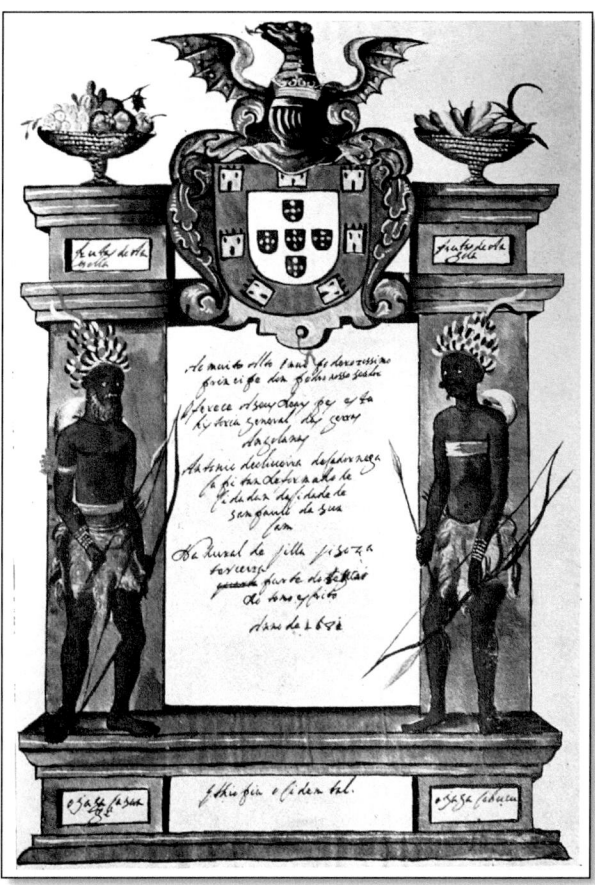

Illustration of native Angolan warriors, from the *História Geral das Guerras Angolanas*, 1681. (Author's archive)

The enemies of the Portuguese would also try to fight during rainstorms in order to prevent their firearms being used. For both the Africans and Portuguese, warfare was largely about plunder, and Portuguese soldiers on the march would frequently be encumbered with booty, slaves and cattle.

In the neighbouring Congo, the Portuguese only began to make real inroads into the lands after 1618, when they struck up an alliance with the Imbangala warlords. The Imbangala, called *Jaga* by the Portuguese, lived in fortified settlements known as *Kilombos* where young male captives were initiated into the group.[62] They were formidable warriors, and the Portuguese found that with their assistance the weak Mbundu and Congo states could be easily conquered. The raids provided the Imbangala with the recruits they required and the Portuguese with a regular supply of slaves for the ever-expanding Atlantic trade. Another objective of the Portuguese in the Congo was to find the legendary silver mines of Cambambe and to control the sources

---

60 Disney, *History of Portugal*, vol. II, p.83.
61 Malyn Newitt, *The Portuguese in West Africa, 1415–1670. A Documentary History* (Cambridge: Cambridge University Press, 2010), p.19.
62 *Ibid.*, pp.16–17. The Imbangala did not allow any children to be born to the group, and instead raided neighbours for women and male children. The young males were initiated with ceremonies that involved ritual cannibalism.

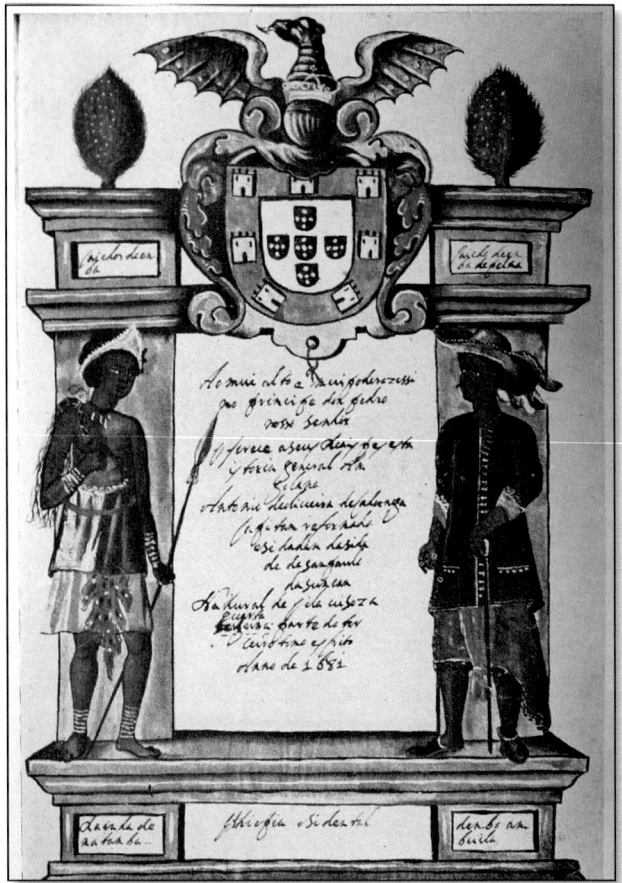

Illustration of a *mbangala* warrior and an African-Portuguese infantryman from the *História Geral das Guerras Angolanas* (1681). Note the soldier on the right wearing a dark blue coat with pale colour cuffs. (Author's archive)

of salt and copper in the region, but by the early seventeenth century the wars had become a broader struggle for regional supremacy between the Portuguese in Luanda, the King of Congo and the independent Mbundu kings. In the 1640s, the Portuguese faced the Dutch and their insidious competition in Africa. In the course of their struggle against the West India Company, the Portuguese tried repeatedly to get the permission from the *manicongos* (kings, or masters) to build a fortress at the Nsoyo port of Mpinda. There the Dutch had been operating with considerable success, often trading with more attractive goods than the Portuguese could provide. Pressured by the Portuguese and still resentful of Lisbon's claims to ecclesiastical patronage, the local leadership began to gravitate to the side of the Dutch West India Company. When in 1641 *manicongo* Garcia II learned that the Dutch had captured Luanda, he decided he could dispense with the Portuguese, believing they would soon be gone anyway. But instead, it was the Dutch who were expelled, and Congo was left to face the full force of Portuguese hostility with no one else to turn to. After the Portuguese recovery of Luanda, the Angola-based Portuguese adopted slaving tactics that were distinctly more aggressive and violent than previously. Relations between Portuguese Luanda and the Kingdom of Congo deteriorated.[63] This occurred under the leadership of a series of particularly energetic governors with backgrounds in Brazil. One of them, André Vidal de Negreiros, having decided that *manicongo* António I had violated his treaty obligations by frustrating Portuguese efforts to exploit Congo's mines, invaded the African kingdom to punish him. Negreiros, who was an able and experienced soldier and a hero of the recent struggle against the Dutch in Brazil, acted on his own initiative and in the interests of the slavers. He paid no more than lip service to the scruples of the government in Lisbon or to the Crown's formal requirements for a 'just' war. In 1665, Negreiros's expedition inflicted a devastating defeat on the Congolese at the battle of Mbwila, at which

---

63 The main problem was the difficulty of determining where the boundaries of the two states lay. Luanda itself was disputed territory as the king of Congo claimed that it was traditionally part of his kingdom, while many of the states on the southern borders of the Congo kingdom only owed a loose and sketchy allegiance to São Salvador. The Portuguese saw this as a kind of no-man's-land and gradually expanded their own control by incorporating these people into the Angolan state. It was one such shift of allegiance, when the ruler of Mbwila recognised the overlordship of the Luanda Portuguese rather than the King of Congo. Further reading in Newitt, *The Portuguese in West Africa*, p.21.

Print dated 1845, depicting João Fernandes Vieira and André Vidal de Negreiros, two of the major leaders during the war against the Dutch in Brazil. Unusually for nineteenth-century iconography, the soldiers' dress is represented fairly correctly. (Author's archive)

manicongo António was killed along with many other Congolese leaders.[64] After the Battle of Mbwila, there was a succession of insecure occupants of the Congo throne, desperate to secure Portuguese backing, and they were in no position to refuse Luanda's demands. Mining concessions were granted in 1667 and again in 1670. In the latter year *Manicongo* Rafael, beset by internal enemies, won the Portuguese governor's support by granting not only mining rights, but a substantial indemnity and permission to build the fort at Mpinda. Portuguese Governor Dom Francisco de Távora, responded by sending an Afro-Portuguese contingent against Rafael's main rival and tormentor, the rebel 'count' of Nsoyo.[65] The Nsoyo were defeated in 1670; but the expeditionary force then went on a slaving and looting rampage and lost all discipline.[66] The Nsoyo warriors had meanwhile re-grouped, and catching the expedition by surprise, they outflanked and annihilated the Portuguese at the Battle of Kitombo. After this battle, the Congo kingdom as such ceased to hold much interest for the Portuguese, while Nsoyo became a relatively powerful state with which they signed a peace treaty in 1690. After this date, the Portuguese abandoned any hope of permanently conquering and incorporating the Kingdom of Congo into their African territories.

Turning to the other Portuguese settlements in Africa, resistance from the locals was almost inexistent. For most of the seventeenth centuries, Cacheu was the principal Portuguese outlet for slaves from Upper Guinea. In 1644, João IV declared the town to be the port where duties on all slaves exported from the region must be paid. It replaced for this purpose the town of Ribeira Grande on Santiago Island, in the Cape Verdes, causing great dismay to the

---

64 *Relação da mais glorioza e admiravel uictoria que alcançarão as armas de El Rey D. Affonso 6o Neste Reino de Angola, contra El Rey de Congo gouernando o senhor André Vidal de Negreiros*(Lisbon, 1665).
65 Newitt, *The Portuguese in West Africa*, p.201.
66 António de Oliveira Cadornega, José Mattias Delgado, Manuel Alves da Cunha, *História Geral das Guerras Angolanas* (Lisbon, 1942), vol. II. pp.280–281.

Rodrigo de Costa (1640?–1690), governor of Goa between 1686 and 1690 (Collection of the Archaeological Survey of India, Goa). Like his predecessor, Costa successfully faced the pressure of Moghul, Maratha and other Indian states on the tiny Portuguese Indian domains.

Cape Verdeans. Meanwhile, *lançados* had also settled on the island of Bissau, which lay south of Cacheu near the mouth of the Geba River. There, as had happened earlier at Cacheu, the trader-settlers were welcomed by the local rulers. Bissau was healthier than Cacheu and was also conveniently located for trade. Its ruler, having been converted to Catholicism by Portuguese Franciscans, gave permission to build a fortress in 1696. Shortly afterwards, Bissau was declared a Portuguese captaincy. On the other hand, in 1694 Portuguese interests secured a new *asiento* to supply up to 4,000 slaves a year to Spanish America. This was a welcome development: for the break with Spain in 1640 had not only dealt a major blow to Portuguese slavers but also threatened to cut off a prime source of Spanish American silver. So important to Portugal was the market for slaves in the Spanish Indies that in 1646 João IV felt compelled to authorise the trade's resumption, even though a war for national survival against Felipe IV was still being waged.[67]

On the other side of Portuguese Africa, in 1620 Dom Nuno Álvares Pereira, *capitão-mor* in Mozambique led an expedition of several hundred soldiers up the Zambesi valley via Sena and Tete to Chicoa, the alleged location of the Monomotapa silver mines. He had been instructed to reinforce Portuguese garrisons en route and to establish new Portuguese settlements, and with this in mind his men were encouraged to bring their families with them. However, it seems that little if any actual colonisation took place. Another official attempt to establish more white settlements was made in the 1630s, 23 experienced silver miners from Spanish Peru were brought in, plus some 200 soldiers from Portugal and 200 settler families. The aim was to secure and exploit the gold and silver mines on the interior plateau.[68] Then in 1637 a substantial reinforcement intended for Mozambique had to be diverted to Goa to counteract a threat from the Dutch in India. In 1677, another Mozambique settlement scheme was formulated, this time with personal support from Prince Pedro. The plan was to ship out 600 troops and some 50 married colonists, the latter to be provided with land and

---

67 *Ibid.*, p.56. In the event, the 1694 asiento was held only until 1701, when the Spanish Crown awarded it to the French.
68 *Ibid.*, p.356. Optimists believed the alleged Monomotapa mines were the richest in the world; but others, more cautious, considered such claims to be mere speculation. In the event many of the immigrants died, such mines as were found proved disappointing and hopes for a quick road to wealth rapidly evaporated.

tools. An expedition was duly dispatched to East Africa, and some immigrants were deposited in Zambesia. However, their actual numbers were very few and their long-term impact minimal. In the next century, further schemes for the colonisation of Mozambique were forced on the government by a range of influential personages, including viceroys, governors and visiting magistrates. Brazilian mestizos, Indians from the sub-continent and Irish Catholics were all suggested as possible settlers. But it seems nothing of substance ever materialised. Existing settlements gradually grew, nurtured by a steady trickle of Indo-Portuguese and Hindu settlers from India.

The Portuguese dream of a great Asian empire lingered on for another two or three decades after 1600. As late as 1637 schemes were being canvassed to move the Portuguese captaincy from Chittagong to Dacca and convert the nearby region to Catholicism. Their expansion encountered the resistance of the Mughal sultanate and the neighbouring Arakanese, and any further attempts were abandoned. Also, at about this time, the Portuguese were beginning to intervene in China. On at least five occasions between 1621 and 1647, expeditions were dispatched to the Chinese mainland from Macao, in response to urgent pleas from Beijing to support the Ming rulers. The first two expeditions were small scale and achieved little, but the last three each involved several hundred men, and in 1647 Portuguese forces played a prominent role in defending the last Ming strongholds in Guangzhou. While these interventions were clearly not the work of soldiers of fortune acting on their own initiative, their status was semi-official at best. All five expeditions were procured by highly placed Chinese Christian converts through the Jesuit mission in Beijing and were authorised not by the Lisbon's authorities, but the Macao *câmara*.[69]

Throughout the whole period, the number of Europeans on Macao and Timor remained tiny. Nearly all the local 'Portuguese' of Timor were actually Eurasians, namely people of mixed race who were known locally as *topasses* or 'black' Portuguese. It was the *topasses* who provided most of the manpower for military purposes and who coincidently constituted the greatest source of political trouble for the Crown authorities. The *topasses* first came to official notice as a problem in the mid seventeenth century, a time when Timor was being vigorously disputed with the Dutch. As a by-product of that struggle, there emerged on the island two rival clans: the *Hornays* and the *Costas*. The *Hornays* were descended from Jan de Hornay, a Dutch commander who had deserted to the Portuguese at Larantuca in 1629 and turned Catholic. Mateus da Costa, a Portuguese captain with a distinguished fighting career against the Dutch, founded the *Costas*. Both men had taken Timorese wives, and from these unions their respective clans had grown. Competition between the two for control of the Portuguese settlements and interests in Timor, and of the lucrative sandalwood trade, began in 1665. First Mateus da Costa got the upper hand; then, after Mateus's death in 1673, António de Hornay, son of Jan de Hornay, held ascendancy until he too died in 1695.

---

69 Disney, *History of Portugal*, vol. II, p.192.

4

Uniforms, Equipment and Ensigns

When a national army was formed in 1641, military uniforms were certainly the least problem that beset the Portuguese government. Contemporary testimonies, both written and pictorial, show Portuguese soldiers wearing the conventional military clothing of this period, and only in the following decades did the Crown take into consideration the establishment of a specific uniform for its army. The Portuguese soldiers' issue of clothing included coat, shirt, breeches and stockings, as well as a hat and shoes, which were distributed once a year, against a deduction in their pay. These items were only issued to the professional troops, while the *auxiliaries*, and obviously the militiamen, would have received only minimal equipment. The first evidence concerning the uniforms of the Portuguese army date to the late 1650s, when the professional infantry is described dressed in *pardo* – tanned brown like their Spanish enemies.[1] It is necessary to use a lot of caution when dealing with Portuguese uniforms in the mid seventeenth century. In the infantry, the use of uniforms in the modern sense was taking its first baby steps, more on the personal initiative of the commanders than by any institutional design. Also, with the cavalry, the adoption of specific uniform clothing came much later before being introduced. Therefore, in Portugal, military equipment and clothing was a significantly later development compared to Spain. Research shows that both infantry and cavalry did not adopt any distinctive colour to differentiate one unit from another. For cavalry it was difficult to introduce specific unit uniform distinctions considering that the equipment introduced in Portugal: long-sleeved buff coat under aback and breastplate, was similar to that used by several European armies in this period and the only distinctive mark was generally in the form of a coloured scarf around the waist, which for the Portuguese was dark green, or more infrequently, white. Moreover, the standardisation of a uniform was hampered by the fact that in Portugal the company continued to be the basic administrative unit for a long time, and this did not favour uniformity of

---

1   *Relación de la frontera de Portugal*, 1664; BN, ms. 9394, f. 427.

UNIFORMS, EQUIPMENT AND ENSIGNS

clothing in either the infantry or the cavalry. Since there were no permanent units larger than the company, to distinguish one unit from another was often considered a luxury by the majority of Portuguese commanders.

The existing illustrations from the 1640s and 1650s show that the Portuguese infantry wore coats, doublets, and *hungarinas* of different colours, with a predominance of brown, grey and other undyed clothes. The style is similar to the one of the low class people of Spain, and perhaps a little more out of fashion, and the shirt retained a wide falling collar. Coloured battle scenes painted on lead depicting Portuguese soldiers and officers before the 1660s show the infantry wearing coats of different colours of brown, yellow ochre, grey, as well as red and green cloth.[2] Some soldiers wear *justaucorps* or shorter coats, and only the headgear is black for all. The style of the miniatures is naïve, and probably certain colours, such as the brighter ones, are products of the painter's imagination, but the non-uniformity of the infantry contrasts with the relative homogeneity of the cavalry, depicted in buff coats and lobster helmets, which is too marked a differentiation for it not to be deliberate.

Weapons and equipment were generally of mixed types and vintage, as the Portuguese army resorted to using material from other countries, especially captured Spanish equipment, or imports from France, the Dutch Republic, Sweden, and England. As a result, the miscellany of equipment must have increased the rough and ready appearance of Portuguese soldiers even more, at least until the early 1660s. There are a large number of portraits dating back to the years of the Restoration War, and among these, the works of Feliciano de Almeida (1635–1694) are very accurate. The artist portrayed the major Portuguese commanders and many of them wear armour or the generic dress typical of military leaders of this age, but a couple of paintings depict less conventional clothing. Luís de Meneses is portrayed wearing a fashionable buff coat with cuffs and ribbons, while Tristão da Cunha wears a *carlino*-style coat of medium brown (*pardo*) cloth lined in yellow (or light grey), over a leather coat. Both the officers carry a wide scarf of dark green silk with silver fringes, and white cravats tied with a black ribbon.[3] The portraits clearly show that the style in vogue in Portugal during this period

Tristão da Cunha, portrayed by Feliciano de Almeida. (Uffizi Museum, Florence)

---

2   See the series of battle paintings on lead sheets preserved in the National Museum of Antique Art of Lisbon.
3   The portraits are dated to between 1659 and 1665 and were purchased by Prince Cosimo de' Medici during his visit to Portugal in 1669. Today the series is preserved in the Galleria degli Uffizi of Florence and comprises 11 portraits.

Luís de Meneses Count of Ericeria, portrayed by Feliciano de Almeida. (Uffizi Museum, Florence)

draws its influence from Spain as well as from the Netherlands, France and England.

As in almost every other European army, the officers could tailor their dress as they saw fit, and until 1665 there is no evidence that the Portuguese officers were dressed in the same colours as their soldiers. There were even some freedoms regarding equipment. Sometimes mentioned in the inventories of the arsenals, the presence of bucklers suggests the continued practice of officers to be equipped like the *rodoleros* of the first half of the seventeenth century. In this respect there are also some contemporary images, like the *azulejos* ceramics preserved in the Palacio Fronteira in Lisbon, where some Portuguese swordsmen with round shields are engaging the Spaniards during the Battle of Montes Claros. They are Portuguese infantry officers, and on the enemy side they are also represented at least once. It should not be underestimated that in 1665, especially on an isolated theatre of war like the Portuguese one, this kind of weapons remained in use, while on other fronts the *rodoleros* had disappeared as early as the 1630s.

Further items issued to infantrymen and widely recorded in the registers were the rests for muskets, the powder flasks, and the bandoliers with the wooden flasks containing the cartridges with the bullets and powder. Usually, each bandolier had 12 cartridges like those issued to the Spanish infantry. Old heavy muskets remained in use for long time in the Portuguese army, and until the 1660s the infantry companies retained rests for more than half of the muskets.

With the initial distribution of uniforms in the 1650s, the government established, very optimistically, to provide the troops with new clothing each year, but it did not follow any actual uniformity in colour and pattern, and occasionally the clothing had a common pattern or colour based on the whatever the supplier could get hold of.[4] Changes in fashion, especially from France, introduced some differences in the pattern of coats, breeches and headgear as the conflict went by. Even in the absence of administrative evidence, from 1660, together with military contingents from France, the Portuguese army received aid in the form of equipment and presumably clothing. According to the testimony of an eyewitness, in 1669 the infantry in Alentejo were dressed completely in grey, except for some units that instead had clothing of different colours.[5] Probably, these latter were *auxiliaries* from

---

4   Jorge de Penim Freitas, 'The use of uniforms during the War of the Portuguese Restoration – infantry, *Guerra da Restauração* (28 February 2017).
5   ASFi, *Mediceo del Principato, Diario di Lorenzo Magalotti*, (s.n.) 1669; p.17.

UNIFORMS, EQUIPMENT AND ENSIGNS

Above and overleaf: Oil paintings on lead sheets, commissioned in 1665 and illustrating the major Portuguese victories of the Restoration War. Despite the naïve style of the figures, these painting are a useful source of knowledge for the Portuguese military dress of this age. (National Museum of Antique Art of Lisbon)

UNIFORMS, EQUIPMENT AND ENSIGNS

Portuguese arquebusiers: left, 1655–1660; right, 1667–70. Contemporary images depict the Portuguese infantryman still wearing more conservative clothing in the early 1660s. The geographical isolation of this theatre of war did not favour the introduction of a new style. However, in the following years the Portuguese introduced for the private infantrymen of the professional army the French style *justaucorps*, usually in grey or blue. (Author's illustrations)

Azulejo of the early 1700 depicting Portuguese infantry. Note the ensign and NCO still wearing breastplates and lobster helmet. (Author's archive)

some still existing companies, but most likely, the grey coat of the professional soldiers were the same *justaucorps* that a few years earlier also began to be distributed to the French infantry. Five years before, the *Mercurio Portuguez* related to the first uniforms of the Portuguese infantry, mentioning the *Terço de Armada* (PI-1), with green coat faced and lined in yellow, and the *Terço Novo da guarnição de Lisboa* (PI-16), with an azure coat faced and lined in red.[6] The same source makes further mention of details regarding the *Terço de Armada*: 'the *mestre de campo*, the officers and some soldiers redressed with more expensive clothing, conforming to the possessions of each one, but the colours are the same for all; and so are the colours (flags) and the drums.'[7] As for the other unit: 'the troops did a similar parade and exercise in the Terreiro do Paço … all of them with blue coats faced and lined in red, more or less expensive, depending on the wealth of the soldiers.'[8] These notices seem to allude to the fact that even the ordinary soldiers could have their uniforms tailored privately, as NCOs and officers certainly did. Some clues suggest that the uniforms possibly followed the contemporary French style, namely the fashion introduced by Count Schomberg. However, in 1664, the French style was not yet the one established at the end of the 1660s, but something between the old and new style existed.[9] However, foreign influence was behind the first signs of the use of uniforms by Portuguese infantry in the 1660s, and helped the spread of military dress in the Portuguese army. English infantry that fought alongside the Portuguese in the 1660s wore red coats probably lined in different colours, and the French regiments, as well as the German and Italian soldiers who changed sides in 1663, wore grey coats.[10] As for the French cavalrymen, they did not wear armour, but had a buff coat and broad-brimmed hats over iron 'secrets' (skull caps).

---

6   *Mercurio Portuguezcom as novas da guerra entre Portugal, e Castella, Começa no principio do anno de 1663* (Lisbon, 1667), April 1664, p.174, and June 1664, p.192. The same source also refers the dress of some mounted lifeguard mounted companies.
7   *Ibid.*, p.174.
8   *Ibid.*, p.192.
9   See Alberto Cutileiro, *O uniforme militar na Armada: trêsseculos de História* (Lisbon: Amigos do Livro Editores, 1983), vol. I, the graphic reconstruction made by the author of the uniform of the *Terço de Armada* in 1664.
10   Jorge de Penim Freitas, 'The use of uniforms during the War of the Portuguese Restoration – Infantry', *Guerra da Restauração* (28 February 2017).

UNIFORMS, EQUIPMENT AND ENSIGNS

Above: Detail from the painting illustrating the arrival of the Apostolic Nuncio Giorgio Cornaro at Lisbon in 1693 (Museu Nacional dos Coches, Lisbon). Two theories have been advanced to identify these troops. The first suggests that they are militiamen of Lisbon, while the other assumes that the soldiers depicted belonged to the *Terço de Lisboa*, which served wearing very informal clothing (thanks to Nuno Pereira for this note).

Below: Portuguese field artillery depicted in an *azulejo* of the early eighteenth century. These artillerymen are dressed and equipped in a very informal way, and this suggests that an actual artillery uniform did not exist in the Portuguese army even in the previous decade. (Author's collection)

Portuguese infantrymen, 1664, copy after *O uniforme militar na Armada: trêsséculos de história* by Alberto Cutilero (1983). The author's reconstruction shows the infantry wearing a uniform a mix of local and French style.

The lack of defensive equipment in the contemporary records means that the use of breastplates was a rarity among the Portuguese infantry, as it was not provided to the soldiers by the royal suppliers. There is little reference to this type of protection in contemporary images either. Usually, only officers, NCOs and pikemen were entitled to wear this type of protection, but the proportions are very low in relation to the specialties existing in a company. According to authoritative scholars who had investigated the Portuguese arsenal inventories, breast and back corselets varied between 0.4 and 7.6 percent; morion helmets between 0.4 and 8.3 percent, and this latter percentage was only reached in 1647, being increasingly scarce in later years. The round shields used by captains are between 0.2 and 0.4 percent, and gorgets between 0.1 and 0.3 percent.[11] In the case of shield and gorgets, the use of these defensive weapons by officers justifies the small number found in the inventories. Captains could choose to fight with spontoon or with sword and shield, or even with musket or harquebus if they preferred. According to the records, the disuse of any armoured protection for the body was an evident trend in the Portuguese infantry. In 1663, the Count of Ericeira reports that 3,000 infantry corselets were adapted for use as cavalry breastplates, as infantry no longer used such protection.[12] Some illustrations from the 1660s show pikemen wearing sleeveless buff coats, and the only metal protections is represented by a morion helmet or perhaps a French-style burgonet. This type of body protection is quite common in those years even on the Spanish side, sometime replaced by coat manufactured with a double or even triple layer of cloth. On the other hand, the use of leather buff coat by the infantry depended on the ability of each soldier to obtain supplies from the war spoils by stripping the dead, the wounded and enemy prisoners, especially horsemen and officers.

Foreign influence appears even more evident in the clothing of the cavalry. In contemporary images Portuguese horsemen are generally depicted wearing clothing very close to the almost contemporary Cromwellian Ironsides. The buff coat and the lobster helmet were common also on the Spanish side, but the combat tactics and equipment seems to confirm that the Portuguese cavalry had chosen the English horsemen as models. Despite a more or less extensive uniformity it is possible to find some cavalry units identified by their equipment.

---

11 *Ibid.*
12 Luís de Meneses, Conde de Ericeira, *Historia de Portugal Restaurado* (Lisbon, 1679), vol. II, p.101.

UNIFORMS, EQUIPMENT AND ENSIGNS

Lobster helmet, Portuguese manufacture, c. 1660 (private collection). This was the universal head protection of the Portuguese cavalry during the Restoration War, and its use continued until the next century.

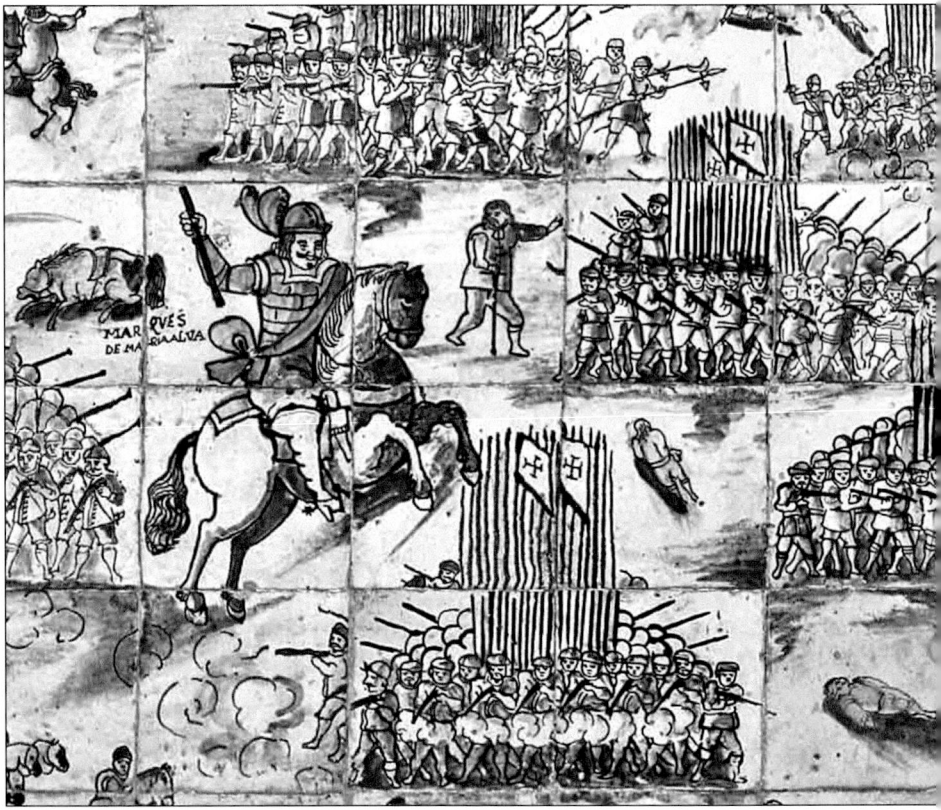

Right: Detail from the *azulejo* depicting the Battle of Montes Claros (1665). Note the Portuguese officers engaging the enemy with buckler and sword. (Author's archive)

Below: Procession for the departure to England of Catarina de Bragança in 1662, after a print by Dirk Stoop. The cortege is escorted by the *Arqueiros*. Contemporary accounts relate that the King's Lifeguard wore green with silver laces. (Author's archive)

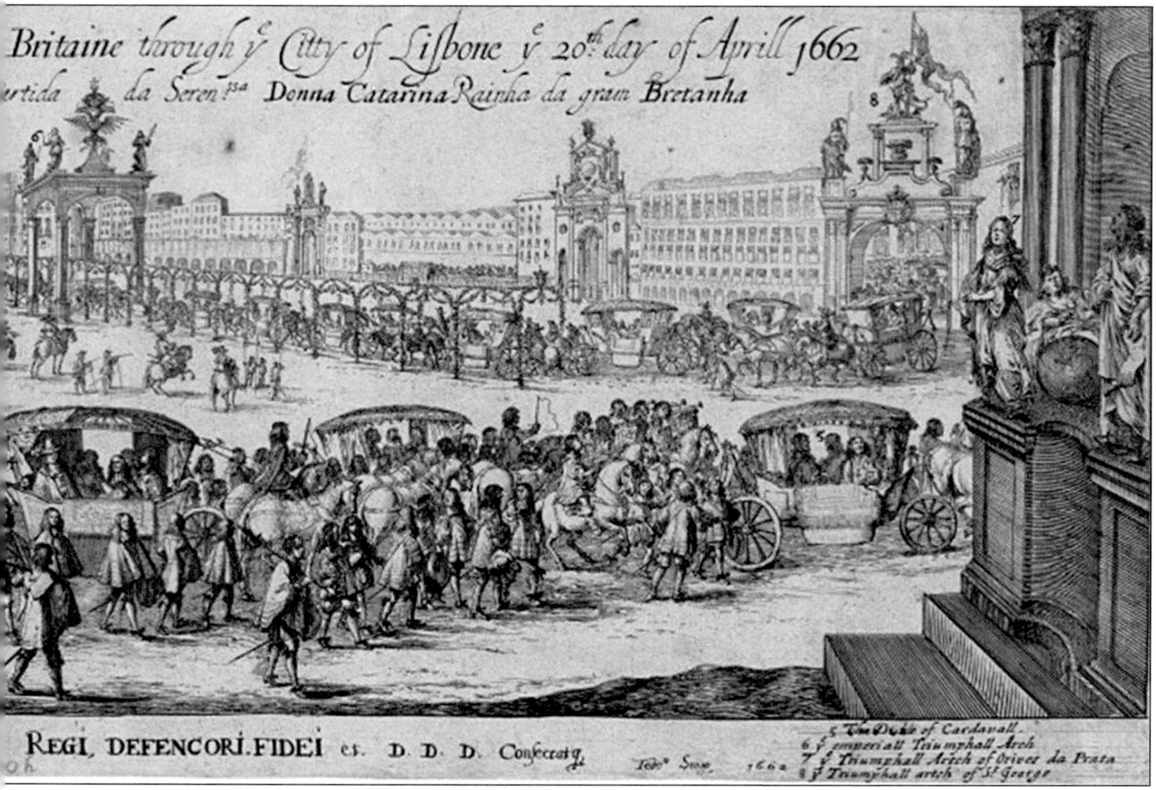

UNIFORMS, EQUIPMENT AND ENSIGNS

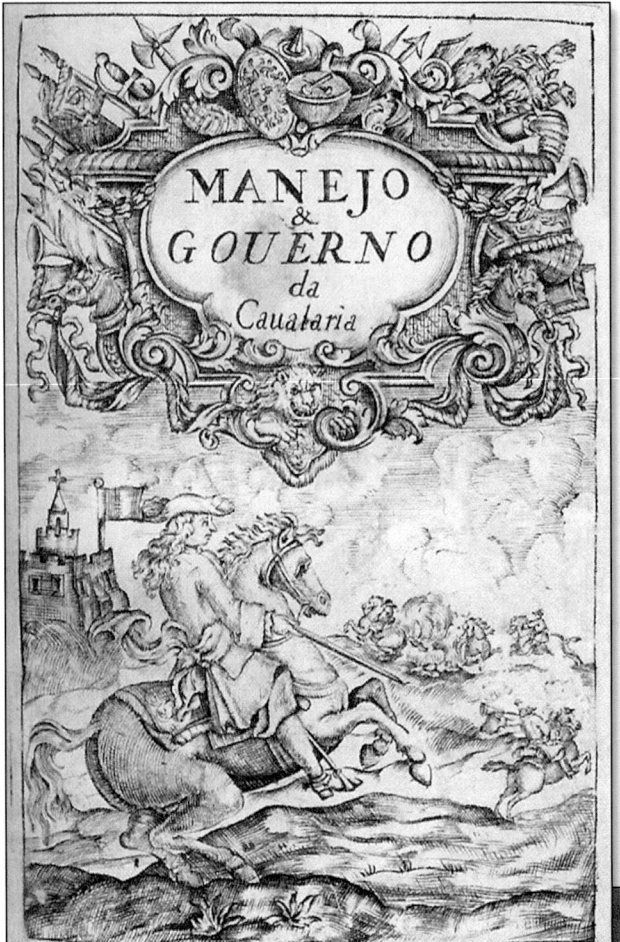

Facing page: Influence from England's military clothing survived for a long time in Portugal. The manufacturing of this equestrian armour is attributed to Richard Holdenin, a job commissioned in 1683 by Pedro II, and it is significant because it is a very late example of this type. This form of armour retains items which date back to the 1640s, like the triple-barred helmet, the cuirass with a bullet proof breastplate, and elbow gauntlet, as was commonplace in England since 1645. Although this type of clothing was intended for ceremonial and symbolic use, the Restoration War epic represented a powerful legacy for the Portuguese kings. (Collection of the Metropolitan Museum of Art, New York)

Left: Cover of the 1707 printed edition of the work *Maneio da Cavallaria* written by Galeazzo Gualdo Priorato with annotation by João Mascarenhas, lieutenant general and general of the cavalry in Alentejo in the second half of the 1640s. The cavalry officers are wearing the classic western European clothing, which gradually replaced the earlier style.

Below: Portuguese (marine?) infantry, early 1680. (Private collection, Lisbon)

UNIFORMS, EQUIPMENT AND ENSIGNS

The fact that this particularity has been registered is a sign that it was an exception. An anonymous letter dated April 1645 mentions the arrival in Ameixial of the new governor of arms of Alentejo, the Count of Castelo Melhor, João de Vasconcelos e Sousa. The document describes the equipment of the armoured cavalry companies raised in 1644, as well as the cavalry and infantry of the province: 'the entrance of the Count of Castelo Melhor happened with crowd and applause never seen in this city. João de Vasconcelos went to wait for Estremoz, in the Alcarapinhais field, [with] ten troops of horses: two of these wore breastplates armed with no more than a sword, and the others with their pistols and carbines.'[13] Some contemporary accounts state that the Portuguese cavalry had approximately the half or just one third wearing breastplates.[14] The cavalry retained dress in much the same style until 1668, with broad cross-belts for carbines and swords. Horse furniture and holsters were of different colours in order to distinguish the companies.

In a minor number of cases, the different units of cavalry are identified precisely by their clothing, but only a minority were Portuguese cavalrymen. During the campaign in Alentejoof 1663, the Lifeguard company of the Count of Schomberg wore a blue coat over their breast and back plate. Two years later, at the Battle of Montes Claros, the same company wore red *casaques* with white crosses, probably patterned on the ones worn by the musketeers of Louis XIV's *Maison du Roi*, since it was a codified clothing for this kind of units.[15] In the same year, the Lifeguard company of the Marquise of Marialva, António Luís de Meneses, *governadores das armas* of Alentejo, wore green coats laced of green and silver, with (green?) *cappotillos* with the Marquis' coat of arms embroidered on both side. The Lifeguards horsemen of Count of São João, and the ones of Afonso Furtado de Mendonça had a similar clothing but in red.[16]

In the following decades, the French style continued to influence military clothing in Portugal. In the 1670s, all the pictorial evidence shows the widespread adoption of the *justaucorps* with the wide flap cuffs, worn with the typical items of the military clothing codified at the end of the seventeenth century. Some obsolete elements survived in the clothing of officers and NCOs, including the infantry, who on active service still wear helmets and breastplates until the early years of the following century.

---

13   Freitas, 'O uso de 'uniformes' na cavalaria', *Guerra da Restauração* (23 June 2008).
14   BNE, *Sucesos 1663*, pp.122–123.
15   Freitas, 'O uso de 'uniformes' na cavalaria', *Guerra da Restauração* (23 June 2008).
16   *Mercurio Portuguez*, p.192.

Portuguese cavalry standard (1662), from a print of the map by Pedro de Santa Columba relating the Battle of the Lines of Elvas (1659). (Author's archive)

The persistence of old fashioned clothing after 1668 was the result of the symbolic meaning inherent in the Restoration War's panoply. In this regard, lobster helmet, breast armour and buff coat belonged to King Pedro II and retained an evident resemblance to the clothing of the Portuguese cavalry of the 1640s–1660s. Equally significantly, apart for the golden decorations and the Christ's cross on the breastplate, iron gauntlet and helmet echoed those employed by the *Ironsides*, and this could allude to the pro-English party of the Portuguese court. From about the 1670s, buff coat began to be replaced by a tailored coat of cloth, but the leather buff coat remained a key part of the horsemen's dress though it was sometimes worn under the cloth top coat.

In the following years, the English and French styles tended to come together, and also in Portugal the fashion of central and northern Europe was welcomed by the aristocracy and upper classes. Some more traditional items survived, mainly in the colonies, together with others of mixed origins. In an interesting painting dating from the early 1680s, a group of Portuguese infantrymen wear dark blue *justaucorps* lined and faced in grey. Equipment and weapons are consistent with the ones distributed to the marine infantry, including the musket, which appears to be a flintlock. The absence of pikemen suggests that they are soldiers belonging to a marine infantry company, portrayed somewhere in the Portuguese archipelago or Africa. Together with them, a mounted *capitão mor* dresses in a style that retains some features of the Portuguese clothing, such as the large black felt hat, and also the horse furniture is typical of the Iberian Peninsula in this period.

UNIFORMS, EQUIPMENT AND ENSIGNS

Ensigns and Colours

Unfortunately, knowledge on this matter is presently rather scarce, since in 1755, the archives of the *Tenência* (Army Arsenal) were destroyed by the great Lisbon earthquake, and in the 1930s, a fire consumed the archives of the *Junta dos Três Estados*, depriving the scholars of precious information about the military ensigns used during the Restoration War. The surviving sources, both written and pictorial, are very fragmented. As for the original items, only one relic from this age has survived, probably a captain general's standard, possibly the one that belonged to the Marquis of Marialva, carried at the Battle of Montes Claros in 1665. Four years later, the ensign was offered to the Church of Nossa Senhora da Conceição, in Vilaviçosa, and there it remains on display.

Captain-General's Guidon preserved in Vila Viçosa. The background is now in azure-blue, which originally could be green, carrying the coat of arms of the royal family with golden embroideries; fringes has possibly been lost. (Author's graphic).

Despite the uncertainty of contemporary items, it is possible discern some differences in the use of the ensign, through the frequency with which these terms are employed. When on 1 December 1640, the 'national revolution' against Spanish domination was proclaimed, the conjurers in Lisbon hoisted a flag, which was called *bandeira de aclamação*. This was a red *Cruz de Cristo* (Christ's cross) on a green field, and this ensign was also used by the army in the first campaigns against the Spaniards. The cross is usually represented in full red, or in white with the outer edge in red. The flags most used by the Portuguese infantry were, as a general rule, square in shape, measuring about 180–190 cm, the vast majority being green or white, with a red or green cross depending on the background.[17]

Similar but smaller ensigns were also carried by the cavalry. In addition to these standards, there was a great variety of ensigns with the coat of arms of the commanders, or that carried a wide variety of painted or embroidered religious images. Among the most frequent religious images, there was the Virgin Mary (Nossa Senhora da Conceição) painted on one side, and the coat of arms of the Bragança royal family on the other. As a rule, only heavy cavalry carried a standard, but in practice, it was common for all the cavalry companies to bear an ensign as well. Sources depict the cavalry trumpeters with small green pennants on the trumpets bearing the King's coat of arms or a red-white cross.

As for commanders' ensigns, Luís de Meneses, Count of Terceira, wrote that, as a general of the artillery of the Alentejo army in 1663, he was accompanied by two ensigns, (possibly these should be guidons), one with the royal coat of arms, probably similar to the one preserved in Vilaviçosa, and another with their own heraldry, 'and next to them a piece of artillery (embroidered or painted), among which there were the motto in gold letters SINE QUA NON.'[18]

---

17 Ernesto Augusto Pereira de Sales, *Bandeiras e estendartes regimentais do Exército e da Armada e outra bandeiras militares* (Lisbon, 1930), pp.10–11.
18 Meness, Luís de, *História de Portugal Restaurado*, 1946, vol. IV, pg. 212. Thanks to Jorge Frejtas for this notice.

Appendix I

Military Governors, Army Strength, and Orders of Battles

Military Governors (Governadores das Armas) of Alentejo

Afonso de Portugal, Count of Vimioso (1640–1641)
Matias de Albuquerque (1642)
Martim Afonso de Melo (1641–1643)
Joane Mendes de Vasconcelos; Vasco de Mascarenhas Count of Óbidos; Matias de Albuquerque; Francisco de Melo (interim) (1643)
Matias de Albuquerque Count of Alegrete (1643–1645)
Joane Mendes de Vasconcelos (interim) (1645)
João de Vasconcelos e Sousa Count of Castelo Melhor (1645–1646)
Matias de Albuquerque Count of Alegrete (1646)
Joane Mendes de Vasconcelos (1646–1647)
André de Albuquerque Ribafria (interim, 1647)
Martim Afonso de Melo Count of São Lourenço (1647–1650)
João da Costa, Count of Soure (1650–1654)
André de Albuquerque Ribafria (interim,1654–1655)
Francisco de Melo, Countda Ponte (1655–1656)
João da Costa, Count of Soure (1656–1657)
André de Albuquerque Ribafria (interim,1657)
Martim Afonso de Melo, Count of São Lourenço (1657–1658)
Joane Mendes de Vasconcelos; André de Albuquerque Ribafria (interim, 1658)
António Luís de Meneses, Marquis of Marialva (1658–1659)
Jerónimo de Ataíde, Count of Atouguia (1659–1662)
António Luís de Meneses, Marquis of Marialva (1662)
Sancho Manuel de Vilhena, Count of Vila Flor (1663–1664)
António Luís de Meneses, Marquis of Marialva (1664–1665)
Friedrich von Schomberg (1665–1667)
Dinis de Melo de Castro Count of Galveias (1667–1668)

APPENDIX I

Military Governors (Governadores das Armas) of Beira

Álvaro de Abranches da Câmara (1641)
João de Saldanha de Sousa (interim 1641–1642)
Fernão Teles de Meneses (1642–1643)
Álvaro de Abranches da Câmara (1643–1645)
Francisco de Mascarenhas Count of Serém (1645–1647)

Partido of Almeida
Rodrigo de Castro Count of Mesquitela (1647–1656)
João de Melo Feio (interim 1656)
Rodrigo de Castro Count of Mesquitela (unified command of both *partidos*, 1656–1658)
Sancho Manuel de Vilhena, Count of Vila Flor(unified command of both *partidos*, 1658–1659)
João Forjaz Pereira Conde da Feira (1659–1660)
Manuel Freire de Andrade (1660–1662)
João de Melo Feio (1662)
Sancho Manuel de Vilhena, Count of Vila Flor (unified command of both *partidos*, 1662–1663)
Pedro Jacques de Magalhães (later, Viscount of Fonte Arcada) (1663–1668)

Partido of Penamacor or Castelo Branco
Sancho Manuel de Vilhena, Count of Vila Flor (1647–1654)
Nuno da Cunha de Ataíde (as *tenente-general da cavalaria*, 1654–1656)
Rodrigo de Castro, Count of Mesquitela (unified command of both *partidos*, 1656–1658)
Sancho Manoel de Vilhena, Count of Vila Flor (unified command of both *partidos*, 1658–1659)
Sancho Manoel de Vilhena Count of Vila Flor (1659–1661)
João de Melo Feio (1661)
Sancho Manuel de Vilhena, Count of Vila Flor (unified command of both *partidos*, 1662–1663)
Afonso Furtado de Mendonça (mais tarde, first Viscount of Barbacena) (1663–1668)

Military Governors (Governadores das Armas) of Entre-Douro-e-Minho

Gastão Coutinho (1641)
Junta of three governors: Manuel Telo, Diogo de Melo Pereira and Gustave Pierre Viole d'Athis (1641–1643)
João de Vasconcelos e Sousa, Count of Castelo Melhor (1643–1645)
Diogo de Melo Pereira (interim, 1645–1646)
Francisco de França Barbosa (interim, 1646)
João de Vasconcelos e Sousa, Count of Castelo Melhor (1646–1649)
Francisco de Azevedo (1649–1650)

Diogo de Lima, Viscount of Vila Nova de Cerveira (1650–1655)
Álvaro de Abranches da Câmara (1655–1657)
Diogo de Lima, Viscount of Vila Nova de Cerveira (interim,1657–1658)
Nuno da Cunha de Ataíde (interim, 1658)
Diogo de Lima, Viscount of Vila Nova de Cerveira (1658–1660)
Francisco de Sousa, Count de Prado and Marquês das Minas (1660–1670)

Viceroys and Governors of Brazil

Jorge Mascarenhas, Marquis of Montalvão (1640–1641)
Junta provisória (Provisional junta), (1641–1642)
Antônio Telles da Silva (1642–1647)
Antônio Telles de Meneses, Count of Vila-Pouca de Aguiar (1647–1650)
João de Vasconcellos e Sousa Count of Castelo Melhor (1650–1654)
Jerônimo de Altaíde, Count of Atouguia (1654–1657)
Francisco Barreto de Meneses (1657–1663)
Vasco Mascarenhas, Count of Óbidos (1663–1667)
Alexandre de Sousa Freire (1667–1671)
Afonso Furtado de Castro do Rio de Mendonça Viscount of Barbacena (1671–1675)
Junta provisória composed of Agostinho de Azevedo Monteiro and other people. When Azevedo Monteiro died, Cristóvão de Burgos (1675–1678) was appointed in his place.
Roque da Costa Barreto (1678–1682)
Antônio de Sousa de Meneses (1682–1684)
Matias da Cunha (1687–1688)

Viceroys and Governors of Portuguese India

João da Silva Telo e Meneses, Count of Aveiras (1640–1644)
Filipe Mascarenhas (1644–1651)
João da Silva Telo e Meneses, Count of Aveiras (1651) (second term): died at Mozambique, en route to India
Governing Council: Fr. Francisco dos Mártires (Archbishop of Goa), Francisco de Melo e Castro, António de Sousa Coutinho(1651–1652)
Vasco Mascarenhas Count of Óbedos (1652–1655); expelled by internal coup
Brás de Castro (1655); arrested by successor.
Rodrigo Lobo da Silveira, Count of Sarzedas (1655–1656)
Manuel Mascarenhas Homem (1656–1656)
Governing Council: Manuel Mascarenhas Homem, Francisco de Melo e Castro, António de Sousa Coutinho (1656–1661)
Governing Council: Luís de Mendonça Furtado e Albuquerque, Manuel Mascarenhas Homem, Pedro de Lencastre (1661)
Governing Council: Luís de Mendonça Furtado e Albuquerque, António de Melo e Castro, Pedro de Lencastre (1661–1662)
António de Melo e Castro (1662–1666)
João Nunes da Cunha, Count of São Vicente (1666–1668)
Governing Council: António de Melo e Castro, Manuel Corte-Real de

Sampaio, Luís de Miranda Henriques (1668–1671)
Luís de Mendonça Furtado e Albuquerque (1671–1676)
Pedro de Almeida, Count of Assumar (1676–1678); Interim Governor
António Brandão, Archbishop of Goa (1678–1681)
Francisco de Távora, Count of Alvor (1681–1686)
Rodrigo da Costa (1686–1690)

Governors of Angola

Salvador Correia de Sá e Benavides (1648–1651)
Rodrigo de Miranda Henriques (1652–1653)
Bartolomeu de Vasconcelos da Cunha (1653–1654)
Luís Mendes de Sousa Chichorro (1654–1658)
João Fernandes Vieira (1658–1661)
André Vidal de Negreiros (1662–1666)
Tristão da Cunha (1666–1667)
Junta provisória (1667–1668)
Francisco de Távora (1669–1676)
Pires de Saldanha de Sousa e Meneses (1676–1680)
João da Silva e Sousa (1680–1684)
Luís Lobo da Silva (16843–1688)

The Army of Alentejo 1642–1665

Date:	Infantry	Cavalry	Overall Strength
October 1642	7,409	1,983	9,342
September 1643	12,000	2,000	14,000
May 1644	6,000	1,000	7,000
August 1645	5,500	1,200	6,700
September 1646	7,200	1,600	8,800
December 1648	5,000	1,600	6,600
February 1652	7,000	2,387	9,387
October 1657	10,000	2,000	12,000
June 1658	14,000	3,000	17,000
January 1659	7,000	2,500	9,500
October 1661	10,000	3,500	13,500
June 1662	12,000	4,000	16,000
June 1664	22,000	6,000	28,000
May 1665	7,000	2,500	9,500

Source: Lorraine White, 'Guerra y revolución militar en la Iberia del siglo XVII', in *Manuscrits* 21 (2003), p. 82.

Army Strength in 1646–1647

In Summer (June–October)		
Province	Infantry	Cavalry
Alentejo	5,500	1,750
Beira	2,000	460
Trás-os-Montes	1,115	220
Entre-Douro-e-Minho	1,000	65
Algarve	550	–
Cascais (Lisbon)	285	–
Peniche (Lisbon)	100	–
TOTAL	10,650	2,495
In Winter (November–May)		
Alentejo	3,200	1,000
Beira	1,150	278
Trás-os-Montes	700	130
Entre-Douro-e-Minho	600	40
Algarve	320	–
Cascais (Lisbon)	175	–
Peniche (Lisbon)	60	–
TOTAL	6,205	1,448

Regular Infantry in the Army of Alentejo (Sept 1661)

	Unit:	Officers & NCOs	Priv. Soldiers	TOT.
PI–02	*Terço* of Pedro Opecinga	104	665	769
PI–04	*Terço* of Francisco Mascarenhas	103	713	816
PI–05	*Terço* of Jorge Henriques	84	248	332
PI–06	*Terço* of João Leite de Oliveira	79	380	459
PI–07	*Terço* of Luís de Meneses	98	919	1,017
PI–10	*Terço* of Pedro de Melo	85	235	320
PI–11	*Terço* of Agostinho de Andrade Freire	114	676	790
PI–12	*Terço* of Pedro Mascarenhas	29	302	331
PI–17	*Terço* of Francisco Pacheco Mascarenhas	75	193	268
PI–19	*Terço* of Fernão de Mesquita Pimentel	84	458	542
–	*Companhias Soltas* (free companies)	17	400	417
	TOTAL	867	5,234	6,101

Source: ANTT, *Conselho de Guerra, Consultas*, 1661, M. 21: *Relação dos Officiais e Soldados de Infanteria e Cavalaria que se acharão neste Exercito – ultima mostra* (22–23 September 1661).

APPENDIX I

Cavalry of the Army of Alentejo (September 1661)

Company:	Officers & NCOs:	Troopers:	Total:	Horses:
Guarda do Governador das Armas	6	38	44	49
Guarda do General da Cavalaria	3	62	65	72
Dinis de Melo de Castro	4	102	106	106
João de Vanichelli (Italian)	4	39	43	48
João da Silva	4	70	74	75
Luís da Costa	6	70	76	77
Couraças do Manuel Luis de Ataíde	6	66	72	76
Couraças do João do Crato	7	77	84	87
Couraças do Duarte Fernandes Lobo	6	34	40	34
Couraças do Miguel Barbosa da Franca	6	32	38	37
Couraças do Gaspar de Paiva	5	33	38	37
Couraças do Manuel de Paiva Soares	4	44	48	44
Couraças do António Coelho de Góis	6	74	80	72
Couraças do Pedro César de Meneses	7	43	50	47
Companhia que foi de Frei Jorge de Melo (died)	4	41	45	32
João de Sainclá (French)	6	37	43	37
Simão Borges da Costa	5	33	38	38
Manuel Mendes Mexia	7	46	53	39
António de Sequeira Pestana	5	31	36	39
Pedro Furtado de Mendonça	5	38	43	45
Manuel Rodrigues Adibe	4	23	27	28
Diogo de Mesquita	6	29	35	38
Bernardo de Faria	4	42	46	36
Gomes Freire de Andrade	6	44	50	46
Aires de Saldanha	6	37	43	44
André Mendes Lobo	5	141	146	135
Estêvão da Rocha	6	42	48	40
António Fernandes Marques	4	36	40	44
Bernardo de Miranda	2	34	36	31
João Furtado de Mendonça	5	47	52	54

Company:	Officers & NCOs:	Troopers:	Total:	Horses:
Jácome de Melo Pereira	4	40	44	48
António Botelho	4	28	32	37
Ambrósio Pereira	6	59	65	60
Henrique Rozendo	5	33	38	43
Frei Rui Pereira	5	41	46	36
Jerónimo de Moura	4	46	50	47
Filipe Ferreira Ferrão	3	38	41	43
Francisco Cabral Barreto	4	41	45	48
Duarte Lobo de Gama	4	40	44	42
Henri de Lamoniére (French)	3	34	37	28
Jorge Dufresne (French)	2	38	40	40
Luís Gonçalves de Azevedo	6	33	39	39
Bartolomeu de Barros Caminha	4	47	51	49
Francisco Henriques	6	32	38	45
Barão de Sauserais (French)	2	32	34	32
Roque da Costa Barreto	6	39	45	42
Filipe de Azevedo	3	43	46	44
José Pessanha de Castro	6	48	54	54
Matias da Cunha	6	34	40	36
Manuel Lobo	4	43	47	38
Luís de Saldanha	5	31	36	41
Herman Ricol (German)	5	30	35	30
João Vieira Mendes	6	44	50	44
La Richardière (French)	5	52	57	49
Rafael de Aux (Catalan)	3	24	27	28
Preboste geral João da Costa	5	49	54	49
Pilhantes de Marvão, Manuel da Fonseca	3	33	36	36
Pilhantes de Nisa, Francisco de Matos	4	39	43	43
Pilhantes de Montalvão, (already under Inácio Correia)	3	56	59	59
Pilhantes de Alegrete, Diogo Rodrigues Tourinho	3	51	54	54
TOTAL	283	2,683	2,966	2,879

Schomberg's Cavalry Regiment (French)

Company	Officers	Troopers	Total	Horses
Companhia do mestre de campo general	7	93	100	91
Companhia do sargento-mor Bogni	1	43	44	47
Companhia do tenente-coronel Jeremias Chavet	7	53	60	60
Companhia do capitão João Salomon	4	54	58	51
Companhia do capitãoBartolomeu de Brand	4	38	42	44
Companhia do capitãoJoão Morignac	2	47	49	21
TOTAL	25	328	353	314

Coronel Monjorge's Cavalry Regiment (French)[1]

Company	Officers	Troopers	Total	Horses
Companhia do sargento-mor M. de Sossé	4	30	34	14
Companhia do capitão Du Mortier	3	12	15	4
Companhia do capitão Labotinière	1	24	25	0
TOTAL	8	66	74	18

Source: ANTT, *Conselho de Guerra, Consultas,* 1661, M. 21: *Relação dos Officiais e Soldados de Infanteria e Cavalaria que se acharão neste Exercito – ultima mostra* (22–23 September 1661).

Infantry of the Army of Alentejo (May 1663)

In Estremoz

Terço da Armada, mestre de campo Simão de Vasconcelos e Sousa (brother of the Count de Castelo Melhor, Escrivão da Puridade of King Afonso VI): 825 men, of which 87 in hospital.

Terço do mestre de campo napolitano Dom Pedro Opecinga: 476 men including 52 in hospital.

Terço do mestre de campo Tristão da Cunha de Mendonça: 287 men including nine in hospital.

Terço do mestre de campo Roque da Costa Barreto: 418 men, including 40 in hospital.

Terço do mestre de campo Lourenço de Sousa: 508 men.

---

1 In September 1661 there were only two French cavalry regiments,. One was nominally under the command of the Count of Schomberg, who was *mestre de campo general* of the provincial army (hence the title of colonel in the regiment was honorary; command on the ground was exercised Lieutenant Colonel Chavet). The second was the very small regiment of Colonel Monjorge, who had suffered from the assault that occurred during the sail to Portugal by the Spanish fleet. The capture of part of the ships carrying the regiment meant the imprisonment of many officers and soldiers, including Monjorge himself. The regiment was commanded by *sargento mor* Sausé. As was customary in most documents of the time, the foreign officers' proper names are in Portuguese.

Terço pago de Trás-os-Montes: 310 men.
Terço pago do Algarve: 457 men (3 companies missing, expected in Estremoz).
Terço de Auxiliares de Santarém: 310 men.
Terço de Auxiliares de Vilaviçosa: 212 men.
English Regiment, Colonel James Apsley: 495 men.
English Regiment, Lt Col. Thomas Hunt: 694 men including 45 in hospital.
Companhias soltas de Italianos: 263 men, including 26 in hospital.

In Vilaviçosa

Terço do mestre de campo Diogo de Faro: 279 men.
Terço do mestre de campo João Furtado de Mendonça: 543 men.

In Elvas

Terço do mestre de campo Francisco da Silva de Moura: 734 men.
Terço do mestre de campo Fernando de Mascarenhas: 550 men.

In Campo Maior

Terço do mestre de campo Pedro César de Meneses: 462 men.
Terço pago de Cascais: 532 men.
Terço de Auxiliares de Avis: 350 men.
Regiment of Jacques Alexandre de Tolon (French infantry): 360 men.

In Portalegre

Terço do mestre de campo Alexandre de Moura: 630 men, including 130 in hospital.
Terço de Auxiliares de Portalegre: 400 men.

(When the list had been compiled, the regular *terço* of Beira had arrived in Portalegre, but its strength had not yet been registered.)

In Mourão

Terço do mestre de campo Martim Correia de Sá: 350 men.
Terço do mestre de campo Miguel Barbosa da Franca: 501 men.
Terço de Auxiliares de Évora: 541 men.

In Moura

Terço de Auxiliares de Campo de Ourique: 600 men.
Terço de Auxiliares de Beja: 350 men.

In Castelo de Vide

Terço de Auxiliares do Priorado do Crato: 320 men.

In total: Estremoz: 5,469 men (of which 1,259 in hospital); Vilaviçosa: 822 men; Elvas: 1,284 men; Campo Maior: 1,704 men; Portalegre: 1,030 (of which 130 in hospital); Mourão: 1,392 men; Moura: 950 men; Castelo de Vide: 320 men.

Source: ANTT, *Conselho de Guerra, Consultas*, 1663, M. 23, *Lista da infantaria que se acha nas praças desta prouincia de Alentejo em 7 de Maio (1)663*.

APPENDIX I

Composition of the Portuguese infantry *terços* at Evora (May 1663)

Arqueb.	Musk.	Pikemen:	Coys:	Officers	Privates	Total
137	176	159	15	21	506	527
99	87	97	12	55	298	353
52	123	2	6	19	254	273
6	120	89	11	36	215	251
–	152	203	9	11	267	278
–	311	167	7	23	274	297
1	394	216	16	25	699	724

Source: BNE, *Sucesos 1663*, pp.122–123

Província da Beira: Infantry and Cavalry Quartered in the District of Penamacor (1663)

Infantry

In Salvaterra do Extremo
Companhia do capitão Fernando de Chaves, 5 officers, 28 private soldiers, total: 33 men.
Companhia do capitão Inácio Arnaut, 4 officers, 19 private soldiers, total: 23 men.
Companhia do capitão Manuel Vieira, 4 officers, 21 private soldiers, total: 25 men.
Companhia do capitão Sebastião de Elvas, now under the *alferes* Manuel Rodrigues, 3 officers, 30 private soldiers, total: 33 men.
Companhia do capitão Luís de Lima, now under the *alferes* Manuel Marques, 3 officers, 28 private soldiers, total: 31 men.

In Segura
Companhia do capitão António Rodrigues de Figueiredo, 5 officers, 35 private soldiers, total: 40 men.
Companhia do capitão Hipólito Cardoso de Moxica, 5 officers, 28 private soldiers, total: 33 men.
Companhia do capitão Martim de Melo, now under the *sargento* Domingos Gonçalves, 3 officers, 21 private soldiers, total: 24 men.

In Rosmaninhal
Companhia do capitão João da Rocha, 5 officers, 35 private soldiers, total: 40 horsemen.

In Zebreira
Companhia do capitão Andrade Gouveia Coelho, now under the *alferes* José de Matos, 3 officers, 34 private soldiers, total: 37 horsemen.

Cavalry

In Penamacor
Lifeguard company of the *governador das armas*, 3 officers, 47 troopers, total: 50 horsemen with 30 horses.

In Idanha a Nova
Companhia do tenente-general Martinho da Ribeira, 2 officers, 30 troopers, total: 32 with 32 horses.

In Salvaterra do Extremo
Companhia do capitão Paulo Correia Rebelo, prisoner in Spain, now under the *furriel* Pedro Fernandes, 1 officer, 25 troopers, total: 26 horsemen with 26 horses.
Companhia do capitão António Estaço da Costa (prisoner in Spain, now under lieutenant Domingos Homem), 2 officers, 20 troopers, total: 22 horsemen with 21 horses.

In Segura
Companhia do auxiliares (*amunicionada*) of *capitão* Manuel de Sousa de Refóios, 3 officers, 13 troopers, total: 16 horsemen with 16 horses.
Total: infantry, 40 officers, 279 private soldiers, 319 overall. Cavalry; 11 officers, 135 troopers, 146 horsemen, with 125 horses.

Source: ANTT, *Conselho da Guerra, Consultas*, 1663, M. 23–A, C. 87 *Efectivos detalhados que existiam no distrito militar de Penamacor, província da Beira*.

Order of Battle at Montes Claros (17 June 1665)

Commanders: *Capitão-General do Reino* António Luis de Meneses, Count of Cantanhede, marqués de Marialva
Mestre de Campo General: Friedrich Hermann von Schomberg
Sargentos Móres de Batalha: Miguel Carlos de Távora, Diego Gomes de Figuereido, João Solva de Susa, Balandrin (French)

Vanguard
Infantry: *mestre de campo* António de Saldanha
Terço de Auxiliares de Comarca de Tomar

Right Wing Cavalry: *general da cavalaria* **Dinis de Melo e Castro**
4 *batalhões* (squadrons) under Roque da Costa Barreto
3 *batalhões* under Simão de Vasconcelos and João da Silva

APPENDIX I

First Line:
Left Wing Cavalry: *general da cavalaria* Pedro César de Meneses
6 *batalhóes* under Francisco and Bernardino de Távora
3 squadrons of French cavalry
3 Squadrons of English cavalry
1 company of the Schomberg's Lifeguards

First Line of Infantry: *mestre de campo* Tristão da Cunha
12 *esquadróes* (battalions)

Second Line:
Right Wing Cavalry: 17 *batalhóes* under Luis da Costa
Second Line Infantry: *mestre de campo* Gonçalo da Costa Meneses
9 *esquadróes*
Left wing cavalry: 17 *batalhóes* under António Maldonado

Reserve:
6 *batalhóes* of cavalry
4 *esquadróes* of infantry: auxiliary *terço* ofMourão, auxiliary *terço* ofAires.

(Approximately overall strength: 22,000 men)

Appendix II

Portuguese Infantry *Terços*, 1641–1668

APPENDIX II

Terços Pagos (Professional Terços)

	Year	Commander - Mestre de Campo	Denomination - Note	Raised in	Garrison -Engagements	History	Uniforms
PI–01	(1618) 1641	Luís da Silva Telles, 1657 *conde de Miranda*, Diogo Gomes de Figueiredo, 1663 Simão de Vasconcelos e Sousa, 1665 Mathias da Cunha	*Terço da Armada Real*	Estremadura (Lisbon)	Castel Rodrigo (1661) Ameixial (1663) Valença de Alcantara, Badajoz (1664) Montes Claros (1665)	(1715) *Regimento de Infantaria de Armada*	(1664) Private: green coat, yellow lining and facing.[1]
PI–02	1641	João da Costa conde de Soure, 1659?Miguel Carlos de Távora *conde de São Vicente*?, 1661 Pietro Pissingo, 1665 Francisco Henriques	*Terço de Elvas*	Alentejo	In Elvas, Nossa Senhora de Graça (1659) Évora, Ameixial (1663) Montes Claros (1665)	Disbanded in 1668	(1660s) Private: grey coat
PI–03	1641	Francisco João de Sousa,		Alentejo		Disbanded in 1645	
PI–04	1641	Nuno Mascarenhas, 1658? João de Zuñiga, 1660 Francisco Mascarenhas *conde de Torre*, 1663? Tristão da Cunha		Alentejo	In Castelo de Vide, Ameixial (1663) Montes Claros (1665)	Disbanded in 1668	(1660s) Private: grey coat
PI–05	1641	Aires de Saldanha de Albuquerque, 1661? João Henriques, 1664 Francisco da Silva Moura		Alentejo	In Campo Maior Montes Claros (1665)	Disbanded in 1668	(1660s) Private: grey coat
PI–06	1641	Miguel de Azevedo, 1650? Manoel Henriques, 1658? João Leite de Oliveira, 1663? Manoel Lobato Pinto		Alentejo	Juromenha (1662) Ameixial (1663) Badajoz (1664)	Disbanded in 1668	(1660s) Private: grey coat
PI–07	1641	(1642) António Ortiz,[2] 1658? Luis de Sousa de Meneses (?), 1662 Fernando de Escovedo,1663? Thomás de Estrada	*Terço de Lisboa*, 1668 *terço do Príncipe*	Estremadura (Lisbon)	Nossa Senhora de Graça (1659) Ameixal (1663) Montes Claros (1665)	(1715) *Regimento de Infantaria do Príncipe*	(1670s) Private: dark blue coat

	Year	Commander – Mestre de Campo	Denomination – Note	Raised in	Garrison -Engagements	History	Uniforms
PI-08	1641	Diogo de Melo Pereira, 1645 Francisco de França Barbosa, 1649 Francisco Peres da Silva, 1659 António Soares da Costa, 1663 António Luís de Sousa *marqués das Minas*, 1665 Manuel da Silva Souto Maior	1657 *Terço velho de Entre-Douro-e-Minho*	Entre-Douro-e-Minho[3]	Galicia (1662) Montes Claros (1665)	Disbanded in 1668	(1660s) Private: grey coat
PI-09	1641	Sancho Manuel *conde de* Vilaflor,[4] 1658 João Fialho, (1665, Sebastião de Elvas as *sargento mor*)		Beira	In Penamacor (1657) Elvas (1658) Montes Claros (1665)?	Disbanded in 1668?	(1660s) Private: grey coat
PI-10	1642	(1658) Pedro de Melo,1665, João Alvares Cravo (as *sargento mor*)		Beira	Montes Claros (1665)?	Disbanded in 1668?	
PI-11	1643	António Hortis de Mendonça, 1648(?) 1659 Agostinho de Andrade Freire, 1663(?) Diego de Faro,[5] 1665 Manuel Lobato Pinto		Alentejo	In Olivença and Vila Viçosa (1645)	Disbanded in 1668	(1660s) Private: grey coat
PI-12	1643	Martim Ferreira da Câmara, 1646 David Caley, 1650(?) 1661 *conde de* Portolhano, 1663(?) Luis da Silva		Alentejo	In Campo Maior and Olivença (1645) Ameixial (1663)	Disbanded in 1668	(1660s) Private: grey coat
PI-13	1646	Francisco Barreto		Entre-Douro-e-Minho		Disbanded in 1646	
PI-14	1646	Francisco de Castelo Branco		Algarve		Disbanded in 1646	
PI-15	1648	Rodrigo de Castro, 1661 Diogo Gomes de Figueiredo, 1663 Bernardo de Miranda Henriques, 1664 Rui Pereira da Silva, 1665 Baltasar Lopes Tavares		Riba-Côa	San Miguel, Monteiro (1658) Badajoz (1664)	Disbanded in 1668	(1660s) Private: grey coat

APPENDIX II

	Year	Commander – Mestre de Campo	Denomination – Note	Raised in	Garrison – Engagements	History	Uniforms
PI-16	1657	Rui Lourenço de Távora, Pedro de Almeida, 1661 Gerónimo Mendonça Furtado, 1663 Roque da Costa Barreto, 1664 Gonçalo da Costa de Marti	*Terço Novo da guarnição de Lisboa*	Estremadura (Lisbon)	In Evora (1663) Montes Claros (1665)	(1715) *Regimento de Infantaria de Lisboa*	(1664) Private: azure coat, red lining and facing.[6]
PI-17	1657	Francisco Pacheco Mascarenhas, 1662 Fernão de MesquitaPimentel, 1663(?) Pedro Cesar de Meneses, 1665(?) Gonçalo da Costa Meneses		Alentejo	In Olivença (1657) Juromenha (1662) Montes Claros (1665)	Disbanded in 1665?	-
PI-18	1657	João de Mello Feio, 1658 Bartolomeu de Azevedo Coutinho, 1663 Manuel Ferreira Rabello, 1665(?)		Riba-Côa	Castel Rodrigo (1661) Ameixial (1663)	Disbanded in 1668	(1660s) Private: grey coat
PI-19	1657	António Galvão, 1658 Manuel de de Castro, 1663Fernão da Mesquita Pimentel		Algarve	Montes Claros (1665)	Disbanded in 1668?	-
PI-20	1657	Sebastião Correia de Lorvela		Azores	Badajoz (1658)	Disbanded in 1658	-
PI-21	1658	Diogo de Brito Coutinho, 1663 Gonçalo Vasquez da Cunha, 1664 João Rebelho Leita, 1667 António Barbosa de Brito	*Terço novo de Entre-Douro-e-Minho*	Entre-Douro-e-Minho[7]	Galicia (1662) Montes Claros (1665)? Umbrales (1666)	Disbanded in 1668; re-established in 1696	(1660s) Private: grey coat
PI-22	1658	Fernão de Sousa Coutinho, 1659 Rodrigo Pereira Souto Maior, 1663 Jerónimo da Silva, Luís Manuel de Távora, 1666 João de Sousa		Entre-Douro-e-Minho[8]	Valença (1658) Galicia (1662) Montes Claros (1665)?	Disbanded in 1668	(1660s) Private: grey coat
PI-23	1658	Manuel Velho da Guerra	*Terço da Armada da Bolsa*	Estremadura		Disbanded in 1668	
PI-24	1658	António Jaques de Payva		Trás-os-Montes		Disbanded in 1659	

	Year	Commander – Mestre de Campo	Denomination – Note	Raised in	Garrison -Engagements	History	Uniforms
PI-25	1658	Gergório de Castro de Moraes, 1664 Francisco de Távora, Diogo de Caldas		Trás-os-Montes	Galicia (1662) Montes Claros (1665)?	Disbanded in 1665?	(1660s) Private: grey coat
PI-26	1658	?	*Terço da Ilha da Madeyra*	Madeira[9]	Elvas (1659)	Disbanded in 1659?	
PI-27	1659	Álvaro de Azevedo Barreto, 1661 Miguel Carlos de Távora *conde de São Vicente*, 1662 Manuel Nunes Leitão, 1666 Diogo Soares Pereira		Entre-Douro-e-Minho[10]	Nossa Senhora de Graça (1659) Galicia (1662) Montes Claros (1665)?	Disbanded in 1668	(1660s) Private: grey coat
PI-28	1659	Fernão Sousa da Silva, 1668 (?) Manuel de Ataíde e Azevedo	*Terço novo da Câmara do Porto*	Entre-Douro-e-Minho[11]	Galicia, São Lourenço (1662) La Guardia (1665) Montes Claros (1665)?	(1763) *Regimiento de Porto*	(1660s) Private: grey coat
PI-29	1661	Sebastião Correa de Lorvela, 1664 José de Sousa Cid	*Terço da Cascais*	Estremadura		(1715) *Regimento de Infantaria de Cascais*	(1670s) Private, dark blue coat
PI-30	1661	Manuel da Câmara *conde de Ribeyra*, 1663 Fernando Mascarenhas, 1666 Martim Correa de Sá	*Terço da Setúbal*	Estremadura	Ameixial (1663) Montes Claros (1665)	(1715) *Regimento de Infantaria de Setúbal*	(1660s) Private: grey coat (1670s) Private, dark blue coat
PI-31	1663	?	*Terço da Junta do Comércio*	Estremadura (Lisbon)		(1763) *Regimento de Lippe*	(1670s) Private, dark blue coat
PI-32	1663	Paulo Freire de Andrade-Castelo Branco	*Terço da Beira*	Beira	Ameixial (1663)	Disbanded in 1665?	(1660s) Private: grey coat
PI-33	1663	Francisco de Moraes Henriques		Trás-os-Montes	Montes Claros (1665)?	Disbanded in 1665?	(1660s) Private: grey coat
PI-34	1663	Alexandre de Moura de Albuquerque		Alentejo	In Portalegre, Ameixial (1663)	Disbanded in 1668	(1660s) Private: grey coat

APPENDIX II

	Year	Commander – Mestre de Campo	Denomination – Note	Raised in	Garrison –Engagements	History	Uniforms
PI-35	1663	João da Costa de Brito		Alentejo	In Portalegre Ameixial (1663)	Disbanded in 1668	(1660s) Private: grey coat
PI-36	1664	João Filgueira Galo[12]		Entre-Douro-e-Minho	Montes Claros (1665)? Galicia (1665)	Disbanded in 1668	(1660s) Private: grey coat
PI-37	1664	Manuel Pacheco de Mello		Trás-os-Montes	Montes Claros (1665)	Disbanded in 1665?	(1660s) Private: grey coat
PI-38	1665	Sebastião da Veiga		Trás-os-Montes	Montes Claros (1665)?	Disbanded in 1665?	(1660s) Private: grey coat
PI-39	1665	Francisco Mendes Homem		Alentejo	In Valença (1665)	Disbanded in 1668	
PI-40	1665	Rui Pereira da Silva		Riba-Côa	In Penamacor?	Disbanded in 1665	
PI-41	1665	Francisco da Cunha da Silva[13]	(Former auxilliary terço)	Entre-Douro-e-Minho	Montes Claros (1665)	Disbanded in 1668	(1660s) Private: grey coat
PI-42	1665	Luís de Sancé[14]	(Former auxilliary terço)	Entre-Douro-e-Minho		Disbanded in 1668	(1660s) Private: grey coat

Auxiliary Terços

	Year	Commander – Mestre de Campo	Denomination – Note	Raised in	Garrison –Engagements	History	Uniforms
PA-01	1643	Francisco de Mello		Alentejo	In Moura and later in Mourão (1645)	Reformed in 1645	–
PA-02	1643	?		Alentejo		Reformed in 1645	–
PA-03	1643	Luís de Almada		Alentejo		Reformed in 1643	–

	Year	Commander – Mestre de Campo	Denomination – Note	Raised in	Garrison –Engagements	History	Uniforms
PA–04	1643	David Caley		Estremadura	Valverde, Vila Nova (1643)	Reformed in 1643	–
PA–05	1643	?		Estremadura	In Alentejo (1643)	Reformed in 1643?	–
PA–06	1644	*Conde de Penaguião,*		Alentejo		Reformed in 1645	–
PA–07	1644	David Caley		Estremadura	In Estremoz	Reformed in 1645	–
PA–08	1644	?		Estremadura		Reformed in 1645?	–
PA–09	1644	?		Estremadura		Reformed in 1645?	–
PA–10	1645	Belchior de Lemos de Britto, 1662? Lourenço Garcez, 1664 Baltasar Lopes Tavares, 1665?		Alentejo	In Olivença Ameixial (1663)	Reformed in 1668	–
PA–11	1656	*Conde de Vimioso,* 1657 Francisco Mascarenhas *conde de Torre,* 1661? Miguel Barbosa de França		Alentejo	In Mourão San Miguel (1658) Elvas (1661)	Reformed in 1659	–
PA–12	1657	Luis Alvares de Távora *conde de São João,* 1665 António Velez Castelo Branco	*Terço de Avis*	Alentejo	In Elvas Nossa Senhora de Graça (1659) Montes Claros (1665)	Reformed in 1668	–
PA–13	1657	Agostinho de Andrade		Alentejo		Reformed in 1658?	–
PA–14	1657	Pedro de Mello		Alentejo	Mourão (1657)	Reformed in 1658?	–
PA–15	1657	Simão Correa da Silva, 1661? João da Castanheyra de Moura		Alentejo	Mourão (1657) Nossa Senhora de Graça (1659)	Reformed in 1668	–
PA–16	1657	Diogo de Mendoça, 1661? –Christovão de Sá de Mendoça, 1662? Francisco de Moraes, 1665 Manoel de Lemas	*Terço de Mourão*	Alentejo	Mourão (1657) Castel Rodrigo (1661) Ameixial (1663) Montes Claros (1665)	Reformed in 1668	–
PA–17	1660	Alexandre de Moura de Albuquerque, 1661 Lourenço de Sousa de Menézes		Alentejo	Juromenha (1662)	Reformed in 1665?	–

APPENDIX II

	Year	Commander – Mestre de Campo	Denomination – Note	Raised in	Garrison –Engagements	History	Uniforms
PA–18	1661?	Balthasar de Sousa		Trás-os-Montes	Galicia (1662)	Reformed in 1665?	–
PA–19	1662	Francisco da Cunha da Silva	(Regular terço in 1665)	Entre-Douro-e-Minho[15]	Galicia (1662)	Reformed in 1668	–
PA–20	1662	Luis de Sancé	(Regular terço in 1665)	Entre-Douro-e-Minho[16]	Galicia (1662)	Reformed in 1668	–
PA–21	1662	Manuel da Silva Souto Maior		Entre-Douro-e-Minho[17]	Galicia (1662)	Reformed in 1665?	–
PA–22	1662	Balthasar Fagundes da Fonseca		Entre-Douro-e-Minho[18]	Galicia (1662)	Reformed in 1665?	–
PA–23	1662	Gonçalo de Araujo		Entre-Douro-e-Minho[19]	Galicia (1662)	Reformed in 1665?	–
PA–24	1662	Pierre de Sanpierre		Entre-Douro-e-Minho[20]	Galicia (1662)	Reformed in 1665?	–
PA–25	1662?	Roque de Costa Barreto, 1663? Francisco de Alarcão		Alentejo	In Evora (1663)	Reformed in 1668?	–
PA–26	1661	Francisco Pacheco Mascarenhas		Alentejo	In Elvas (1661) In Moura (1663)	Reformed in 1668	–
PA–26	1661	?	*Terço da Comarca de Castelo-Branco*[21]	Alentejo	Castel Rodrigo (1661)	Reformed in 1667?	–
PA–27	1661	António de Saldanha	*Terço da Comarca da Guarda*[22]	Alentejo	Castel Rodrigo (1661) Montes Claros (1665)	Reformed in 1667?	–
PA–28	1661	Francisco Banha de Siqueyra	*Terço de Volantes da Guarda*[23]	Alentejo	Castel Rodrigo (1661)	Reformed in 1665?	–
PA–29	1662?	Martim Correa de Sá		Alentejo	In Serpa Juromenha (1662)	Reformed in 1668	–
PA–30	1663?	Antonio de Cunha		Estremadura		Reformed in 1668	–
PA–31	1663?	Marcos de Noroña		Estremadura		Reformed in 1668	–

	Year	Commander – Mestre de Campo	Denomination – Note	Raised in	Garrison – Engagements	History	Uniforms
PA-32	1663?	Fernão de Miranda		Estremadura (Setubal)		Reformed in 1668	–

Terços of Militia

	Year	Commander – Mestre de Campo	Denomination – Note	Raised in	Garrison – Engagements	History	Uniforms
PM-1	1663?	Simão de Miranda Henriques		Estremadura (Lisbon)		Disbanded in 1668	–
PM-2	1663?	Luis Coutinho		Estremadura (Lisbon)		Disbanded in 1668	–
PM-3	1663?	Fadrique de Camera		Estremadura (Lisbon)		Disbanded in 1668	–

Footnotes

1. *Mercurio Portuguez* (Lisbon, 1667), April 1664, p.174.
2. Meneses, conde de Ericeyra Luis de, *Historia de Portugal Restaurado* (Lisbon, 1679),Vol. I, p.432.
3. Gastão de Melo de Matos, *Os terços de Entre-Douro-e-Minho nas guerras da Aclamação – esboço de História Orgânica*, in 'Revista de Guimarães' N. 50 (Special volume published for the Centenaries of the Foundation and Restoration of Portugal,1940), pp.209–219.
4. Meneses, *Historia de Portugal Restaurado*, vol. I, pp.374–375
5. Geronimo de Santa Cruz, *Declaracion que por el Reyno de Portugal ofrece el doctor G. De Santa Cruz a todos los Reynos, y Provincias de Europa* (Lisbon, 1663), p.35.
6. *Mercurio Portuguez* (Lisbon, 1667), June 1664, p.192.
7. Melo de Matos, *Os terços de Entre-Douro-e-Minho*, pp.218–220.
8. *Ibid.*, p.220.
9. Meneses, *Historia de Portugal Restaurado*, vol. II, p.151.
10. Melo de Matos, *Os terços de Entre-Douro-e-Minho*, p 221.
11. *Ibid.*, p.222.
12. *Ibid.*
13. *Ibid.*, p.223.
14. *Ibid.*
15. *Ibid.*

APPENDIX II

16 *Ibid.*
17 Meneses, *Historia de Portugal Restaurado*, vol. II, p.431.
18 *Ibid.*
19 *Ibid.*
20 *Ibid.*
21 *Ibid.*, p.353.
22 *Ibid.*
23 *Ibid.*

Colour Plate Commentaries

Plate A: Portuguese Infantry, 1660s

1. Infantry *Mestre de Campo*, 1664–1668
This figure is based on the portrait of Tristão da Cunha, preserved in the collection of the Galleria degli Uffizi of Florence. Da Cunha held the command of a Portuguese infantry *terço* at the Battle of Montes Claros and was later appointed as artillery general in 1668. He wears a *carlino*-style coat over a leather waistcoat, following a style becoming usual in Spain and Portugal in these years. The green scarf secures the coat, which has short cuffs laced of silver: an uncommon feature in this age.

2. Musketeer, *Terço de Armada*, 1664
In 1664, the *Mercurio Portuguez* recorded some of the first uniforms of the Portuguese infantry, mentioning the *Terço de Armada* wearing green coats faced and lined with yellow. According to the research of Alberto Cutileiro in the 1980s, the coats have much in common with the Spanish *casaca* rather than the French *justaucorps*. However, in the following years, the Portuguese infantry received grey coats presumably tailored in French style.

3. Pikeman, Unknown Unit, 1665
Contemporary accounts state that Portuguese pikeman had discarded their armour by the 1650s. In 1663, the Count of Ericeira reports that 3,000 infantry corselets were adapted for use as cavalry breastplates, as infantry no longer used metal armour. In images of the 1660s, some pikemen are portrayed wearing jackets or buff coats without sleeves, and these latter could be jupons manufactured with more layers of cloth.

Plate B: Infantry, 1670–1680

1. Fife, *Terço de Lisboa*, 1670s
Reconstruction after Cutileiro's *O uniforme militar na Armada: três séculos de história*, where he proposes a Portuguese version of the infantry uniform for musicians, with chequered lace in silver and green, the colours of the Bragança' livery.

COLOUR PLATE COMMENTARIES

2. Officer, Early 1680s
The *capitão mor* Manoel Damaral Carral is portrayed in an early 1680s painting preserved in a Portuguese private collection. The painting is a very interesting source illustrating the evolution of military dress of Portugal. The Western European style is mixed with Portuguese features in a very original way.

3. Marine Infantryman, 1680s
In the same painting from which the previous figure is based, three infantrymen are depicted, armed with flintlock muskets and ammunition pouches. This suggests that they could be marine soldiers serving with the fleet. Portugal's military involvement in their overseas domains continued until the next century, and the fleet did not decrease in its importance as happened with the field army.

Portuguese regular troops and militia were also supported by African soldiers, since in the 1680s, the King agreed that no distinction be made between 'whites, mulattos' and 'free negroes'. These Africans were recruited among the Guinean *lançados* and the Angolan *empacaseiros* and other free people.

Plate C: Portuguese Cavalry, 1660s

1. Senior Officer, 1660s
The portrait of the famous commander and historian Luis de Meneses, Count of Ericeira, shows with great detail the dress of Portuguese cavalry officers in the last phases of the Restoration War. The buff coat is adorned with silk ribbons and presumably is tailored with the better quality calf leather. The black broad brimmed hat appears in the portrait, though a lobster-style helmet was probably worn in action.

2. Cavalry Trooper, 1660s
This figure is based on the horsemen depicted in the battle scene painted on the lead sheets preserved in Lisbon, illustrating some episodes that occurred in the Restoration War. Portuguese horsemen are generally depicted wearing clothing very close to the almost contemporary Cromwellian Ironsides. The buff coat and the lobster helmet were common also on the Spanish side, but the combat tactics and the equipment seems to confirm that the Portuguese cavalry had chosen the English horsemen as models. This dress remained popular in Portugal since the equestrian clothing of the Portuguese kings was also manufactured after this model.

Plate D: Trumpeter

Trumpeter, Portuguese Cavalry, late 1650s–early 1660s
This figure is a reconstruction after the painting on sheet lead preserved in the National Museum of Antique Art of Lisbon, illustrating the conquest of

Vila Nova del Fresno. Although the episode occurred in 1643, the figures are dressed in the style of the following decades. Sashes were usually worn as distinctive sign since green or white were the colours generally worn by Portuguese officers as well as NCOs. However, in the painting a couple of trumpeters wear red sashes similar to the ones worn by the Spanish.

Plate E: English and French Soldiers in Portuguese Service, 1661–1680

1. English Musketeer, Portugal 1663
English regiments serving alongside the Portuguese in the 1660s wore red coats probably lined in different colours. Usually, in the 1660s, the English infantry retained the dress of the Cromwellian period, although breeches were usually of grey or other undyed colour. However, the full red uniform is stated by several eyewitnesses. The English infantry gained a considerable reputation in Portugal, contributing to the successes in the major field engagements after 1662. This figure is a reconstruction after the *azulejo* depicting the Battle of Ameixial, preserved in the Palacio Fronteira in Lisbon. The English infantrymen are portrayed wearing the 'Puritan hats', jackets and short open breeches.

2. English Infantry Officer, Portugal 1662
The Restoration style of the English aristocracy derived from the Dutch and French clothing, which comprised a doublet, Rhinegrave breeches and broad-brimmed hat, of the high 'Puritan' model the most used in the early 1660s. This officer must have aroused the curiosity of the Lisbon residents upon his arrival with the English contingent in the spring of 1662, since this kind of military dress was almost unknown in Portugal. In all likelihood, in the following months his elegant clothing was replaced with dress much more suited to the harshness of the Alenetjo frontier territory.

3. French Musketeer, Regiment *Schomberg Allemand*, 1661–63
Mazarin and later Louis XIV gave substantial support to Portugal during the Restoration War. In 1659, after the Pyrenees' Peace, France sent troops to Portugal under the German general Friedrich Hermann von Schomberg, despite the raise of troops was impeded by the articles of the treaty. However, in 1660, a small contingent of 400 French cavalry, 80 among officers and volunteer gentlemen and engineers sailed to Portugal. In Lisbon, on 11 November, the cavalry was reviewed by the court, which hoped for further military aid, but until 1661, this was the only French contingent to serve in Portugal. In the next summer, a complete regiment of infantry landed to Lisbon. It was the German regiment *Schomberg Allemand* raised on 20 December 1657 by the count Friedrich Hermann. There are just a few clues about the dress of this regiment, which very probably wore the first version of the French *justaucorps*, possibly in medium grey. This kind of coat considerably echoed in the early 1660s, since in the Iberian Peninsula it took the denomination *chamberga*. This figure is a reconstruction after a drawing

of Sébastien Leclerc dated 1660, representing a French Guard's cadet wearing a coat with short sleeves and flap cuffs. Note the large stockings in undyed textile fixed on the breeches with strings, to preserve the clothing from mud and dust.

Plate F: Portuguese Infantry and Cavalry Ensigns

1. Infantry Ensign, 1640s
This flag is represented in a painting attributed to the Dutch artist Dirk Stoop depicting the Portuguese infantry during a muster in Lisbon. The same colours, but with the diagonal cross of Saint Andrew are represented in another contemporary painting, illustrating the encounter of Alcavariça in 1646. This has generated a debate concerning the reliability of the source, because the flags are very similar to the Spanish ensigns bearing the Burgundian cross.

2 and 3. Infantry Ensigns, 1660s

Plate G: Portuguese Infantry and Cavalry Ensigns

1. *Bandeira de aclamação*, 1650–1660
This flag became the first military ensign carried by the Portuguese troops as early as the 1640s. This pattern is represented as a main Portuguese ensign in the painting on lead illustrating the battle scene of the Restoration War, along with the cavalry standard.

2. Cavalry Standard, 1650–1660

3. Cavalry Standard, 1662
This standard is a notable variation of the classic pattern, and appears on a print dated 1662, which depicts the Battle of the Linhas de Elvas, fought on 14 January 1659. The colours of the main field are graphically represented on the print, but unfortunately the colours of the edges are not specified.

Plate H

A painting depicting the arrival of the Apostolic Nuncio Giorgio Cornaro at Lisbon in 1693 (Museu Nacional dos Coches, Lisbon). The carriage of the Papal Ambassador is met by formed troops, albeit in a variety of coat colours. Two theories have been advanced to identify these troops. The first theory suggests that they are militiamen of Lisbon. The second argues that the soldiers depicted belonged to the *Terço de Lisboa*, which served wearing very informal clothing (thanks to Nuno Pereira for this note).

Select Bibliography

Archive Sources
Arquivo Nacional da Torre do Tombo (Lisbon)
Conselho de Guerra, Consultas
Arquivo Histórico Militar (Lisbon)
Arquivo Histórico Ultramarino (Lisbon)
Instituto Arqueológico, Histórico e Geográfico Pernambucano (Recife, Brazil)

Contemporary Printed Works
Brandao, Francisco, *Dell'Istoria delle Guerre di Portogallo*, vols I–III (Rome, 1724)
Langres, Nicolas de, *Desenhos e plantas de toda as praças do Reyno de Portugal Pello Tenente General Nicolao de Langres Francez que serviu na guerra da Acclamação* (Lisbon, c. 1661).
Meneses, *conde* de Ericeira Luís de, *Historia de Portugal Restaurado*, vols. I–II (Lisbon, 1679)
Santa Cruz, Geronimo de, *Declaracion que por el Reyno de Portugal ofrece el doctor G. De Santa Cruz a todos los Reynos, y Provincias de Europa* (Lisbon, 1663)

General Documentary Sources
Chalby, Claudio de (editor*)*, *Synopse dos Decretos remettidos ao extinto Conselho de Guerra*, Vols. III–V (Lisbon, 1869)
Disney, Anthony R., *History of Portugal,* Vols. I–II (Cambridge, Cambridge University Press, 2009)
Magalhães Sepulveda, Chistovam Ayres de, *Historia Orgánica e Politica do Exercito Portugués*, Vols. I-V (Lisbon, 1908)
Newitt, Malyn, *The Portuguese in West Africa, 1415–1670* (Cambridge: Cambridge University Press, 2010)
Ribeiro, Ângelo, *História de Portugal: A Restauração da Independência-O início da Dinastia de Bragança* (Porto: Quidnovi, 2004)
Schedel de Castello Branco, Theresa M., *Vida de Francisco Mello Torres, 1º Conde da Ponte, Marquês de Sande. Soldado e Diplomata da Restauração, 1620-1667* (Lisbon: Livraria Férin, 1971)

Military History
Borges Salvado, Emília, *A Guerra da Restauração no Baixo Alentejo (1640–1668)* (Lisbon: Colibri, 2015)
Cutilero Alberto, *O uniforme militar na Armada: três séculos de história* (Lisbon: Editorial Estúdios C. Amigos do Livro Editores, 1983)
De Oliveira de Cadornega, Antonio, *Historia Geral Das Guerras Angolanas 1680* (1681), vols I–III (Lisbon, 1942)
Dores Costa, Fernando, *A guerra da Restauração 1641–1668* (Lisboa: Horizonte, 2004)

SELECT BIBLIOGRAPHY

Dumoriez, Charles François, *Campagnes du Maréchal de Schomberg en Portugal depuis l'année 1662 jusqu'en 1668* (London, 1807)

Espírito Santo, Gabriel, *Montes Claros, 1665: a Vitória decisiva*, (Lisbon: Tribuna de História, 2003)

Espírito Santo, Gabriel, *A Grande Estratégia de Portugal na Restauração, 1640–1668* (Lisbon: Caleidoscópio, 2009)

Freitas, Jorge Penim de, *O Combatente durante a Guerra da Restauração, 1640–1668. Vivência e comportamentos dos militares ao serviço da coroa portuguesa* (Lisbon, Prefácio, 2003)

Freitas, Jorge Penim de, *A cavalaria na Guerra da Restauração: reconstrução e evolução de uma força militar, 1641–1668* (Lisbon: Prefácio, 2005)

Gonsalves de Mello, José Antônio, *João Fernandes Vieira, mestre-de-campo de terço de infantaria de Pernambuco* (Lisbon: Comissão Nacional para as Comemorações dos Descobrimentos Portugueses, 2000)

Matos, Gastão de Melo de, 'Notícias do têrço da Armada Real (1618–1707)', in *Anais do Club Militar Naval* (Lisbon, 1932)

Melo de Matos, Gastão de, *Um soldado de fortuna do século XVII* (Lisboa, 1939)

Oliveira Cadornega, António de, José Mattias Delgado and Manuel Alves da Cunha, *História Geral das Guerras Angolanas*, Vols. I–III (Lisbon, 1942)

Pereira de Sales, Ernesto Augusto, *Bandeiras e estendartes regimentais do Exército e da Armada e outra bandeiras militares* (Lisbon, 1930)

Riley, Jonathon, *The Last Ironsides. The Portuguese Expedition to Portugal, 1662–1668* (Solihull: Helion & Company, 2014)

Articles and Essays

Alves, José Lopes, 'Através das 'Memórias Arqueológico-Históricas do Distrito de Bragança' por Francisco Manuel Alves (Abade de Baçal)', in *Revista Militar* N. 2446 (November 2005), pp.11–32

Cosme, João, 'Mazagão em 1677', in *Arquipélago-História*, 2ª série, VII (2003), pp.79–98

Childs, John, 'The English Brigade in Portugal', in *Journal of the Society for Army Historical Research* Vol. 53, N. 215 (Autumn 1975), pp.135–147

Dores Costa, Fernando, 'Formação da força militar durante a guerra de Restauração', in *Penélope. Revista de história e ciências sociais*, XXIV (2001), pp.87–119

Dores Costa, Fernando, 'Governadores das armas, mestres de campo e capitães-mores no Alentejo durante a Guerra da Restauração: inovações na administração e centros periféricos de poder', in *Centros Periféricos de Poder na Europa do Sul (Sécs. XII–XVIII)*, (Lisbon: Publicações do Cidehus, Edições Colibri, 2013), pp.199–228

Fonseca, Teresa, 'The Municipal Administration in Elvas During the Portuguese Restoration War (1640-1668)', e-JPH, Vol. 6, number 2, Winter 2008, pp.1–15

Freitas, Jorge Penim de, 'War abroad: English, Scot and Irish officers in the Portuguese Army, 1641 to 1657', in *Arquebusier*, vol. XXIX/III (2005), pp.2–11

Freitas, Jorge Penim de, 'Propaganda, experiência, liderança. Sobre o contributo dos militares estrangeiros ao serviço da Coroa portuguesa, 1641–1668', in *Actas do XV Colóquio de História Militar*, Comissão Portuguesa de História Militar, vol. I (2005), pp.237–252

Freitas, Jorge Penim de, 'A batalha de Montes Claros vista por um oficial Inglês. "A Relation of the last summers Campagne in the Kingdome of Portugal, 1665" (by an Anonymous officer of an English Regiment of Horse), 23 June 1665 – The National Archives, London, State Papers Portugal, SP 89.7', in *Lusíada*, Série II, N. 5-6 (2009), pp.341–355

Freitas, Jorge Penim de, 'Armas e praças fantásticas: efectivos, armamento e equipamento das unidades estrangeiras ao serviço da Coroa portuguesa no período inicial da Guerra da

Restauração (1641–1645)', in *Actas do XXI Colóquio de História Militar, Lisboa, Comissão Portuguesa de História Militar* (2012), pp.475–503

Freitas, Jorge Penim de, 'Estatuto social e hierarquia militar, uma difícil conciliação: a conduta operacional do Exército Português na batalha de Montes Claros', in *Callipole, Revista de Cultura*, N. 23 (2016), pp. 135–149

Freitas, Jorge Penim de, 'A estratégia de defesa da raia alentejana e a capitulação de Olivença em 1657: o caso Stéphane Auguste de Castille', in *O Pelourinho - Boletín de Relaziones Transfronterizas*, N. 20 (2nd Series, 2016), pp. 47–66

Freitas, Jorge Penim de, 'O sentido de «pertença» na raia alentejana durante a Guerra da Restauração: identidades e fidelidades num clima de conflito', in *Revista de Estudios Extremeños*, Badajoz, vol. LXXIII, N. III (September–December 2017), pp. 2611–2623

Freitas, Jorge Penim de, 'Ascensão e queda de D. João de Azevedo e Ataíde, comissário geral da cavalaria do Alentejo e tratadista militar (1641–1647)', in *Alentejo Restaurado, Conferências Internacionais de Elvas* (2019), pp.67–105

Hardacre, P. H., 'The English Contingent in Portugal, 1662–1668', in *Journal of the Society for Army Historical Research*, vol. XXXVIII (1960), pp.112–125

Lemos Pires, Nuno, 'Guerra global portuguesa: a restauração', in *Revista de História das Ideias*, Vol. 30 (2009), pp.337–353

Melo de Matos, Gastão de, 'Os terços de Entre-Douro-e-Minho nas guerras da Aclamação – Esboço de História Orgânica', in *Revista de Guimarães* N. 50 (Special volume published for the Centenaries of the Foundation and Restoration of Portugal,1940), pp.203–225

Morais-Alexandre, Paulo, 'A moda e o traje militar no século XVII' in *Comissão Portuguesa de História Militar* (November 1991), pp.169–174

Moura, Rui, 'Presença militar estrangeira no Exército Português, do século XVII a Napoleão', in *Congresso Internacional de Arqueologia e História – CIAH, As Linhas Defensivas entre o Século XVII e Napoleão* (1–2 September 2017), pp.1–20

Pires, Lemos, 'A Batalha de Montes Claros e o Conceito de Armas Combinadas', in *Armas Combinadas – Revista Militar da Escola das Armas* (first semester 2014), pp.6–11

Silva Duarte, António Paulo David, 'Para uma Tipologia da Guerra no Século XVII – A Batalha das Linhas de Elvas', in *Revista Militar* N. 2451 (April 2006), pp.285–307

White, Lorraine, 'Guerra y revolución militar en la Iberia del siglo XVII', in *Manuscrits* 21 (2003), pp. 63–93